WILD
AND
HEARTY

WILD
AND
HEARTY

KEVIN SCOLLANS

PALMETTO
PUBLISHING
Charleston, SC
www.PalmettoPublishing.com

Paperback ISBN: 9798822954168

Contents

Acknowledgements

loved writing this book; it energized me to take a deeper look into what makes my life "Wild and Hearty." At my core is a life brimming with good fortune, adventure, and risk-taking. This very essence is what propelled me to write this book and share my experiences with the world.

I am so proud to release this book into the bigger world while keeping in mind that none of this would be possible if it were not for the great people who were always there for me on my way (and stray) through a very exciting and wonderful life.

A special thanks to my friend Joe McLaughlin, a professional writer. Joe is currently the Senior Director of Leadership Communications for Seton Hall University and the lead writer for its president. Joe generously gave his time both as a sounding board and as one of my editors.

I would be remiss if I did not thank my wonderful wife, Kathleen, who became a "writer's widow" while I spent an enormous amount of time in my man cave writing this manuscript. Then there are my two precious daughters, Colleen (an English major) and Tara (a Journalism major), who were always there to listen to another story while offering praise and guidance. An additional big thanks to Colleen for volunteering to do a final edit and Tara who jumped in to assist since they both know me best from my childhood stories to this day.

And then there is my wonderful son, Brendan—a Harvard Baker Scholar, who was both supportive and helped me solidify why I was so focused on this book. He would say, "*Dad, don't you think it is time to relax? Why do you always have to be on a roll?*" Writing this book was an obsession for me, and the only answer that came (and still comes) to me is, "*Son, that is who I am, and when that stops, so will I.*" Doing what we love is what energizes us to do more. We will keep going, as long as we can hear the tick of the big clock.

A special big thanks to Erin Miller at Palmetto Publishing and her team for their counsel, great work editing, and bringing this book to fruition from the very beginning. She diligently worked with me through every aspect of the process, and I could not have done it without her.

In a life as rich and long as mine, there are far too many to thank, so I will use this book as an opportunity to say a big thanks to all who helped me on my way through life. Without each and every one of you, there would be many fewer pages in this book. To all who helped me, please accept my gratitude in its abundance.

Introduction

A thrilling story that covers a broad spectrum of Wild and Hearty stories, form growing up in this very poor rural part of Ireland that formed this young adventure's mind. An endless list of stories and adventure, including the local political environment. The ongoing struggle for freedom in the homeland played a significant role in developing the young mind to always push the limits in every aspect of a much fulfilled life. With an uncanny drive to maximize every opportunity that life offered, where it always appeared that there was gold to be found at the end of every Rainbow. With a trail of great stories from a very poor upbringing in rural Ireland to London great town, where he lived for three years and then immigrated to the US where he got drafted into the US Army where he excelled served with distinction and awarded the United States Army Certificate of Achievement. Then moved on to a very successful intriguing career in civilian life while attending night school to further his education on the very generous GI bill. With a great family life, he could take on many enormous challenges that were always fulfilling while very demanding, requiring long hours and time away from home. A marriage of fifty-four plus years to date. Three wonderful children and five wonderful grandchildren and one Step-grand. How lucky we are, where family was always what mattered. Life was not always easy and there were many challenges, but every challenge when confronted with gusto, many times, turned into something positive, and that always made the overall effort worthwhile. It is now that he is heading towards the sunset and felt incumbent on telling his story. In particular, for his grandchildren, friends and all who enjoy a repertory of exciting story based on a long and wonderful life of excitement, adventure, achievement and success that is far beyond his wildest dream. If he had to live his life all over, there is not one thing to change. Indeed, a charmed life and for that he is so grateful to family, friends, the beautiful country where he was born and loves and spent his younger days, London, great town, the US Army and this great country that he also loves. God bless the United States of America, the Land of the Free and the Home of the Brave

CHAPTER 1

The Border

Growing up on the border between the Republic of Ireland and Northern Ireland from the 1940s to 1960 instilled a deep love of country. My parents were born and raised in British-occupied Northern Ireland and settled down across the border in the Irish Republic after they got married. My dad and his family were all Irish rebels; he wanted to raise their children to be Irish citizens rather than British subjects.

In this unique part of Ireland, nature has lavished the bounties of a beautiful, rugged landscape. There are hills, dales, mountains, rain, and glistering blue lakes surrounded by lush green fields, with forty shades of green and the beautiful sky and gorgeous clouds hanging overhead. There are heathery moors that carpet the bogland, which is brown with its beautiful soft purple cloak. There are rushes, furze bushes with their beautiful yellow blossoms that add a glow of beauty to the hills, and hawthorn hedges with beautiful purple flowers where the brown thrush sways and trills all along the roads and hedges. There are berries and fruit everywhere—wild strawberries, raspberries, blackberries, bilberries, blueberries, blackthorn sloes, wild apples, crab apples sweet and sour, and delicious wild plums. These wild berries are unimaginable and capture the souls of all who love nature's beauty, where wildlife and birds feed. In my childhood, the children loved to pick and sell the delicious bounty in the marketplace, where it brought in a little money—but a little money went a long way. The berries, rhubarb, and apples were used for making delicious jams, cakes, and pies from the home recipes that were handed down from mother to daughter over many generations. In this region of northwest Ireland, the women of the house were great bakers and cooks.

Most of the meals were made from nature's resources from the farm, as there was little money to buy comfort foods. Although the lifestyle was very poor, it was very rich in culture and diverse in many ways. Living so close to the boarder, there were pressures on our day-to-day survival too. Political strife was a way of life, along with living under an oppressor that only took from the Irish people and gave so little back. Policing the border was an exercise for the Irish Republic on the south side and British paramilitaries on the northern side. It was incumbent on the Irish government to provide the necessary policing on the south side of the border in order to demonstrate to the British government that Ireland was a good neighbor and not aiding or abetting the rebel forces. Otherwise, the British military would come into the republic in search of the rebels who were inflicting guerilla war tactics on the occupying forces. Policing on both sides of the border created a very politically charged, tense environment for the inhabitants of this rural border village and the surrounding area. The purpose of the policing on both sides of the border was to restrain would-be IRA rebel freedom fighters from blowing up the British army and customs posts at the border and to restrict their movement into Northern Ireland's countryside and towns, where they would plan their next attack on the British military establishment. The rebels would hide out in countryside safe houses and mountain terrain on both sides of the border, where they would spring surprise guerilla-type attacks on the British paramilitary establishment. Without the wall, the British military would come into the republic in search of the rebels who were inflicting guerilla war tactics on the occupying forces. The purpose of these attacks was to maintain a continuous level of antagonism in the region. They also wanted to maintain a constant reminder that there would never be peace until the oppressive occupiers picked up and left forever. In many ways all these paramilitary exchanges were welcomed by the local rebel supporters and made life somewhat exciting in this rural, very tranquil environment when there was a surprise attack on the British establishment by the IRA. The young—and in particular those influenced by rebel sentiment—had young minds that could quickly become engaged and get drawn into what was referred to as the cause (of freedom).

This lifestyle and political climate started challenging the young mind at a very early age. A ten-year-old child living in this environment could tell you more about the politics and who was in control than seasoned politicians in other parts of the world. In this environment the young established their loyalty to the cause of freedom at a very young age, which was why every generation grew its own new brew of freedom fighters.

Each new generation of freedom fighters became even more determined than those who went before them. They too were determined to fight for their freedom and to throw off forever the yoke of the tyrant oppressor. One might ask what motivated the young mind to pick up arms with the will to fight and die, when so many generations before them had fought for the same cause and failed in their daring mission. This was a tough cause—the occupying force was always too overpowering for the small rebel forces. Those early freedom fighters were out-manned and outgunned by the largest colonial empire known to man at that time.

Much of the reason for this "will-to-fight" can be tied to the conditions of the time. The lifestyle in this rural area was extremely poor for most of the people. The main livelihood for the people who inhabited these areas was farming; there was virtually no industry or market to create jobs. The farms were very small, and the land that ran along the border was poor-quality mountain land that had limited tilling capability for planting large crops.

The farmers would seek out plots of bogland that could be cultivated and tilled manually by using a manual spade rather than a plow to plant the necessary life-supporting crops.

Most of these little farms were created in the mountains after the farmers' eviction, by the British, from their own fertile fields and homes in the lowlands.

Plows and other machinery did not function well there, where there were a lot of rocks and clay with no more than an inch or two of fertile soil, or in many cases only bog peat residue.

The land was also very wet and soggy during rainy periods, when the clay underlayer had poor permeability and slowed down the rate of the soil percolation and was not good for many of the crops that the inhabitants needed to survive.

In the late '40s and '50s, the Irish government offered small grants to farmers in rural areas for land reclamation, including field drainage systems to improve the land for tillage to culti-vate better grass and hay fields. Crops would not do well in wet, soggy land.

In some cases, the crops would rot during wet seasons, and there would be very little to harvest. The same went for the hayfields and grazing land, where wet and soggy was not good for grass or hay. The poor farmers did not have money to purchase fertilizer and therefore used the animal manure, which they composted for their crops in large piles until it was ready to be used. As the Irish economy improved a little during the earlier years, the government offered small grants to fertilize. This was the best thing ever and paid off in a big way, as tillage and hayfield yields improved significantly and there was much greater product quality. When the land was properly fertilized, the poor farmers could increase their herd counts and crop production. The government also provided farm animal subsidies for sheep and cattle as a method to keep young farmers on the land.

Despite the welcome help from the Irish Government, there was very little money to be made in farming, since most of the markets for farm goods were in Britain and the British used their power over the new Irish Free State by controlling the marketplace. It was not until 1973, when the Irish government joined the European Common Market (EU), that the Irish Free State got its first break.

Entry into the EU created an economic environment for a New Ireland that was life changing. This economic boom, known as the "Celtic Tiger", saw large U.S, corporations, with significant investments, establish operations all over Ireland creating new good jobs and prosperity.

As a result, the Irish Republic today can be counted among the nations of the world that are prosperous, with a great standard of living and quality of life. It also has an excellent national health system and an educational system that is second to none.

Now it is very interesting to see that Britain competes with the rest of the world for Irish food products and Britian is Ireland's biggest export market, which is estimated at about 60 percent of all goods exported from the Republic of Ireland. Ireland's ability to freely compete on the world open market for the first time in its long history has propelled the republic to be a real success story; it really rose from the ashes of hundreds of years of tyrannical oppression.

CHAPTER 2

The Penal Laws/
Catholic Emancipation

The Penal Laws began in 1691 and continued until the days of the Catholic Emancipation in 1829. During this time, the nationalists, who were mostly Catholics, were evicted from their land and replaced by British and Scottish loyalists who were loyal to the Crown. The new arrivals were planted on the land where the indigenous people had lived before being evicted. The reason they were evicted was that they were not willing to give up their Catholic faith, join the Anglican Church, and pledge allegiance to the Crown. The evicted farmers fled to the mountains and foothills, where they carved out and reclaimed small patches of mountainside terrain and built little thatched mud huts as refuges where they tried to create a new existence.

During this tyrannical period, there were very large families—ten, twelve, or more children was not unusual. When evicted, many died from starvation at the hands of the oppressive tyrant occupier. When families were evicted, their friends and families would come together and help them build these little stone-and-mud thatched cottages as a portion of their survival. Even today, it is not uncommon to find the ruins of the mud huts and small graveyards on the sides of mountains and foothills. You would not expect to see these ruins of old homesteads where families lived for generations.

Remote graveyards were established so the peasant farmers could bury their dead with some level of respect and dignity. The tyrant occupier did not allow any type of public gathering or movement of the native people. Burials had to be carried out in hidden areas where the oppressor could not easily detect movement. The ruins of these graveyards can be found today. The land is dotted with old headstones that were cut from the rough fieldstone slabs dug up from the rocky fields and sculpted by the peasant farmers to honor their dead. These graveyards and headstones are preserved and valued as part of the Irish and EU historical preservation.

The ruins of these hidden graveyards that are situated in the valleys and dells of the Irish mountain foothills and bogs are a reminder of the suffering imposed on the people of Ireland by a cruel and ruthless occupying tyrant that prevailed for many generations. The farm I grew up on consisted of three small farms; one ran up to the foothill of the mountain where the ruins of the old structures known to the locals as "John Andes's auld walls" are still there. There are also the ruins of an old fieldstone fort. The fort was placed there to both secure the residences and to hide the little graveyard with its old headstones.

Today, this is an area where tourists and history buffs visit during the summer. In pictures and movies of the old Ireland, you can see little stone-and-mud thatched cottages, usually consisting of two or three rooms. There was no running water or bathroom facilities; the bathroom facilities consisted of maybe an outhouse hut that was not very comfortable or pleasant to use. These little thatched cottages, with their whitewashed walls, could be seen all over the hills and mountainsides of Ireland. In later years, what remains has become a tourist attraction, in particular for droves of Americans who love to trace their Irish ancestry; they love to rent these beautiful little cottages and tell their children and grandchildren about the great time they had tracing their roots. However, the tourist cottages of today are luxuries in comparison to the cottages of old; there is now hot and cold water and most of today's comforts.

This was a very sad period of Irish history, when these little white cottages dotted the hills and mountainsides of Ireland and from which many native inhabitants imigrated to distant lands in search of better lives.

When the old people passed away, the little mountain patches of land grew barren and desolate. The oppressor built castles and mansions all across the rich, fertile heartland of Ireland while the natives died from starvation in the mountains. They lived lives of luxury with butlers and servants while the victims of eviction in many cases were starving. It always amazes me how any of the native victims were able to survive these incredibly cruel times that lasted for centuries. Living in the mountains during the winter months, when the weather could be harsh, with long-lasting snow, was a death sentence for the old and sick.

Those who lived in the castles and mansions were the landlords and barons of Ireland. They imposed the farm rent and rates on the peasant farmers living in their makeshift mountain farms, which they had to build from fieldstone and mud with thatched straw roofs, while the landlord lived a life of luxury with slave servants. During these rough times, food from crops was so scarce it is said that the people had to eat grass to survive hunger at the hands of the tyrant.

It was not until later years, as younger generations emigrated and older folks died off, that many of these little farms and homesteads were abandoned to history. My grandmother on my mother's side of the family was one of seven children raised on a small mountainside farm patch. As she and her siblings came of age, all of them immigrated to the United States in the mid- to late 1800s. Eventually, all of them went back to Ireland except for one who stayed in the Bronx, New York. Those that came back did so with their little earned fortunes. The boys all bought little farms and raised families, and the girls married local farmers.

During her time in the United States, my grandmother spent about six years in New York City's Hell's Kitchen as a domestic servant. She loved America and loved to talk about her days in Hell's Kitchen and all her great friends and good times, but she always wanted to come back home and raise her family in Ireland It is in Ireland where she met my grandfather through what was said to be a matchmaker.

The mountain farm where my grandmother and her siblings grew up became a barren part of the mountainside, and when her parents died, there was no one to stay on the old mountainside farm. My grandmother loved that little mountainside farm, and although no one lived there, she loved to visit occasionally; although she had grown up very poor, she had fond memories of her parents and siblings. She would walk around the old homestead ruins like she was searching for a valuable jewel; that always brought a tear to her eye. When my children visited Ireland, a special treat was to take the quad up the mountain to visit the old homestead.

The Irish people have an uncanny love for the land as well as their country. The reason young people left the land and families they loved was not because they wanted to, but out of desperation. It was that or face a life of poverty, oppression, and possible starvation during those times. There was a time in Ireland when people lived under the terms of what was referred to as the Act of Settlement of 1652, after the Cromwell conquest of Ireland. (An additional Act of Settlement was passed by the British Parliament in 1701, mandating that successors to the English and Irish Crowns could be Protestants only.)

The oppressor drove the natives from their fertile farms and planted that same land with its own people; these were mostly Scottish, some British, and some Welsh who shared Cromwell views and were loyal to the Crown. During the penal days, people were not just robbed of their land and possessions, they were also not allowed to attend church, school, or any other type of assembly. There was what was called the hedge schools period, from 1702 to 1718; during this period school was illegal, and the only place dissidents could set up school was in remote places, such as behind tall hedges or ditches.

This is where the term "hedge school" originated. The imperial power's objective was to create an illiterate society where there would be fewer capable leaders to rise up and start an insurrection. This very oppressive period where there was no public schooling had a devastating effect on the nationalist population. Most of the nationalist farmers who had large families were ejected into a life of illiteracy, misery, and starvation.

Their land and livestock were confiscated by the occupier; it was again during these times when many Irish victims emigrated all over the world, and a large percentage came to the United States to escape hunger and starvation. In America, there was a strong British influence that was wielding the same cruel hatred and depraved annihilation upon the Irish immigrants. British colonialism in Ireland was no different from communism and other autocratic, sadistic, dictatorial regimes that ruled over people all over the world, where the natives lost all their rights and possessions.

CHAPTER 3

The Famine

The real cause of the so-called Irish potato famine from 1845 to 1849 was not the blight itself, but rather the British government. This was one of the greatest atrocities of all time because of how the British inflicted this horrific level of genocide, illiteracy, and destruction on the people of Ireland For many the only relief was to get out of the country, an option only available for those who were physically able. This is exactly what the British occupier wanted: to cleanse the country by getting rid of the Catholic/nationalist population and replacing it with Scottish and English Anglicans who were loyal to the Crown strengthening their hold on the island of Ireland.

During these catastrophic times, the British government confiscated Irish crops and food supplies and shipped them off to Britain to feed her loyal subjects. Across the channel, there was a raging crop blight that started in Britain around 1845 and spread to Ireland by 1846.

This act of aggression caused one of the greatest atrocities of that time; the number of deaths by starvation was estimated in the millions. The death toll was far reaching. People not only died at home, but also on ships bound for foreign lands. The ships that provided passage for the Irish emigrants to America and Canada and other foreign lands were referred to as "coffin ships" because of the numbers of fleeing emigrants who died on the voyages. Many of the dead were buried at sea, where their families never knew what became of them or if they were alive or dead. Because there were too few doctors on the coffin ships, as people died, many were simply thrown overboard in great numbers.

When they landed, they died in great numbers along the roadsides and were left to die, and in many cases, they lay there until eaten by wild animals. If the wild animals did not get the corpses, they were buried in mass graves.

Many who survived the voyage, died soon after they landed. When the ships landed in the United States, there were not enough doctors and medical services on the mainland to attend to the sick and dying. On land there were so many sick and dying it could take weeks for immigrants to see a doctor or get medical attention, and as a result they died. The roads were littered with dead bodies in such great numbers that in many cases they had to be dragged and pushed into mass graves along the way. They died from pure starvation, malnutrition, and disease caused by the hunger imposed on them by a heartless oppressor. In the United States and British colonies, the starving immigrants, who survived the coffin ships, found themselves dealing with the same evil-empire handlers, who were completely indifferent to their very basic survival needs and, in many cases, wished them only ill.

This was not a potato famine, as was published in the British press as part of its propaganda and deception narrative. In many cases, when the Irish arrived in the United States, they were met by the same people who had evicted them out of their land in Ireland and now showed their profound hatred for the unfortunate immigrants who were at their mercy.

To his credit, the British Prime Minister Tony Blair, in June 1997, made a public apology at a festival in County Cork commemorating the Irish famine. He stated that those who had governed in London at that time had failed their people. A gross understatement in my opinion. The Irish prime minister at that time, John Burton, welcomed Tony Blair's statement and admission of the past crimes against humanity. He recognized that millions of Irish people had died from starvation at the hands of the British occupier.

Some would say this apology was too little too late, which I do not agree with for a variety of reasons—in particular, it is now on record. I believe that the statement of apology and acknowledgment by the British prime minister will help in a somewhat philosophical way to make public the wrongdoing in the history books for future generations. A reprehensible genocide of this magnitude, where the Irish population dropped from 8.4 million to 6.6 million from 1845 to 1852 or thereabouts, can never be erased from history.

An honest and sincere acknowledgment by a government leader can establish time for future generations to heal. Now there is an opportunity to rewrite history and correct this shameful injustice, and to write a new chapter in Irish history for present and future generations.

Because I am something of a history buff and love to research history, it was a little surprising to read that the Irish, English, Scotch, and Welch share much of the same gene pool. It makes perfect sense, since the same Celtic tribes plundered all of the British Isles, followed by the Norse and Norman conquerors, who also plundered all of the British Isles, including Ireland, for hundreds of years. There also has been mass movement of people back and forth across the channel, including conquering forces, and then there was the plantation of Ireland by the British. I recently discovered that one of my own ancestors on my father's side was English in origin and moved to Ireland somewhere in the mid-tenth century from around Lancashire, England. It is said that they were lords and barons. It is more than likely that they too moved to Ireland as plantation barons.

Not surprisingly, my DNA has an Irish, Scottish, English, and Scandinavian mix as there is "No ethnic purity in Ireland." Although a lot of emphasis is put on Irish historical names like Murphy, Kelly, and Donovan—and the list goes on—in fact there is a very large segment of the Irish population in the north and south where the names are a mix of many different nationalities, in particular Scottish, English, Scandinavian, Norse, and Norman. I believe diversity is a good thing and makes nations stronger. However, it would have come to my dad, a rebel at heart, as a big surprise to discover British blood was running through his veins.

Many of the Irish rebellions were instigated by names such as "Pearse", "Tone" and others who were Protestant and came from the English aristocracy. Even though they had British roots, they were Irish freedom fighters—and believed in a united Ireland.

CHAPTER 4

Love of Country

The love of one's country is a magnificent manifestation of how one feels about one's country to the point where a person is unconditionally willing to fight and die to defend and protect the country and its freedom. As stated in the lyrics of the Irish ballad, The Patriot Game, "the love of one's country banishes fear with the speed of a flame and makes us all part of the patriot game". The ballad is set in the period following World War II and is about fighting and dying for one's country. There is no greater calling than that which inspires and inflames the minds of so many that wish to free their country from the yoke of imperialism. Those brave men and women are willing to make any sacrifice, including their own lives, for a cause that is greater than life. During the 1950s, the IRA launched a new campaign to bring about the reunification of Northern Ireland with the Irish Republic. Again, the occupiers learned very quickly the strength and will of the Irish people to free their country from the yoke of imperialism.

The determination to fight for one's country's land and life, where each new rising is always more determined and ferocious than the previous one, or at least it seems to be that way, was very evident during the Troubles from 1968 to 1998. The occupier cannot underestimate the manifestation of the love for one's country to death and the last man standing, which has been demonstrated in countries all over the world when they are occupied by a foreign invader.

Nowhere in the world was this manifestation demonstrated more magnificently than in the United States of America after 9/11. The events of 9/11 enflamed young men and women, who signed up in droves for the US military, including the great Pat Tillman, who was an outstanding football player and scholar who left the National Football League as a young, prominent star to enlist. He enlisted in the military following the September 11 attacks to fight for his country. Again, look at the determination and bravery of the Ukrainian people, young and old, who are willing to fight and die for their beautiful country, none finer. These people put their country first and their own lives and family second. What better example is there of love of country? Despite all that is heard about the apathy of young people in the United States, when it came to defending their country, 9/11 proved that nothing has changed. Young people were more patriotic than ever and ready to pick up arms and fight at the drop of a hat to defend the country they loved. It is a shame that it takes incidents like world wars or 9/11 for people to see how patriotic our young men and women really are. Our young people of all races and creeds are just as brave and patriotic today as any of those who came before them when it comes to defending their country against a foreign foe. It is this very concept that the enemy must understand; there is no greater demonstration of love of country than the willingness to fight and die for its freedom. These young people are willing to impose great suffering and hardship on themselves and their immediate families and loved ones to fight and protect their country.

I have great admiration and believe that there is no higher honor than the desire to fight and die for the freedom of one's country, whether it be the country where you were born or your adopted country. There were many Irish uprisings with the objective to rid Ireland of occupation. Some of the first major uprisings to be documented were as follows:

1780   Napper Tandy was a revolutionary, plotting against the Crown.

1798   The United Irishmen uprising was led by Wolfe Tone.

1803   A few years later, Robert Emmet led an uprising.

1848   That was followed by the Fenian Rising.

1916   Easter week uprising; Irish independence. The Irish Free State was established in 1922.

One of the challenges and quagmires that remained after the Irish Republic was declared was that Ireland was partitioned; six of the thirty-two counties stayed under British occupation. A large percent of Irish nationals wanted England completely out of Ireland and vowed there would never be peace until that objective was accomplished. The partition of Ireland was the root cause of the Troubles, and not Catholic-versus-Protestant hatred.

The British were notorious for creating division everywhere they ruled to weaken the overall will of the people. It was always they who tried to label the Troubles as a Catholic-versus-Protestant sectarian conflict to drive their propaganda scheme to mislead the public. In reality, it was a war of equal rights and justices with the desire to unify the country into one independent nation of Ireland.

For the most part, the Irish people are extremely tolerant when it comes to religious preferences.

When it comes to selecting political leaders, the Irish people all through the ages have demonstrated time and again that they vote for who they believe is the best person for the job, rather than choosing any particular denomination or sector. Many of the great Irish patriots who died for Ireland were Protestant, with at least one English parent who lived and grew up in Ireland.

Although 95 percent of the population in the Republic of Ireland was Catholic, they still elected many non-Catholic leaders, starting with Mr. Childers, who belonged to the Anglican Church of Ireland. He was president from 1973 to 1974, and he died in office. The Catholic-versus-Protestant conflict was pure propaganda created by the British in Ireland. This false narrative was carried over to the United States, in particular during the famine. It was during this period that the saying "No Irish Catholics need apply" arose. This depraved slogan was seen all over the United States where there was a vacancy or hiring sign.

This inhumane treatment added to the horrific suffering of the desperate famine victims who after having nowhere to turn, came the US, and ended up in the same quandary they had originally tried to get away from. The irony of this heinous genocide is that while one nationality was trying to rid the other, they were in fact not different, but of the same bloodline. Today, through DNA testing, we know that the Irish, the English, the Scots, and the Welsh share a common bloodline.

In addition to President Childers, there were several other high-profile leaders of diverse backgrounds elected in Ireland. Let me just mention a few: Mr. Briscoe, who was Jewish, 1956 to 1957, lord mayor of Dublin, who again served a second term as lord mayor of Dublin, 1961 to 1962; Mr. de Valera, 1917 to 1973, president of the new Republic of Ireland, who had an Irish mother and a Spanish father; and the list goes on.

The above political record speaks very well of the Irish people and their ability to be objective rather than biased when it comes to selecting the best political leaders for their country. The record shows that they vote for whoever they think is the best leader rather than on religion or any other affiliation. The British government tried to portray the Irish in its media propaganda as narrow-minded Catholic ideologues to fit its disingenuous narrative.

During the mid-1950s there was a small-scale Irish uprising that escalated in 1969 into what was known as the Troubles. The IRA militants, freedom fighters during the period, launched a guerilla tactical-type warfare whose strategy was to make surprise guerilla attacks on the British establishments throughout Northern Ireland and the British mainland and beyond. The objective was to inflict as much destruction and chaos as possible to rid the British occupier from the island of Ireland and unify the six northern counties under British rule with the Irish Republic.

During the Troubles there were shameful deeds committed against innocent people on both sides of the divide in Northern Ireland, where innocent people were maimed and killed as part of a fierce war and retaliation by both sides. Both parties were willing to commit heinous crimes against their opponent, which tragically often included innocent citizens.

It was much like what we see going on in Gaza as a result of the October 7th incident. Although war is never just or fair, it was especially unconscionable that so many innocent families became victims and that most of the unfair victimization was perpetrated by the British army and its paramilitary forces as part of the British strategy to deter young recruits from joining the rebel cause. However, that strategy did not work and only inflamed the minds of the nationalist youth who joined the IRA freedom fighters in droves, resulting in all-out war in Northern Ireland and across the British mainland. The guerilla war spread to other places where there was a British presence, such as Gibraltar. The objective was to prove that there was no safe zone within the British Empire in which to hide.

This was one of the most corrupt and nasty wars ever, where the British intelligence forces were totally corrupt and totally unethical in their mission to get the upper hand over the IRA freedom fighters. There was no regard for the innocent people on both sides who got hurt, killed, and maimed. The British army and paramilitary groups colluded with the Ulster Unionist Party (UUP) to kill and maim groups of innocent people on a mass scale. The British intelligence forces selected innocent targets to be murdered; this approach prompted European humanitarian groups to get more involved because they vigorously condemned this type of action, which was in violation of international law and the Geneva Conventions. When the humanitarian organizations from Europe and the United States published their findings, they depicted shocking, gruesome, and unacceptable violations under the terms of all war crimes guidelines.

Because of the horrific injustices and crimes against humanity that were now made public by the humanitarian agencies in the news media and world press, there was an outcry, and great pressure was exerted on the British government by the U.S. and European governments and humanitarian organizations to resolve this conflict. What is still shameful today is that British Parliament's recent legislation approved a Northern Ireland reconciliation bill. The purpose of the reconciliation bill is to prevent lawsuits from being brought against the British army for the collusion and killings and atrocities against innocent people, all of which was in violation of the Good Friday Agreement. The bill has faced strong condemnation from the Irish government, the United Nations, the Council of Europe, and the U.S. Congress. It was during the 1998 Good Friday Agreement that the nationalists (Catholics) and unionists (Protestants) came together in a power-sharing agreement. The power-sharing agreement for the most part brought an end to the conflict. Peace and a reasonable level of prosperity came to this war-torn part of Ireland. The Good Friday Agreement has made way for a more level playing field and created an environment for more prosperity, which improved the lives of those who suffered so much. The Good Friday Agreement peace dividend has already improved the lives of a great number of the people in Northern Ireland in many ways: there are more good jobs and a fairer system, including housing and the elimination of the ongoing gerrymandering of the voting system, which has led to 2022's Sinn Féin victory, making it the leading elected political party in Northern Ireland.

There will be a whole new array of opportunities from new global investors that will now feel safe to invest and set up operations in Northern Ireland. Britain will be expected to invest more in social programs—in particular, health, education, and infrastructure. The most important part of the peace dividend will be a great effort by the people on both sides of the divide.

They will have to work together for the common good rather than continue fighting and destroying the fabric of this beautiful province, Ulster.

Other parts of the world, where freedom fighters are fighting similar types of wars and have similar ideologies, may be inspired by the Good Friday Agreement outcome. They too may try to end their conflicts in a similar way. Freedom fighters all over the world who are fighting for the freedom of their country or occupied land have a common thread that often brings them together.

Countries outside Ireland had difficulty understanding the Troubles. There was a massive propaganda spin launched by the British media that labeled the Troubles a Catholic-versus-Protestant sectarian war. Labeling the war a sectarian conflict distracted world opinion away from the real problem, which was exactly what the Brits wished for. This was totally disingenuous and contrary to the real issue of the occupation and oppression imposed by the British on the nationalists to keep them down and controlled, just as they did during the hedge school period and well into the twentieth century. This method of deception was used against the Irish people for centuries and did nothing but prolong the incentive for each generation to rise up and fight for freedom, as they so bravely did all down through the ages. The outside world did not understand what the war was really about, and as a result, did not take it seriously.

The real struggle was about British occupation and oppression, the gerrymandering of the voting system, and unjust labor laws where people were imprisoned without trial for years, and in some cases for decades, in Northern Ireland and on the British mainland. These unfair, unjust laws were imposed on the people in what was a police state similar to the USSR.

Only property owners could vote, which led into their sinister narrative that if you did not own property, you were ineligible to vote. There was a very unfair and unequal distribution of public housing by the government to again disqualify nationalists from voting.

The unfair public housing was part of the gerrymandering of the voting system in order for the establishment to maintain control and prop up its puppet government in Northern Ireland.

In addition to the unfair housing, there were unfair discriminatory labor practices.

All the nationalists were forced to live in what was a police state that was in collusion with the Ulster Unionist Party, making sure that they stayed in control and loyal to the Crown. Nationalists living in Northern Ireland had fewer rights and a higher level of oppression by far; it was worse than that of communist countries or South Africa's apartheid. Nationalists could not move around freely without continual harassment by British paramilitary extremists. Innocent people on their way to church services would get held up, searched, and harassed by British troops and other paramilitaries.

This was a deliberate attempt by the British paramilitaries and the army to make them arrive late or completely miss their church service. Again, it was not until the outside world started to understand the magnitude of the collusion and injustices that were imposed on the nationalist minority that change finally began.

Many of the very influential American congressmen and senators that formed the Irish National Caucus demanded that there be a high-level investigation into all the grievances of the nationalists in Northern Ireland. The British government fought this investigation tooth and nail but to no avail, due to the level of incriminating evidence and the power of the Irish National Caucus in Washington, D.C.

The Irish National Caucus, established by Father Sean Mc-Manus, consisted of some of the most powerful people in Congress and the Senate. The findings of wrongdoing, collusion, and deliberate crimes against the nationalists were extraordinary, and a demand for change was raised.

These high-level powers of the American and European governments put pressure on the British government so it could no longer hide behind its wall of propaganda and deception. That was when meaningful things started to happen, and the very impressive British propaganda network started to crumble and to some degree lose its voice. As the old saying goes, when you lose your reputation, you lose everything.

The purpose of the British deception was to keep the nationalists down by not letting them have jobs or housing and tarnishing them as troublemakers/terrorists/religious ideologues rather than the true freedom fighters they were. The nationalists were fighting for equality, justice, and freedom in their own homeland. It must be recognized that the IRA also carried out some heinous crimes against innocent people in its struggle for freedom and equality. I cannot condone crimes against innocent people, no matter what the cause or motive might be. In my heart, I have the deepest sympathy for all the innocent people on both sides who were maimed and murdered. The innocent are the real victims who suffered so much and lost loved ones that will leave a void and a pain in their hearts that will never go away. It is yet more unconscionable to learn that the British paramilitaries and British intelligence forces perpetrated the majority of the most heinous crimes on the people that they were supposed to be protecting and now they want a reconciliation bill to let them hide and walk away from their horrific crimes against humanity while giving amnesty to thugs and murderers. The British authorities, as always, betrayed the people that relied on them for security and protection.

It was the British forces and paramilitaries that were for the most part the problem, colluding and committing the worst type of heinous crimes against the people instead of providing some level of protection and security for the innocent people on both sides of the divide. It was the British army and paramilitaries that launched their own campaign of the most vicious types of heinous crimes of all against the innocent people living in nationalist and Catholic neighborhoods who were not involved in any way with the struggle of the freedom fighters.

Finally, the free world became aware of the real problem in Northern Ireland, and none more than the great Father Sean McManus, a founder of the Irish National Caucus.

The Irish National Caucus in Washington, D.C. played a major role in getting a large number of United States representatives on Northern Ireland's side, including President Bill Clinton and his envoy, Sen. George Mitchell. They played a major role in the peace process and formed a high-level negotiating committee that paved the way to the 1998 Good Friday Agreement. As a result, the Irish people give much credit to Clinton and Mitchell as major players in establishing the agreement. There was no better man, once he got on board, to lead the peace process than President Clinton. He deployed Mitchell, one of his most able political negotiators, who did an incredible job against all odds and deserves great credit and gratitude.

The British Prime Minister Tony Blair and the Irish Prime Minister Bertie Ahern also played a major role and were instrumental in providing the necessary support for making things happen. All the above leaders provided a mechanism to keep the initiative on track. The Republic of Ireland played a very important role in bringing about a sense of linkage in pursuing a common goal. There were benefits for both the north and south to break down that cursed border that had divided Ireland north and south.

For close to a century, there was no official commerce or trade between north and south other than by smugglers from the time the border was put in place. That both the north and south were part of the European Union during those years also contributed to the success of the Good Friday Agreement.

With all that said, and with all the very impressive leaders, this agreement could never have been brought to fruition if it were not for the Reverend Ian Paisley, first minister of Northern Ireland. In spite of all odds, he came to the table and worked with the negotiators. He was one of the most ardent unionist leaders who spewed hate and contempt against nationalists and demonized the IRA but became one of the most significant players in the breakthroughs of the peace agreement. He surprised most people on both sides of the divide by eventually agreeing to support the Good Friday Agreement.

In spite of great opposition from his own party, he had the will and the courage to do what was right and deserves a great deal of credit; he will go down in the annals of Irish and world history as a man of character and courage despite the inflammatory oratory of hate and division by which he led his people for decades.

Many other British leaders had attempted to resolve the ongoing conflict, but when it came down to making a deal to resolve the conflict, they always sold out the nationalists.

This was never more evident than when Prime Minister John Major found himself in a politically difficult situation in his bid for reelection in 1997. He too sold out the nationalists to get the unionist vote in order to rein in more seats for his bewildered fledgling Tory Party. He still lost the election and deserved to.

Any man or woman who does not have the courage to stand up for his or her own convictions does not deserve to lead the people he or she represents.

With that said, British prime minister Tony Blair was a major player in the peace process, and for the first time in Irish history, he was an honest and a very effective British leader who worked with the Irish government and all the players in bringing about a resolution that to this day has delivered a great peace dividend.

In spite of the great odds, for the first time in history, the people of Northern Ireland are, for the most part, living in peace; sectarian violence is down to the lowest level in years. The people of Northern Ireland on all fronts are demonstrating a concerted effort to live in peace and harmony with their neighbors. This is a wonderful accomplishment in which all the people of this part of the island of Ireland are winners. The peace dividend has delivered a much better lifestyle for all the people of Northern Ireland, where there is a better future for their children and generations to come.

As new foreign investment comes to the region, creating jobs and opportunity, there will be more prosperity for all the people, which to some degree will help to mend the scars of the past. When there is poverty, there is strife, and when there is strife, there are no winners. All the people in the region will be elated at seeing the level of prosperity that peace can bring.

In the world of business, two of the most important factors are stability and reliable, conscientious workers who want to work hard and bring prosperity to themselves and their employers. For the first time in decades, children can play in the streets of Northern Ireland without fear and disruption. The tanks and guns that raced up and down the streets of Belfast and other Northern Ireland cities and towns and created an environment of fear and intimidation are for the most part gone. All the great leaders who played an important role in the Good Friday Agreement's success are to be commended for their great work.

Most of all, their commitment and dedication to peace and justice in a land that has suffered so much at the hands of the oppressor were yeomen's work and more than admirable.

We must keep in mind that all the countries that colonized all over the world left similar destruction and savagery behind them; none came to improve the natives' lifestyle, but rather to take all they could and in many cases rape and plunder. None were worse than the Norsemen. Below are some of the words of the Irish king Brian Boru, who conquered the Danes at Clontarf in 1014.

Stand ye now for Erin's glory! Stand ye now for Erin's
cause!
Long ye've groaned beneath the rigors of the Norsemen's
savage laws…
They have razed our proudest castles—spoiled the
Temples of the Lord—
Burned to dust our sacred relics—put the Peaceful to
the sword—
Desecrated all things holy—as they soon may do again,
If their power today we smite not—if today we be
not men!

Today in Ukraine, its déjà vu, man's inhumanity to man,
where war and destruction from another tyrant occupier have
engulfed the country. The savagery goes on all over the world,
in particular today in a number of the African and South American countries.

We thought mankind was getting smarter and more civ-
ilized, but find this idea no longer holds true because we see
the horrors of war and destruction in so many places throughout the world. It seems that mankind is going backward. Then
there are the great world powers that spend large percentages
of their budgets on weapons of mass destruction, including nu-
clear weapons. That begs the question, "Where will it all end?"

CHAPTER 5

The Smuggler

One of the small economic benefits of living in a pre–European Union border community in a time when everyone was very poor was that it provided small opportunities. Smuggling provided an opportunity to make a little extra money selling farm and other products across the border for a higher price; that opportunity would not exist farther north or south of the border. Smuggling became a way of life for people trading back and forth across the border. Although smuggling was illegal on both sides of the border, that fact did not seem to deter the traffickers. Smuggling offered a significant advantage for farmers when they could smuggle their products across the border. The products would be traded on whichever side of the border was paying more.

There was always the risk of the smuggler getting caught by the Northern Ireland or Irish Republic customs authorities. There was also a significant risk if the smuggler got caught—not only would the product be taken, but if a vehicle was involved, it would be lifted and not returned. The products being smuggled included everything—groceries, farm livestock, household appliances, farm machinery and equipment, fertilizer, and so on.

Despite the risk, smuggling was a worthwhile effort, since most people started at a very young age and knew how to evade the authorities. At the local town markets, there would be people as young as ten years of age selling smuggled farm products, while the elders would be selling smuggled cattle, sheep, pigs, horses, donkeys, and anything else where there was money to be made. The smugglers' task was made easier by the fact that most of the participants lived along the border and knew the terrain very well.

Most of the smugglers had family or close friends on both sides of the border who could help them work through the process; they would provide a staging area where the product would get picked up and transported to the local market.

What also made the smugglers' quest very interesting was that Protestants and Catholics, who were at great odds from a sectarian political point of view, would trade as partners, and in many situations great friendships were developed on an ongoing, prolonged basis.

When it came to doing business, they were all friends, and all the barriers came down, at least when there was money to be made.

In these border town communities, the locals, including the young, could pick out which side a stranger traveling through the area was on—without knowing anything about the person—better than some of the intelligence forces. Each group had an uncanny intuition where they could immediately identify the opposition 95 percent of the time although they may never have seen the stranger before. This level of intuition was generated through the intense brainwashing on both sides from a very early age. Some of the clues for identifying strangers were the clothes they wore, how they wore their hair, their demeanors, and other factors that people were cognizant of and observed somewhat differently in their culture.

When it came to smuggling, nobody cared about religion or politics; they cared only about how they could work together to complete their transaction and make a little money.

It was very common for those on both sides of the divide to share common trading partners and smuggling intelligence, such as where the authorities' hideouts were.

The smugglers were very loyal to one another, with no religious or political barriers. They would risk the possibility of being charged for aiding and abetting should they get caught and end up under oath before a magistrate of the court. It was said that many of them would commit perjury to protect one of their coconspirators.

The smugglers were like a cult that socialized and met up in the pubs, telling their war stories. When fellow smugglers got wind of danger that lay ahead, they would immediately let their comrades know using all kinds of primitive, but creative, communications at a time when there were no cell phones or any type of radio equipment that was affordable or, in many cases, available. Although the method of communicating at that time was primitive in nature, they improvised and came up with methods that were extremely effective and alien to the authorities.

The border was monitored by the Irish Republic's customs agents on the south side. On the other side, Northern Ireland's customs agents and B-Specials, who were a paramilitary group supporting the British customs establishment, and the Royal Ulster Constabulary (RUC), another paramilitary group, on guard around the clock. That made smuggling much more challenging. The customs personnel would hide out in the ditches and bushes all along the border and up in the mountains.

The Northern Ireland B-Specials were known to fire on fleeing smugglers, which created the greatest fear for the smugglers.

The astute smugglers had mapped out routes through very challenging terrain, and in the winter, there could be heavy snow in the higher mountain ranges. The smugglers knew the terrain better than the law enforcement groups, since they grew up in the area and knew all the hiding places and potential trouble spots. They also knew all the escape routes and the treacherous terrain where there were sinkholes and quicksand that they would lead the pursuing authorities into in order to escape; it was said that some law enforcement personnel got lost and were never seen again. The most common smuggled products would range from eggs, butter, and groceries to farm products, cattle, sheep, horses, household appliances, and farm equipment. Large farm equipment was very difficult to move through the mountains during inclement weather. The mountain bogs were wet, swampy, and treacherous for the on-foot smuggler.

Many methods were used to transport the very heavy commodities, although most of the smuggling was done on foot through the mountains.

Some smugglers were big, strong men who could carry large loads on their backs. The heavy materials, such as household appliances and farm equipment, required a truck to transport them, which was very risky, and if the smugglers were caught, the vehicle would be seized as well as the merchandise. A smuggler would have spotters in the dark of night with high-powered flashlights scoping out the route. If the spotters saw any indication of trouble when the smuggler was getting close to crossing the border, they would raise the flashlight in the air and swirl it around. The flashlight code would signal to the smuggler that there was danger ahead. When smugglers saw signs of trouble, they would turn back and take a different route, where there would be the same or similar surveillance by another spotter group that would use the same high-powered-flashlight-code technique. The spotters could not be easily distinguished from the many hunters who used high-powered flashlights to blind rabbits and hares so the hunters' trained dogs could easily grab the prey and bring it back to their masters. It was also said that when the smugglers were planning a large transaction of equipment or machinery, they would have spotters in a far-off secluded area who would fire off gunshots to distract law enforcement; the law enforcement personnel would all run in the direction of the gunshots, creating a window of opportunity for the smugglers to get through. If the customs authorities caught the spotters giving any type of signaling, they could be charged with aiding and abetting the smugglers and brought in front of the local magistrate to testify under oath. Aiding and abetting the smugglers was considered a crime, but there was no documented history of such charges ever being made to stick.

Smugglers had a macho reputation and very rarely got caught. There were extensive war stories of escape and evasion in the mountain wilderness during the dark of night while holding on to the smuggled goods. There were many stories where an unarmed customs official chased the smuggler and ended up in a boghole, never to be seen again.

Many times, officials got beaten up and dunked into large bogholes; they also came close to drowning in the wild mountain terrain where there was no one to come to their rescue. It was not until the word came down that customs officials and police were allowed to carry and use firearms in self-defense that the smugglers had to refrain from any type of confrontation with law enforcement. There was also a very stiff jail sentence for any type of confrontation with law enforcement. These macho tales gave a great deal of incentive to the young smugglers, including me, to be as good as or better than their older predecessors. This was an exciting adventure for the young smuggler where adrenaline was always flowing at the maximum due to fear of getting caught by the authorities on both sides of the border. Many times, the smuggler had to hide out in haunted old graveyards, fortresses, bogs, and old peat bog holes where peat was removed and harvested for home heating. Many times, the smuggler would hide for hours in a boghole full of water after hiding the products from the eyes of law enforcement by covering the goods with heather camouflage and other bog debris. Many smugglers ended up with serious illnesses due to the wet and cold suffered while in hideouts; although they were young and strong, some endured fatal illnesses such as pneumonia and tuberculosis. The smugglers had many gruesome ghost stories to tell while hiding out in graveyards, fortresses, ruins of old structures, and caves. Although the smugglers were tough people, according to the folklore of that time, many also got lost. They got lost in the rough mountain elevations where there were huge snowdrifts that could be up to twelve feet.

Then there was dense fog and rain (known as the mist) where visibility was so poor that if the smuggler put their hand out, they would not see their hand right in front of them. A good sense of direction and good mountain navigation skills, including knowing when to take shelter, could be lifesaving. It was easier to navigate during daylight, when the fog lifted and bad storms passed by. In life many times there is only one chance to get it right, and if we do not, the results can be catastrophic. There were smugglers who lost their way and walked into very deep bog sinkholes that were like quicksand, got swallowed up, and were never seen again. There were also stories where some ran so far into mountain caves to hide from law enforcement that they lost their way and were never found.

The area locals would spend months searching for the missing smuggler who got lost in the mountains and caves but was never found dead or alive. It was said that in the mountains the wild, human carcasses could have been eaten by a wild mountain animal. Each tragedy would add another page to the smugglers' folklore stories. The stories would be exaggerated to the maximum with all the gruesome details of good storytelling. These stories were repeated over and over during long winter nights by some of the best storytellers of their time, around a big peat hearth fire that would warm the cockles of your heart, where tea, soda breads, or Irish scones would be served by the matriarch of the home. In some ways these were very sad stories, but mostly they were very spirited, full of adventure, where the makeup of the smuggler for the most part was full of adventure while the smuggler was living on the edge with the phenotype of the next hero smuggler who would be remembered and would add to the many legends of smugglers in folklore and history.

CHAPTER 6

A Border Town

Life on the border as a young lad was a wonderful experience. Despite the struggle to survive on a small farm, I would not trade my childhood for the most lavish lifestyle money can buy. Every day was an adventure and something new. Although we were as poor as church mice, we never felt poor because everyone else was in the same boat. No one had any money, and riches were measured by the amount of land, cattle, sheep, and all other entities on the farm, including farm equipment.

How well you ate was based on how well you managed your farm and the crops that provided the main source of food for both the family and the animals. The crops that were harvested had to last until the next harvest crop was ready for consumption, and that was part of survival. Growing crops successfully is a science where extensive knowledge and know-how are required to have a successful crop. Yield and quality are very important to feed family and livestock, which was necessary for survival. Although no one had any money, the people never complained; they were as happy and proud of their farms, family, and lifestyle as if they were all millionaires.

When we were planting a particular crop, it was important to select the right soil and manure in order to have the right chemistry and nutrients to grow a healthy crop. In those days there was little commercial fertilizer, and the poor farmer could not afford to buy what was available, and therefore the farm livestock manure was the only source of fertilizer available for use. There was cow manure, horse manure, pig manure, and fowl manure, which all had different applications. Again, each manure type had to be properly selected; this was critical in order to have successful crops that were so essential. One could always tell when passing a crop field if the proper manure and quantity had been used.

My dad was very conversant and knowledgeable when selecting the right manure for each of the designated crops. When a fine, healthy crop appeared, it was also important to know and understand what type of preventive measures were required at different stages of growth to prevent fungus or black blight or other diseases that could kill the crop. This lesson was reinforced by the horrors of the Great Famine during the mid-1840s.

As a result of the famine, farmers became more creative and started to make up their own limestone- and bluestone-type sprays, which were used to control fungus and blight.

Lime kilns were built all over the farm countryside to make limestone and bluestone limes that could be used to make a spray solution to spray the crops to prevent another devastating blight. In today's world, pesticides and herbicides such as Reglone are widely used. Again, a high level of knowledge was required to get the right effective crop spray mix, which had to be thoroughly applied to the tops of the stalk leaves, where it would travel downward into the stalk stem. During these early years, there were no overhead spray machines or equipment to apply and measure the proper spray mix.

A very primitive homemade brush made from long heather stalks with a fine bushy head material was used to apply the spray. The applicator would apply the spray using a back-and-forth throwing motion to get an effective level of spray on all the leaves and down to the stem of the stalk. However, applying the spray correctly was very important because too much spray could burn the leaves and kill the plant, and not enough spray might not protect the crop, and that was where due diligence was imperative. My father was very knowledgeable in the spray application and would mentor friends and neighbors on the proper mix and application. He took great pride in his abilities and loved his work. He worked from dawn to dark every day except Sunday, when he only did what had to be done, such as checking on livestock.

Friends and neighbors would say, "Your dad is a great man who works day and night and never tires." He would stock all kinds of harvested farm food supplies in great quantities. He was always happy, and you could hear him singing his favorite rebel songs while working in the fields. He loved his family and work, never complained, and always wore a welcoming smile of contentment. The supplies would not only feed his own family but also let him have a little extra should a friend or neighbor be in need, and in particular poor people living in the little local village. If he knew someone in need, he would have us drop off a little of whatever was needed on their doorstep on our way to school.

He was a very proud, generous man and a wonderful father whose whole life was his family, which he was extremely proud of. He was always very positive and liked to see people doing well and feeling good about themselves. If a neighbor, friend, or poor person needed food to survive, he and my mother would never send them away empty-handed and would always say, "What God gives, God can take."

He would say how important it was to share, even if it meant a little less for oneself.

He had great intuition and could tell when something was wrong or if something was bothering a family member, a friend, or a neighbor. When someone in the family or extended family needed help, he would be the first there to help in any way he could.

Because of his hard work, we always had plenty of food and turf to keep the house warm during the cold winter. Although there were ten mouths to be fed on the somewhat small farm, he would never apply for any type of government assistance. When he reached the age of seventy, he was entitled to the old-age pension but did not apply until he was well into his seventies. It was not until friends and family encouraged him to collect the old-age pension that he did so. His friends would say, "Look at all the young, strong, healthy men collecting everything the state has to offer."

He was happy with a very simple life where he smoked his pipe and enjoyed a pint of Guinness now and then but always said, "With a family of ten, I cannot afford to drink."

His entertainment was visiting his only brother and two living sisters and their families, with whom he was very close. He loved to read and had a great knowledge of current events. He was very interested in what was going on in local politics but never got involved other than to help as needed. He had only a third-grade education but was self-educated by reading, and his great interest in community and world affairs made him one of the people sought out by friends and neighbors when there were rumors of uncertainty in the community or the world.

He was a man of great depth, loyalty, and a very rich intuition in everything that mattered. I am sure if he'd had the opportunity to get a better education he would have excelled in the business world. When people tell me "You are just like your dad," I am humbled and have to tell them I have not yet reached that pinnacle. He loved to talk about local football, which he and his brother played as young men. His great grasp of Irish politics and world affairs made him the go-to guy for world politics and current events. When the more educated visitors would come by, he loved to get into conversations about world affairs that would surprise the visitors with the depth of his knowledge. The strangers would gaze at his grasp of the detail, which made him sound much more educated than what would be expected of a peasant farmer. He was always very concerned about the well-being and success of his children and was always there to support us in everything we did. One of his favorite sayings was "It is not how well we do as parents that we will be judged by but how well our children do." He was a big believer in a good education and continually preached the importance of education. He pushed his children to do well in school, although I would never study much as a young lad and did not like school.

However, I will be always grateful for his encouragement and pursuit of education for his children. Although I did not always listen to his advice as a young lad, and it was not until later in life I realized the necessity of education and how important my dad's advice was, I am sure it was my parents' insistence on education that inspired me as I got older. The price I had to pay for not listening was that I had to do a lot of making up for lost time, as stated in later chapters.

My mother, while taking care of a family of ten, was also very industrious and a tireless, hard worker. She took care of the family, and in those days, farmhouses did not have running water, so the water had to be carried in a bucket from an outside spring well.

The water had to be heated using a pot that was hung from a fireplace iron crook over a wood or peat fire to wash clothes and for other domestic uses. The clothes had to be washed by hand, using the old scrubbing board; for a family of ten, that was no small task. When the clothes were washed, they had to be dried on an outside clothesline. In a damp climate, it could take days to get a few dry days where there was a good drying breeze with some sun to dry the clothes. When the clothes felt somewhat dry, they were brought into the family kitchen, where they were put on another clothesline, where there was always a big turf fire to remove any remaining dampness.

My mother also raised and took care of all the housed animals and fowl. She fed them and cleaned out their quarters. As we got older, we would help her to do the cleaning and other chores, while my dad was always busy planting and harvesting the necessary, life-sustaining farm crops, no small task for one man. My mother would sell turkeys, chickens, geese, and eggs at the local farm markets. If the market was better across the border, the products would be smuggled and sold across the border. The little money that she made selling her products took care of most of the household needs.

The other source of income was milk. My parents would have milking cows whose milk was sold at the local creamery.

My mother was very smart for her generation and the environment she grew up in, where she and most of her peers left school at fourteen years of age or younger. She went only to seventh grade; however, her ability to deal with numbers was extraordinary. She could rattle off answers to complex math problems without ever putting a pen to paper. She loved to read everything she could get her hands on. When we were young, she loved to read to us and loved to listen to whatever we had to say. When we were doing our homework, she loved to help us understand and solve problems.

My mother was naturally very smart, a great mentor, and would have made a great teacher. She was always a terrific help when it came to our homework. She enjoyed reading our schoolbooks and would teach us how to read and recite poetry. She loved poetry and was always reciting her favorite poems that she learned in the primary school system as a young girl, and as a result I can still recite every poem I ever learned. There are so many that my kids will say, "How you can remember all these rhymes that you learned so long ago?" My mother always knew the answers and was great at explaining complicated math problems; she had a natural ability better than that of many teachers during that period. She loved children and had the perfect personality for teaching. She was a very proud woman and always wanted her children to look neat and clean. When we went to school or church, she gloated when neighbors would comment on how nice and neat we looked. Since there was very little money and clothing was very expensive, we would have to take good care of our Sunday best clothes. We were not allowed to play in them or get them soiled. Clothes were handed down from older siblings and had to be kept clean, neat, and ironed so they stayed looking new.

We would have to take off our Sunday best clothes as soon as we got home and put on our farm clothes. She was always mending and patching the farm clothes. The good clothes could not show any patches, since patched clothing meant that we were poor, which we were, but she did not want the world to know, since we were a little better off than those who surrounded us in this poor farming community.

She was very creative and could make clothes from all sorts of used garments. If something was too big, she would make it small, and if it was too small, she found a way to make it bigger. She was always sewing—every spare moment she had, she was either mending clothes or making new ones out of whatever materials she could find. We would get only one outfit that had to last all year, including shoes. When the soles of the shoes would get worn to a thread and many times would have holes, my father would cut out pieces of rubber and make insoles that would slip into the shoes to protect our feet from the ground. My mother was not too concerned about the condition of the shoe soles, since no one could see the soles. Tears or torn upper parts could be seen and were a major concern. If the shoe uppers were in bad condition, we could not be allowed to go to church until there was money to buy new ones. Appearances were very important and had to be maintained. She was a very proud woman with high standards within her realm.

My mother was for the most part the disciplinarian, and my father got involved only if there were major issues. My father did not relish having to get involved in discipline. Although he did not like being the disciplinarian, he would do what had to be done to support my mother. When my mother was a young girl and left school after seventh grade, she went to work in the local village for a well-to-do family as a domestic worker. The family were lovely people, and my mother loved working there.

My mother was a very smart, tireless worker, and they appreciated her hard work and treated her like family. She had wonderful memories from those days when she was a young girl, and she loved to reminisce and talk about the good times with all her friends. Her boss had what was considered in those days to be a good job as the manager of a creamery that processed milk supplied by local farmers. She stayed with the family until she married my father.

My father was twenty-five years older than my mother, and she was only twenty-two when they got married. My father, I am told, looked very young for his age, had a good personality, and was considered very handsome. He had land and cattle, which made him a good catch in those days when an eligible bachelor's worth was measured by the amount of land and cattle he owned. My mother was a very attractive young woman, so I am told.

Her experience working with a big family who had young children provided great training for her and prepared her well to raise her own family and help my father in every way. My mom never complained, loved life, and had little tolerance for those who liked to complain and would always remind us how lucky we were. She managed the house and the family finances, which were very scarce; however, she was very talented and had great skills in making very little go far. As a result of her ability to prudently manage how to make very little go far, there was always enough to meet the basic needs of the family. In many ways she was the matriarch of the family but had great respect for everyone and liked to make people feel good about themselves.

When money would come in from selling livestock and farm goods, mom would do a great job managing these funds and making every penny count. Now that I have my own family, I can appreciate how talented she was at getting the most out of every penny. Selling farm goods or cattle was the only way to make money.

Farm goods had a very limited and competitive market, and the price of cattle depended on foreign markets. Ireland exported its meat and farm products all over the world, but England was its biggest and most important market. Although my family had farm supplies in abundance, they were used very sparingly, and whatever was not used was sold at the market. My father used to say, "Do not waste anything, because if you do you may later have to follow a crow to try and get it back." Our kids get a big kick out of that old saying.

It was very common for farmers to kill their own pigs, lamb, and chickens for meat, but again, the meat was used very sparingly, with the emphasis on selling as many cattle, sheep, and pigs as possible to pay whatever bills came along. In the Irish Republic, there was a carryover from British colonization where there were land rates and rent.

These tariffs put great strain on families to pay when the occupier was giving nothing back in return. In a few years, after Ireland became independent, a little relief came when the rent was removed and only the land rate remained, a much more manageable level, and there was no immediate eviction if a farmer could not pay on time. As the state became more stable and the new government was able to get rid of the rent tax so that only the land rate tax remained, this was a great relief for the farmers. However, if farmers failed to pay the land rates on time, they could still lose their land, but every effort was made to get people through a rough patch and not let them lose their land. The new government was much more considerate and would work with them to get them back on track and meet their commitments. The good news was that as soon as the state was able to get rid of the farm rate tax that too ended. During the early years, land could be taken over by neighbors for back taxes or rates. This was a very rare occurrence with the new government; however, when this happened, the neighbor could take over the land.

The confiscated land would be taken over for whatever back tax was levied by the state.

Neighbors who took over other neighbors' land by paying the back taxes were resented, scorned, and referred to as land grabbers, and in many cases, they became outcasts within the small communities. *Land grabber* was one of the most derogatory and inflammatory slurs one could use.

The land grabbers were scorned and hated by the whole community. No one would talk to or associate with them. Their nickname from then on would be *grabber*, which would stick with that family for generations to come. This was a great deterrent: in most cases no good neighbor would take over land or property for back taxes, especially in these very congruent farm communities where friendships and family were everything, where being ostracized was like spending time in purgatory or worse.

CHAPTER 7

Poor Times

In 1944, the Irish government's Children's Allowances Act was established for the first time. This was a token relief for families with many children and was very well received across the country, although it was a political ploy by Éamon de Valera to win an upcoming election. This children's allowance started out where each child would get a half a crown (one-eighth of one pound sterling, which at the time had a buying power of over eight dollars) in today's money. As little as the children's allowance was, families made these pennies go far to survive.

The children's allowance was a very successful government program and was initiated by Fianna Fáil, the newly elected party at that time. This entitlement program helped the party leaders stay in office for many years to come. Irish politics is no different from the politics in any other democracy, where the politicians are always looking for some giveaway program that will endear them to the electorate.

The children's allowance, as it was called, was one of the most popular programs ever enacted in the Irish Republic. During the early 1950s, Irish people living on very small rural farms had a very simple peasant lifestyle; however, they were full of life and always looking for a good story to tell or listen to. During these times, very few homes had televisions. Only the rich merchants and professionals, such as doctors, lawyers, merchants, and big farmers, had such luxury.

The local people living in poor rural areas more than compensated for television or any other media-type entertainment. In those days people made their own entertainment by visiting neighboring homes to play cards, play music, and tell stories into the early hours of the morning.

Although the gambling stakes were usually very low, since people had little money, the card games were taken very seriously. Only the most skillful players were allowed to play. For new players to qualify and be considered for the game, they first had to observe other players for a period of time, and then they would be let in on a trial basis as subs. How well the new subs played their hands would determine if they would be considered for the team. The most popular games were poker, twenty-five, rummy, and blackjack.

After many card games were played and the losers were out of money, the women of the house would serve tea and Irish soda bread or maybe scones. When the teatime was over, the stories would start, from gossip about a crazy neighbor who was long dead to a wide variety of issues. Then came the tall stories about the giant men of old and other far-fetched tales. These stories took on a very high level of exaggeration to add excitement and to get the adrenaline flowing, almost like playing out a stage act.

By the time a few of the stories were told, the young children would be scared so badly they would be hanging on to their parents, scared out of their wits and scared to go to bed, but they loved the stories and excitement and always wanted more. Although the children were scared, they could not wait to hear the next story, which of course had to be more dramatic than the previous one. This was a form of homemade theater at its best. Many of the best storytellers were invited to parties and all types of events to entertain.

This was a wonderful form of entertainment with great characters that had a level of charisma equal to that of Broadway actors. A great storyteller was referred to as a seanchaí; these were the ones with the greatest stories and charisma. The leprechaun has become a part of Irish folklore all over the world. Around St. Patrick's Day in the United States, the lore of the leprechaun becomes very much alive in Irish communities.

There are the leprechaun posters and symbolism—everywhere you go, you can see the mythological character that has become bigger than life. Then there is the banshee, which also has a huge mythological aspect to it. One dark, damp evening when my brother and I were on our way across the fields to Grandma's house for a visit, we heard this very lonely, extremely loud wail that rang out across the hills and dale. The loud wail rang out through the grazing pastures and the trees like something we'd never heard before; the hair literally stood up on our heads. The cry seemed to move away from us at a very fast speed as we got closer to the point of origin. The cry sounded like a very old woman wailing in a very distressed way, as if she had been brutally attacked or hurt, like if she just broke her leg or something catastrophic.

Then we thought the cry might be a neighbor's son, who was a big prankster—which was big in those days, putting on an act to scare young people. We started to throw rocks in the direction of the cry. As each stone landed in that destination, the cry seemed to rise toward the sky and get louder and more intense, or so it seemed. When we got to Grandma's house, we told Grandpa the story, and he got annoyed at us for throwing rocks. He scolded and said, "Don't you lads know that this was the banshee, and that some member of the family was going to die, maybe in America or somewhere in the world?" Sure enough, the next afternoon the news came from America that my mother's first cousin who had immigrated to the Boston area when she was a very young girl had died of old age.

The path the banshee followed was the same path she'd traveled as a very young girl when on her way to church or when going to the village store to pick up items for her mother. The path ran from her home at the foothill of the mountain to the village down in the valley.

Although in many ways I am a doubting Thomas, to this day I often wonder where that awful, scary, lonely cry came from. It was bigger than life and very scary for two young lads, one around ten and the other eleven years old. The fact is that I can still hear that cry more than a half century later as if it were yesterday. This conundrum makes one realize that we are not always the master of our own universe and maybe there is something out there bigger than any one of us. Was it all just a coincidence that the next day my mother's family was informed that their cousin in America had passed away? I guess we will never know.

This is a question I am sure my brother and I will take to our grave unsolved.

The banshee's lonely wail was so loud and so scary when it moved away so swiftly in the dense dark of night, leaving behind a feeling that was not only scary, but also somewhat cavernous and mystical. In those bygone days, these types of ghost stories would keep coming; some were based on what seemed to be real and some might be somewhat questionable. However, the stories always had a level of sincerity that epitomized the poker face mentality of the great storytellers such as the old Irish seanchaíthe (the Gaelic for "storytellers"). The mythology of the ghosts is that they are spirits who one day will enter heaven but for a time are in limbo, doing penance for their sins when on earth. These stories were very believable, especially for children and young people in general. The storytellers would stop at no boundaries to entertain their audience young and old.

Here in the United States, when our children were growing up, I would tell them these stories, and they would be so scared and intrigued they would invite their friends over to hear the stories and could never get enough, and now our grandchildren, too, cannot get enough and always beg for more and more. On recounting my childhood banshee story, my grandson, five at the time, described the banshee as something you would not believe is real, but he believed it was real because I, his grandpa, had heard it. Needless to say, of course I love entertaining the kids; I get as big a treat as they do. In my view anything that can put an enthusiastic smile on a child's face lifts one's heart to where there is nothing better. Then there is a ghost story I like to tell about when my granduncle passed away.

My granduncle was my mother's uncle on her mother's side and in his day a big personality and a great storyteller. He lived just down the old boreen (lane) from where we grew up in rural Ireland. My two brothers and I went to his wake, and a very fine Irish-style wake it was, where hundreds of people came from far and near to pay their respects.

We were very young—I was around twelve, and my two brothers were each a year older (typical Irish twins, one might say).

Around two in the morning, my two brothers and I decided to leave the wake and go home, which was less than one mile up the old, lonely, cobblestoned Hawk's Wood Boreen, which was lined with big trees on both sides and was very lonely as noises whistled through the trees and the beautiful bright moonlight seemed to swirl in different shades of light. We came to a turn in the lane where there was a large old fieldstone farm barn with a rusty galvanized roof where the gable was open in order to store hay and large farm equipment. As we were passing by, there was what appeared to be a huge white object that suddenly appeared in the large barn gable opening and seemed to be moving. All three of us got a glimpse of it and got so scared we ran for our lives, and as we were getting closer to our house, the rooster crowed three times.

In Irish mythology, if the cock crows three times before daybreak, that is a danger signal that something bad is going to happen. The rooster's crowing amplified our fear and adrenal rush. What was even scarier was that when we got home, my father was at the door with a worried look and asked, "Did you lads hear the cock crow?" Then he scolded us for leaving a wake before daybreak, when all kinds of evil creatures roam the earth.

Storytelling was a coveted gift, and if you were a great storyteller, you had to tell the best and most scary stories that you had in your bag to obtain that bucolic honor. When our children were young, they loved to bring their friends over to hear their dad's scary stories. Their friends would also be scared out of their wits but would keep asking for more and more, which

I enjoyed, and when they went home and told their parents, I would get calls wanting to know if I would come to some of their parties and tell stories.

Now that my children are all grown up, they ask me if any of those stories that I used to tell were true. The only answer I can give is that these stories were passed down by some of the best storytellers of their time in the area where I grew up.

In Irish folklore, it was the responsibility of elders to pass on their best stories and keep the great stories alive for generations to come. My kids would say, "Dad, you seem to have a pretty good repertoire of your own." Then one day my youngest daughter, a grade-school teacher, asked me if I would come in on ethnicity storytelling day and tell some ghost stories to her class. Needless to say, I was elated. The class of fourth graders, with a large ethnic mix, was full of lovely children, and of course not knowing the culture made it more challenging, and although they loved it, they were so very scared. The next time I saw my daughter, she said, "Dad, it was great, but you did not have to scare the bejesus out of them." The magic of storytelling is that when passed on to the next generation it gets a new flair, which can take the story to the next level.

I treasure these stories, and I am sure our children and grandchildren and their friends at least to some extent also do. There would also be stories about fairies appearing in the dark of night on white horses. The fairies would scoop up anyone walking alone in these very rural, lonely places during the dark of the night. There were a number of areas in every rural, lonely locality that the residents were advised to avoid by the storytellers once the dark of night came down. These were areas where the fairies were supposed to have been spotted. Areas such as old fortresses and ancient burial grounds were to be avoided after dark.

One story that the storytellers loved to tell when I was a young lad was about a local man who took an ancient graveyard headstone home to make a bridge over a small stream by his little old lonely house, where he lived with two old sisters.

When he went to bed that night around midnight, there was a very loud, lonely wail that was coming from the direction of the where the gravestone had been moved and was now installed

This wail was so loud and so scary that the two older sisters were terrified, and not until the gravestone was returned to its original graveyard location, and properly placed at the ancient grave site, did the late-night cry stop.

Another commonly told story is that there was a tribe known as the Fir Bolg that inhabited Ireland in ancient times and was conquered by another tribe, the Tuatha Dé Dannan. The Fir Bolg, were known as a tribe that was very small in stature and were conquered by the Tuatha Dé Danann, a much bigger and more powerful tribe.

It is then said that after the conquest, the Fir Bolg went under the green hills of Ireland into caves, caverns, and dens, and when they died came back as fairies and leprechauns who traversed the Irish rural wilderness after dark. There is another fairy story that the storytellers like to tell about a beautiful young woman who was on her way home one dark night when along came the fairies on a white horse and swept her up, and she was never seen again.

It is told that a passerby was traveling the same path at the foothill of the mountain one moonlit night where the young woman was allegedly abducted, and she was sighted on a white horse in all her beauty. The horse was in a fast trot when passing by. The passerby tried to talk to her, but she just stared ahead as she kept moving on.

These storytellers would have a litany of stories that would go on for hours, and one would be much scarier than the previous one. These storytellers were so popular that in early Irish radio they had a storytellers' hour every night called the seanchaí.

The seanchaí hour was on Radio Erin for many years and later became a TV series. This form of entertainment was great in those primitive days and people loved it. Today in Irish communities throughout the United States, storytelling and old Irish comedy are making a comeback. The seanchaí entertainers from Ireland tour all over the world, and particularly the United Kingdom, United States, Canada, and Australia, and they are using the very same lore and language as the old storytellers. Halloween in Ireland is a church holiday and a bank holiday on which it is told that the spirits roam free after midnight, and there are many stories of sightings. There are scary tales of people walking home in lonely areas and seeing someone who has been dead for some time pass them by in the dark of night. The dead person allegedly looks exactly the same as when they were alive and is in the same type of attire. It is said that although the dead look the same as when they were alive, they do not speak and only stare ahead. It is said that the spirits are doing their penance on this earth, wandering around in the bitter cold and dark of night. There are religious services in churches throughout the country where people who have lost loved ones pray for the dead and light candles. At midnight is when the spirits are said to appear.

Folklore tells us that the spirits wander around the exterior of house after midnight in areas where they lived while on earth. On Halloween the young people would also come out after midnight and play pranks by crawling around houses and crying like banshees, trying to scare the people inside the houses. The pranksters would engage in all kinds of mischief, especially if there were a cranky old man or woman who was very mean to young people. The prankster would climb onto the roof of the house after blocking the entrance door. With the door blocked, the prankster would dump a little water down the chimney, enough to cause smoke from the open fire to fill the house and cause a little panic. With the door blocked, the people would have to climb out the little windows to get out of the house and open the door. The police and religious organizations cracked down on the pranksters who were inflecting suffering on older people. If pranksters got caught doing something that was considered unsafe or harmful, they could face prosecution and could be locked up for a period. Other types of pranks were common where young people would crawl around a house where older people lived and make loud cries. The cries would sound like the banshee wailing and would make older people worry that someone was going to die, either a family member or a close friend. Most of these acts were innocent in nature, and those who were targeted were rarely, if ever, injured in any way. In most cases the pranks were carried out on curmudgeonly targets who were not friendly toward young people and in general not popular in the community. There was one old curmudgeon in particular who was very cranky, and if anyone came close to the old man's property, he would shoot his shotgun over the heads of trespassers while threatening them with a vengeance. Fortunately, no one ever got hurt, though the pranksters loved to get the old man so excited that he would be shooting into the air and the sky would be a blaze of light like a Fourth of July fireworks show.

CHAPTER 8

Rural Ireland

During the forties and early fifties, house dances were very popular in rural parts of the country where there were a lot of young people. These dances were in many ways what young people now call parties. The house dances were a wonderful source of entertainment for young people during this era. Some households would get the reputation of being the best, where young people would come from all over the countryside. The best houses would get all the fun people; the music and refreshments would also be very good, which became something of a status symbol for the households.

The music would consist mostly of accordion, fiddle, violin, mouth organ, and the great spoon players and crooners. The spoon players were unique and in big demand; their music was a melodious folk-type music. The crooners would come from all over the community and would travel many miles. Some of them were so good with their big tenor voices that they could compete on today's *American Idol.*

These céilidhs (parties) would be very festive and spirited, and of course, when there would be a great event, it would become the talk of the village for many weeks to come.

The house dance was then replaced by the open-air dances that were a huge hit in the early to mid-fifties. These events were held at crossroads and major country road intersections.

Young people would come from all over, and again there would be all types of entertainment, similar to those of the house dances. In some cases, there were kegs of beer hidden in the roadside bushes since it was illegal to have alcohol at these outdoor events where there were large numbers of underage people and no chaperones. This was where the open-air parties got a little out of hand. Some got rather wild—young people would be smoking cigarettes, drinking beer, and going wild.

This was so much fun, going wild with great friends outdoors where everyone felt so carefree, sowing their young oats, and just having the time of their lives.

The local farmers became alarmed and concerned that the young boys and girls were wooing and courting while smoking cigarettes and using the farmers' hay barns for shelter and to get away from the intersection crowd. The farmers were afraid that these young people could set the hay barns on fire if they were smoking and not properly extinguishing their cigarette butts. The hay barns could easily catch fire from a lit cigarette spark or improper quenching of a cigarette butt. Many of the farmers lodged complaints with the local police and complained to the parish priest, hoping to stop the open-air hooleys. The clergy became more aware of what was going on at these wild parties, where wooing and carousing would go into the wee hours of the morning. The clergy came out on the church pulpits at Sunday Mass in every community condemning these open-air dances as a temptation for sin, and where young girls could end up in life-changing trouble. Ireland had no laws on the books at that time where law enforcement could legally stop open-air gatherings, since the road intersections were public domain, and as a result law enforcement could only increase their patrols and become much more visible to stop any rowdiness and trespassing onto private property.

The church referred to the open-air dances as venues for bad behavior where young people, male and female, would get in trouble. The clergy revved up their condemnation and labeled these events as immoral and out of control. This situation concerned parents who had teenage youngsters, and as a result there was a major crackdown. Although there was a scaling back on the scope of these events, the kiss of death was when the local clergy got involved and would show up and walk around monitoring the scene. Needless to say, when the clergy showed up, the young people did not want to be around.

By the mid-fifties, Ireland again came alive with a new era of dance and dance halls.

The large dance halls became an instant hit that young people flocked to on weekends, which became a nice replacement for the house and the open-air road dances. These dance halls and music became so popular that a whole new period of modern music and big show bands took Ireland's young people by storm. Every Saturday and Sunday night, these halls would be crowded with young people who would travel far and near to hear their favorite show band.

Just about every little village or hamlet would have a dance hall, including church halls, and the larger towns would have large dance halls that sprang up all over the country As automobiles became more plentiful, the young people were able to travel far to their favorite events, and a new industry of taxi service became popular for those who did not yet have a car or motorbike. During this time motorbikes also became very popular.

Although these were very poor times in Ireland, it was the beginning of the new, more modern Ireland, even in the most rural of areas, where modern music and pop music were everywhere. During this time, Elvis Presley was the heartthrob among the young girls, and although he never visited Ireland, it was part of his bucket list, since one of his great-great-grandmothers came from County Wicklow, where he wished to visit.

Elvis's picture was posted all over, and when his name was mentioned, the young girls went wild. During this time very few people in rural Ireland had TVs—radios and newspapers were the main source of news—but for some reason there was no shortage of news, including the latest trends.

CHAPTER 9

A Republic Was Born

In 1922 the Irish Free State was formed, which was also later known as the Irish Republic, though the Irish Republic was not officially formed until 1948. After eight hundred years of British rule, the Irish Free State had to start from scratch and build a nation that was completely ravaged by the occupier, who took everything and gave little back. During the penal days, schools were forbidden, which left a huge educational deficit that continued to be very substandard during British rule. The newfound freedom became a beacon of light in the eyes of the Irish people, and in particular the young. A new beacon of hope for the first time brought new opportunity and a new sense of optimism. This new optimism could be seen on the faces of the young and could be seen in every Irish place of assembly. There was a new sense of pride in the new Free State that now could take its place among the nations of the free world. This was a hard pill for the British to swallow, but as they still occupied Northern Ireland's six counties, to the chagrin of Irish nationalists north and south, they were still embedded in Ireland. Northern Ireland was where most of the heavy industry was located, and people from the Irish Republic were not allowed to hold jobs in the British-occupied north, and there was no direct trade north and south of the border. The objective of the British was to demonstrate to the people of the Irish Free

State that there was a much better living in Northern Ireland, where there were more industrial jobs than in the new republic. The British government would also subsidize the Northern Irish farmers and gave them all kinds of grants so they would be better off than their southern counterparts.

The Northern Ireland children's allowance was also much more substantial because the British could much better afford to fund generous social programs. The new free state had very little industry or markets where people could sell their goods. The new government was working hard on developing new markets other than its old enemy Britain, which it was dependent on for the export of most of its agricultural products, and this was not a good situation because the Brits took the full opportunity to make life as tough for the new Irish Republic as possible. The Free State also maintained the old British currency system for several years until it was able to float its own currency, the punt, at a discount compared to the British sterling. During this period Britain could wield its economic yoke of control over the new Free State as well as the six northern counties that it still ruled. The Irish Free State was created with what was known as dominion status in 1922, following the Anglo-Irish Treaty. In 1937, a new constitution was adopted in which the state was named Ireland and effectively became a republic, with an elected nonexecutive president. It was officially declared a republic in 1947, to be followed by the Republic of Ireland Act 1948. Although the British still had significant influence in the new Irish Republic, they soon found out that the new Irish government was pretty shrewd and progressive. It revitalized the old education system to where it became very competitive and in the top twenty of the world rankings. This approach gave

Ireland a world-class workforce, which today has propelled the country into many of the high-tech industries, including health care, medical technology, manufacturing/research, software, and electronics manufacturing. Today Ireland has one of the highest GDPs per capita in the industrial world. The new initiatives spread to the countryside as well as the cities. The new wealth created by great global jobs enriched every community in many ways all across the land, where new big homes could be seen.

The big turning point in Ireland's economic standing was its early entry into the European Common Market, which opened the door to global trade.

Global manufacturing and research developed collaborative agreements with the Irish universities, making Ireland world class and well-funded. Now the present Irish government is funding Northern Ireland, which is lacking funds for some of its very important academic programs in areas such as nursing and others.

The Republic of Ireland became a member of the United Nations in December 1955 and joined the European Common Market in 1973.

When the European Common Market was first established, the Republic of Ireland joined and was one of the first six countries to join. This was one of the best decisions that the new Irish government had made. Joining the common market opened up new markets for Ireland, where it became a global player and was able to avail itself of the very lucrative farm grants and subsidies that the EU allocated to poorer countries with large impoverished rural areas. The Irish roads and infrastructure were poor. From 1973 up to 2018, Ireland was a net recipient, in nominal terms, of over €40 billion in EU grants. The country is now a net contributor due to its outstanding economic growth.

This was a windfall opportunity for the Republic of Ireland and as a result made Ireland one of the most successful and competitive small countries within the EU.

Foreign industries flocked to Ireland to take advantage of this new gateway into the European Common Market. When the EU established a single currency, Ireland was one of the first countries to adopt the new currency. This became one of the brightest periods economically in the history of the Irish Republic's commerce. In those early days before Ireland joined the EU, there were very few cars on the roads in Ireland, although young people would travel far and near to hear the latest entertainment idols performing.

The big bands played at dances and concerts to which people traveled on bicycle and on foot, and that included me and my friends. It was very common to see a gang of young boys and girls traveling on bicycles on their way to one of these events, which might be up to ten miles away. The mode of transportation was mostly bicycles, with very few cars. Many of the young girls would ride on the crossbars of the boys' bicycles; you could hear the laughter and glee of these groups of young people on their way to these fun events.

Although miles away, riding on hilly narrow roads, the young people were enjoying their young lives to the max, where nothing was going to hold them back. Needless to say, young people have a way of making the most of every situation and turning it into a fun event, and none more so than the young Irish, who were always looking for fun and excitement. During and after the Elvis period, rock and roll was the new norm; the big bands came, followed by the Beatles and some of the great country and western performers, who all came to Ireland because they knew the young Irish would come out in great numbers. All the large cities, Dublin in particular, as well as Cork, Galway, and Limerick, were always big destinations for world-class performers of all types, and that was where they would see mass crowds attending their events with great enthusiasm.

During the fifties, sixties, and seventies and into the early eighties, the dance halls became very popular in Ireland and in Irish communities all around the world, particularly the United States, where I met my wife, Kathleen, at the City Center Ballroom in midtown Manhattan. In the Irish communities throughout the United Kingdom, including London and all the large cities, the streets were alive with Irish dance halls and Irish pubs, which would be jammed every weekend.

I lived in London from 1961 through 1964. I loved London. It was a great city during those days—clean and safe, with so much to do. New York City, the greatest city, just like London, was also alive with Irish dance halls and Irish pubs.

There was an Irish dance hall in each city borough. This new Irish way of life spread to every city, big and small, across the United States where there were Irish communities. You can find semblances of these Irish pubs and taverns with their traditional Irish music and song all across the world—in most of the larger cities all across Europe, the United States, Australia, New Zealand, and so on. In the Irish dance halls, the girls would line up on one side of the hall, and when the band would start playing its rock and roll, the boys would move quickly to find their favorite girls to dance with. If they hit it off on the dance floor, he might invite her to join him at the bar for a drink. If that went well, the young man would then ask for her phone number and maybe a date for the following weekend, or sometime later there would be a follow-up, a phone call. It all worked for me, and I am sure for many others as well. When I met my wife at City Center Ballroom in New York City, she was nineteen, and I was in my early twenties. She played hard to get, but with a little persuasion, there was an exchange of phone numbers that led to a relationship that started more than half a century ago. These were great carefree times where the youth enjoyed life to the fullest. And boy did I, and now it is great to reminisce with old friends on all the hell raising and the fun we had. Salaries were very small, but food and rent were very reasonable. Everyone was working and had enough money to spend on what was considered to be the good life—and yes, it was; I would not change any of it for all the money in the world. My wife and I dated for about three years, which included the time while I was serving in the military. The plan was to get married after I got out of military service. I got discharged (ETS) from the military on November 6, 1969, and got married in April 1970. Since we both had little money after furnishing our little house, on our honeymoon we toured Washington, D.C., into the Carolinas, driving an old 1963 Ford Falcon, carefree, and had a wonderful time with little money until the next paycheck.

CHAPTER 10

The Dowry

The dowry was commonplace in rural parts of Ireland up until the early to middle part of the twentieth century. It was very common for the father of daughters to give a dowry to each of his daughters when they got married, to the extent that it was expected based on the father's financial standing. During these times matchmaking was very common, and when a farmer's son would be looking for a wife, the dowry was very much in play, and that was where the skilled matchmaker could do good work, mediating what was best for both parties. Families with daughters would work very hard trying to accrue enough money to provide a dowry. As in every other situation in life where there is an entitlement of any kind, the dynamics of the process could get very serious and go off in many different directions.

In the absence of a matchmaker, when a prospective husband would become interested in a farmer's daughter, he would meet with the future father-in-law and ask him for her hand in marriage. When the father agreed, the future son-in-law would ask the father-in-law-to-be what the dowry might be. The future father-in-law would explain that he had three daughters, and that the younger one would get much less than the oldest one since the oldest one had worked harder and for a longer period of time and therefore was entitled to a little more. Many times, in addition to being the oldest daughter, she might not be the best looking of the three, and he would want her married off first. By offering a larger dowry, he might entice the bachelor farmer, who might need funds to improve his farm and increase livestock and might settle for the older daughter. A generous dowry would give him a head start. The cash infusion would give him and his new wife the opportunity to start a family right away, since the bachelors were typically ten or more years older.

Therefore, the bride-to-be would want to start preparing for a family right away.

In some situations where the prospective father-in-law did not have any money, he would offer the prospective husband one of the farm animals. If the girl was young, pretty, and in demand, there might be very little or no offering. The bachelor farmer and father would start bargaining back and forth until they would come to an agreement and agree on a dowry and as to which one of the daughters would become the farmer's wife, which could get a little tacky.

Then there were the matchmakers, who were very popular in those days and were in every community, always looking out for situations where they could make a match. The matchmakers had a keen eye for what was going on in the community. They would know all the eligible bachelor farmers and all the farmers' daughters who were seventeen years of age or older and looking for an eligible bachelor. The effectiveness of the matchmakers and their reputations in the community were based on their success in making matches with good results, such as big dowries and/or girls who were young, good looking, hardworking, and smart. They knew how to manage the process and would meet with both parties to get the lay of the land before working on a match. If either party seemed difficult, the matchmaker would try and work out the details before moving forward, and in some situations, they might walk away telling the difficult party that they were not ready to sit down and work out what was reasonable. Later, when the difficult party came back to the matchmaker, it was often too late.

There are stories that on the wedding day the farmer's daughter that showed up to get married was not the one the bachelor farmer had in mind. Being so busy negotiating a dowry deal, he did not quite lock in his choice of which girl he would be marrying.

When the girl that showed up to get married was not the one the bachelor had in mind, now he had to deal with some confusion and a little disappointment, but it was too late to start all over, and there could be others in the wings for this girl, since there were not enough eligible girls to go around in the broad farm community. This was where the matchmaker had to subtly get involved to work things out. However, to prevent a great embarrassment for both parties on the big day of the wedding, the event would go on, and things would get worked out. Sometimes the priest would get involved and smooth things over. In some situations, the father of the bride would have to up the dowry to keep things quiet and to smooth the way for the newly wedded couple and both families. The matchmaker would tell the bachelor farmer that he was better off with the more mature girl. He would try to convince the future husband that the pretty one would be too busy keeping herself pretty rather than helping him with the farm work. The dowry became a thing of the past around the late 1940s. In many situations the young girls would rather immigrate to a foreign land than end up marrying a farmer who could be ten years or more their elder. Many times, these young women had tough lives where they had little in common with their much older partners. In a time when divorce was unheard of, they had to make the best of their situation for the sake of the children and the family name. In those days, if a woman left her husband, not only would she be shamed, but so would her immediate family, and if there were siblings eligible for marriage, they would be shunned. However, the matchmakers still live on, and up until this present day there are those who enjoy taking part in some form of matchmaking. They find their efforts very rewarding in that they play such an important role in bringing people together. Without the matchmakers, some of those people would have never found each other. In rural areas there were eligible bachelors who were well off financially, with large farms and a lot of cattle, but in some situations would have no interest in getting married.

The confirmed old bachelors could find the matchmakers intrusive and meddling in their private lives. Bachelors who valued their privacy would do everything they could to avoid the matchmakers, while the eligible older unmarried women (referred to in those times as spinsters) would be hunting them down, hoping they would have someone in mind for them to marry. Many times, the reason why the older woman was not married was that her expectation was too high. The eligible spinster was hoping that she would find a well-off farmer and as a result missed out, and the matchmaker could not help, since most of the eligible bachelors wanted the younger girls. The matchmaker studied an eligible bachelor to be well informed on who he was and what his lifestyle might be able to provide, with the goal of convincing a prospective bride and father of the great catch. In rural Ireland, where the community thrived on gossip, the matchmaker and all the prospective parties, men and women, created great conversation about who was going to marry whom and when.

The prospects of a match being made within the community raised a furor of talk and gossip. Women would talk for hours, speculating on who was going to get married next. What started as a whisper would take off like wildfire, and all kinds of assumptions and contrived ideas could enter into the gossip, where rumors started to fly. It sounds crazy, but matchmaking gossip was a major part of the rural Irish culture and was far more exciting to people than anything that they saw or heard on radio or television. They created their own soap operas from the imaginings of what might come true. To them there was nothing like raw gossip; they just could not get enough of it. In most cases the gossip was not malicious and did not hurt anyone other than by creating this major air of romantic speculation that could impact the privacy of the potential bachelor or bride-to-be. Most of the bachelor farmers did not appreciate the gossip and would much rather have lived their lives in complete privacy than be the subject of conversation on every corner.

When barefaced, brazen neighbors approached the bachelor with personal questions regarding false rumors, it become torturous. They did not want to be rude but felt violated when the gossipers were spreading fake information based on assumptions and without any merit.

Back in those days, people did not have enough to do to keep themselves busy, and as a result they used their idle time gathering information, which in many cases was fake news.

To this day in many communities, if you want to know what is going on, there is always that certain someone who seems to know and becomes the one that people go to for the latest gossip. The gossiper becomes empowered by having more information than anyone else in the local community. The gossiper, by virtue of providing the latest gossip, is very popular. Then there are those people who are very private and will shun the gossipers and consider them a nuisance and not very reputable.

CHAPTER 11

Christmas in Ireland

When I was a child growing up, Christmas in Ireland was very festive in a very simple way that made it so real and original—it was just magnificent. These treasured memories will live with me until my dying day. As Christmas across the free world became commercialized, the spirit of Christmas and the magic of the season were somewhat stolen from the children.

The real meaning of Christmas is not about cartloads of gifts where some of the gifts will never be used. Most of the gifts that children receive are broken or destroyed within hours of being opened. Children love gifts, but the craze of parents and relatives showering young children with so many gifts that they do not know which one to open first has overshadowed the real meaning of Christmas giving.

Most of the toys and materialistic things that children receive have little memorable value. When our children were growing up, my wife and I were no different from other parents. We, too, bombarded them with all kinds of toys on Christmas morning, including the dog, who could not be left out—he too would get doggy gifts.

We think this is the American way. I am not sure that this is what our forefathers had in mind. Our forefathers were wise, thoughtful, and generous. It is my belief that they would much rather see every American family sharing its surplus with those less fortunate rather than going overboard spending on an abundance of useless toys during the Christmas season. Most of the toys and gifts end up in the garbage dump within a few days, adding to the heaps of unwanted waste that has a negative effect on the environment. It makes much better sense to take that money and invest it in a child's education, or better yet, share with poor children who are less fortunate.

Although we live in the richest country in the world, many children do not get a Christmas meal and go to bed hungry. Our biggest efforts should be putting in place programs to ensure that no child ever goes hungry. The real joy of Christmas should be for all of us to give to those who are less fortunate. By giving to others, we instill in our children a higher level of common good that is less selfish and more sharing. Sometimes I reminisce about my childhood days in Ireland, when there were no Christmas toys and only a package of candy or a bar of chocolate, if you were good. Only the rich children got toys— they would get a truck or a doll, but that would be it. It is the parents and society, as a whole, that set expectations for what their children should get for Christmas and not the child. If we teach our children to give rather than receive at Christmas, then they, too, will be givers, and the world will be a better place. We were not rich growing up. In fact, we were very poor but we did not know we were poor and in no way felt underprivileged. We were very happy with our candy and all the wonderful Christmas cheer. It was the spirit of Christmas that lit up every home in a very special way that was uplifting and festive. In those early days growing up, everything about the Christmas season was warm and festive, although we had very few material things.

The Christmas preparation would start about two weeks before Christmas. My mother would start baking all kinds of cakes and pies that we as children would long for and could not wait to feast on. Most of the ingredients were from the farm, fruit orchards, and garden. The aroma of my mother's cooking seems like yesterday; those precious times were so full of the season's spirit. There was a wonderful magic about the season that uplifted the hearts of everyone until you felt that this was as good as it gets. My mother would be in her glory, knowing that it was she who was the heart of the Christmas spirit within our home. She was on cloud nine with the Christmas spirit and her wonderful cooking and decorating the house. The wax candles and beautiful holly with red berries lit up the house; that seemed so magical to me as a child. In life many times it is the little things you remember and not the big splashes – which can be empty. My mother, while taking care of a family of ten, would be exhausted from all the preparation but would tell everyone how much she loved the Christmas season and all the festivities. For her all the work and preparation was a labor of love that she thoroughly enjoyed with our dad and her family. On Christmas Eve the house would be decked with holly and endowed with an abundance of red berries and candlelight throughout the house; it was just beautiful and glowing. Everyone was in such a festive mood, and that made it just magnificent and forever memorable. My dad would say it was Mum who made Christmas so special, and it was her very special time of year.

Midnight Mass was one of the highlights of Christmas Eve; everyone dressed in their go-to-church best and went to midnight Mass. The streets of the small village would be full of people, including dozens of horse- or mule-drawn carriages for the elderly who traveled long distances—they came down from the mountains, glens, and dells, along the little cobblestone boreens, where they traveled many miles along picturesque terrain with narrow pavement and paths. In many cases they traveled three or more miles in distance to reach the village at a time when there were very few, if any, automobiles.

The village streets were lit with beautiful carbon and kerosene lanterns that hung from doorways along the street where the village became so alive, welcoming, and cheerful, where everyone was enjoying the Christmas spirit. The village merchants would give their loyal customers Christmas gifts, and the pubs would give everyone who came in a Christmas drink, and everyone would lift a glass in a toast.

The toast would wish all a merry Christmas and a happy New Year. It is a shame that these customs have gone away in the modern world, forever not to return.

When we got home after midnight Mass, my mother would prepare a big Christmas Eve meal with all kinds of her great baked treats that we loved as children. With so few material things, we felt we were riding on top of the world because we had everything that money could not buy. We were a large family of ten, with wonderful parents who were always there and made all of us feel so special in knowing that they were there for each of us and so proud of their family that they referred to us as God's gift. The day after Christmas, which was St. Stephen's Day in Ireland, was a very exciting day when every home waited for the wren-boys to come and play their melodious music, sing, and dance in the big farmhouse kitchen/living area for hours. One of the wren-boys would walk up to one of the young girls in the host house and dance around the kitchen with her in order to raise the festivities to the highest level by including the family as part of their entertainment, and the young girls would be in their glory. At the end of their entertainment session, the head of the house would present them with a token of gratitude. The small gift at that time was commonly a crown, five shillings, which was one-quarter of a pound, or sixty pence sterling. For those who could not afford five shillings, they gave a half a crown or whatever they could. As the wren-boys left and walked down the path from the house and on to the next stop, they played their instruments and all the melodies that personified the Christmas season. By early morning, when everyone was tired out, the wren-boys would go home and count all the money they'd collected and buy a keg or two of beer or whatever they could afford, and they would party, sing, and dance, and young lads and lassies would come from all over the countryside far and near to join the hooley. If they raised enough money and they could buy enough beer, the hooley could go on for days.

One St. Stephen's Day afternoon, a visiting New York Irish Yankee came by who was an old school friend of my father and had done well in America. The old Yank dropped in to see my parents, at which time the wren-boys were playing their music, singing, and dancing. Everyone was having such a great time, and the Yank loved it; however, he had to leave, but he threw a big money gift into the wren-boys' basket. The Yank was a lovely man whose donation was more than their total collection for the day. Needless to say, that big infusion bought a lot of beer and a huge party that went on for days. There is another big story to tell, and one that was talked of in the town— though keep in mind, most Irish stories become bigger than life. Each group of wren-boys would always try to outdo the others. Their objective would be to have the biggest and best party in the area so that people would be talking about it for weeks and months to come. The Christmas season was a time that included family get-togethers and parties that would go on until what they called Little Christmas, which was January 6. During the twelve days of Christmas, friends and neighbors would drop in to have a drink and a cup of tea with some of Mom's delicious cake, pies, and scones as a way to celebrate the Christmas season. They would welcome in the New Year and wish everyone well, rekindling and appreciating new and old friendships. Elderly special visitors would also be offered a glass of Irish whiskey and maybe a little poteen (moonshine) for the older gentleman and a glass of port or cherry wine for the lady. What a great tradition, where there was so little money and so few material things yet so much heart and joy expressed in a very simple way. This traditional way of celebrating the Christmas season brought warmth and joy to families and friends that created a bond of friendship and loyalty that lasted a lifetime. The biggest concern that people would have been had was not to leave anyone out when making their rounds, especially the old and infirm.

I will always cherish those memories as some of the fondest when I look back at my childhood days. As children, we wished that the Christmas season would never end.

CHAPTER 12

The Irish Embrace

When it comes to expressing love or affection toward loved ones, the Irish people have their own way of expressing their deepest feelings. Most find it very hard to show touchy-feely warmth, but down deep you know there is that internal warmth that can be felt coming from the heart. There was no hugging or kissing. Parents would take small children on their knees and show affection up until about age four or thereabouts, and after that, suddenly, you were told that you were too big for that kind of attention.

They believed that the touchy-feely display of love made sissies out of the boys, and it was believed that mollycoddling made children more dependent. In today's world psychologists may differ with that theory; however, I never had any reason to question the devout affection that was always there until the day both of my parents passed on. They demonstrated their love by caring and always working hard to provide and do the best for each one of us. There was no end to how far my parents would go to be there for each one of us in a way that was expressed more by actions than by words or deeds.

This lifestyle is part of our culture, and we are very comfortable with it, and I will go as far as to say that back in those days all of the British Isles and northwest Europe, where there was a strong Celtic, Gallic, and Viking influence, had similar characteristics. And I can vouch that when I lived in London, I found many of the British to have the very same characteristics. As a result of growing up in this un-touchy-feely culture, I am sure my children also had some of the same experiences. We were not as touchy-feely as some of our children's friends' families seemed to be, but we got a little better at it as time went on. I am convinced that our children do not need any affirmation when it comes to their parents love. It is my belief children want to know that that their parents are there for them at all times.

How we express these feelings is immaterial as long as they are there and real. All children need to know is that their parents' love is unconditional and always there. Love cannot always be measured by words and promises; sometimes it is measured more by their knowing you are always there for them in good times and bad. Love can be measured by the profound commitment and unconditional love that is always there until the day we leave this world. Putting our children's well-being before our own is the best example of parental commitment and love. It is my belief the true measurement of our success is not how well we do in life but how well our children do. There was an old man who lived down the road from my grandparents and was somewhat desolate living by himself. Although this old man was eccentric, he was very funny in many ways that made children laugh. His name was James, and he became very ill until he could not take care of himself, and he had no close family because all his siblings had immigrated to the United States at a very young age.

My grandmother on my mother's side took James into her home and brought him back to health. James was forever grateful. She treated him to some extent like family and would yell at him in order to keep him on the straight and narrow. After James got over his illness, he asked my grandmother if he could continue living with the family.

My grandmother told him that they would fix up his little house to make it more comfortable, and then he could go back to his own home, but he would come to her every day for his meals and personal needs, which made him very happy. Despite my grandmother's being somewhat tough on him, he knew she was always there for him, and as a result he had a great admiration and respect for her and would do anything for her.

When my grandmother took ill and passed away suddenly, he was devastated.

James said to my grandfather, "My life will never be the same," and within six months James passed.

Although my mother, her sister, and her brothers were good to James, he knew life would not be the same. Again, poor James felt alone, with no one to watch over him, and as my grandfather would say, it is better to be bickering than to be lonely. This was very true when it came to James. Although highly intelligent in many ways, he needed someone to be there for him, almost like a child. James was an avid reader, very intelligent, with a great breadth of knowledge on current events, and could talk about any subject, but he could not adequately take care of himself. My grandmother was one of seven children who were raised on a small patch of land on the side of the mountain where people were very poor. More than likely her family back in those days were evicted from their land by the occupier and ended up on the side of the mountain, where they reclaimed a patch of a heathery moor for a place to live. She and all her five siblings immigrated to America at a very young age and lived in

New York City, Hell's Kitchen, in the late 1800s. The girls did domestic work, and all the boys worked on the Hudson River ice barges harvesting the ice, which they cut ice for cold storage that was used by New York businesses and domestic families. These were very tough times in America, and the workers had to work very long, hard hours—ten to twelve hours a day, six days a week—for very low pay. My grandmother on my mother's side went back home to Ireland very early in the 1920s after about six years in the United States. It was said she had saved a significant amount of money—all being relative, for the times, but it was considered a small fortune when there was little money anywhere, including the United States. She met my grandfather, who was a farmer, an eligible bachelor; it was said that they met through a matchmaker. Matchmaking was very common in those days when the matchmakers were waiting for such opportunities to match people up, in particular when they had a little money.

When they met, they were very close in age and hit it off right away and got married within a year. My grandfather's small farm needed capital, and my grandmother's little fortune, that she'd scratched together as a domestic worker in America, helped to give them a little start. My grandmother was a great money manager; she was the matriarch of the family and ran everything with an iron fist. People used to say that America made her tough, which was probably true to some extent. Behind that crusty exterior was a very gentle and kind woman who was always reaching out to help others. Because of her generosity and always reaching out, family and neighbors were very fond of her. Her house was always full of people visiting, playing cards, telling stories, and socializing, and she would treat every visitor to tea and some of her fine baking that she was known for. My grandmother was very smart although she had only a third-grade education. She was a great talker, and with her travel experience she was like a celebrity in this rural and poor part of the country. She had a lot of very interesting tales to tell from America, in an area of Ireland where most people never traveled more than a ten- or fifteen-mile radius from where they lived. At that time the only mode of transportation was walking or riding a horse or a bicycle. My grandparents had five children. One died at birth; then there were the remaining two boys and two girls, of which my mother was the oldest. When my grandmother and all her siblings except one went back to Ireland, the boys all bought farms, got married, and raised families, and my grandmother's sister also met a farmer through a matchmaker when she went back. She too had a little fortune that gave her and her husband a little start. They all made a habitable existence on the small farms; by Irish standards at that time, they were poor, but they were somewhat comfortable and a little better off than those who did not have that same opportunity. The little fortunes they made in America were all put to good use, and all her siblings eked out a living.

They raised big families that also emigrated all over the world. One of her brothers and his wife, a lovely woman, had twenty-three children. My grandmother was a very hard worker, driven and very resourceful, whereas my grandfather was very easygoing and went along with the program. She always treated him with kindness and the utmost respect, and they were very close—he would say, "If it were not for her, I might not be here." James was a big man and considered very handsome as a young man, but he was somewhat clumsy in many ways, and he loved young girls in a very harmless way. When he would meet up with young girls, his eyes would light up, and he would love to chat with them and be all talk. The girls enjoyed James and got a kick out of him. Although James by this time was old and eccentric in many ways, he was still very elegant and had a great command of the English language. He too had little schooling other than a few days here and there, but he was a great reader, a champion speller and self-taught. He had a great knowledge of history, geography, and world politics and loved sports. For many of his friends and family, he was a great resource for information; friends and neighbors would call on him for current events and what was going on in the world, including sports. He loved to visit our house, and my father enjoyed him because they both loved to talk football and politics, which could go on for hours. James was a simple man with a great outlook on life. If James had gotten the proper education, he would have been a great professor with a great ability to explain complicated matters in great detail.

He had a photographic memory and was always very positive and saw only the good side of people. He always spoke very kindly about everyone and loved young people; he was in his glory when conversing with the young, studious type. When someone would say something that was not complimentary about another person, James would look up toward the ceiling and say, "Ah, now we have to look for the good in people."

He would not contribute anything negative or get into the typical type of gossip that was so prevalent in these tight-knit communities where everyone knew one another's business in great length. When James would come to our house, he would always take off his boots as soon as he sat down, I think more for personal comfort than for house hygiene. I was a little boy about five years of age at that time, and when I saw James take off his boots, I thought it was very peculiar, since no other visitors took their shoes off when they would come into the house. I got the idea that it would be pretty funny to put some water in James's boots, which was when my mother caught me peeing in James's boots. She was horrified and shouted, "By Jesus, I am going to kill you. You are a real tinker. Whatever put this in your head?" She continued yelling and said, "This brat is possessed by the devil," and sent me outside until James left for home.

All James would say was "Ah, now look for the good in the little lad. He is only a cub." (*Cub* was part of the colloquialisms used for young boys approximately between the ages of two and fourteen). After the shock of this incident was over, the story was told over and over, and I was forever labeled as the bad boy with the evil mind that was always up to no good. My father, who also liked to play pranks, but always of a harmless nature, got a kick out of the whole episode, with me so young and going the extra distance to get everyone's attention.

My mother would yell at my father for encouraging me by laughing when I would do something bad, and she would say, "You are encouraging him." When I was a young lad, our childhood was full of adventure and devilment; we were always living on the edge, where there was never a dull moment. Our parents were very big on school and made sure every one of us completed our school homework after we got home in the evening. However, we rushed through it so we could go outside and be part of whatever was going on. Many times, there would be a number of our school friends waiting outside for us to join in whatever was going on.

We might be playing our favorite sport, Irish football, or hunting, fishing, cave exploring, and so on. There were also the farm chores, which included checking all the cattle and sheep to make sure they were all accounted for and OK. There was the planting of crops, where the children helped however they could. There was the weeding of the crops, which was a task we despised and if possible, tried to avoid. There was also the cutting and harvesting of the turf (peat) for the home fire.

Harvesting the turf in the peat bogs was a very strenuous task, and there were many levels involved in achieving a good turf supply. The turf kept the family warm during the long, cold winter nights and was useful for cooking, baking, boiling water, and drying clothes with the heat from an open-hearth fire. Later, the turf- and wood-burning stoves became popular in these rural areas; they were a nice improvement because several tasks could be performed simultaneously. The hot water they generated could be circulated to clothes-drying hot press cupboards and so on.

Harvesting the turf was a long, drawn-out task performed over several months, especially if there was a rainy period in which the turf had to be raised above the ground to dry out before the pieces could be stacked and taken home, where they would be stored in an open turf shed and used sparingly so they would last until the following year's turf came online.

When the harvest came around, there were all types of harvesting chores. These chores would go on forever, and every member of the family had to contribute and help. The biggest chore was during the hay-harvesting season, when all hands had to be on deck. It was extremely important to successfully harvest enough hay to feed all the livestock over the winter season, since the livestock were where most of the farm income came from. With all the chores, there was still enough time to squeeze in time to play all the sports, mostly Irish football, which all young people loved.

Our hobbies were fishing, hunting, and exploring caves, mountain climbing, raiding apple orchards, and anything that offered a major challenge of adventure and excitement.

We also loved chasing wild horses in the mountains, trying to catch them and ride them if we could. When growing up in this type of an environment, young people become very creative; as the saying goes, necessity is the mother of invention. We used to build our own bicycles from scrap parts that we would find along the rivers and dump areas. Then we would use the rigged bicycles in the fields and take them up the side of the mountain, where we would take wild rides down the mountain's steep slopes. One lovely spring evening, there was a crowd of family and friends, all kids six to about fourteen, taking turns riding the bicycles down the very steep mountain slopes, when my older brother's bicycle wheel came loose. He was thrown into the air and landed, hitting his head on the ground so hard he suffered from what we now know to be a mild concussion. At that time, we did not even know what the word meant—all we knew was he could not remember what happened until the next day. This was a very serious situation that fortunately turned out to be OK by the next day. As children we thought it was funny and never told our parents until years later, when they heard the story as we were reminiscing and having a laugh.

In reality, this incident was no laughing matter and could have been very serious. My mother was horrified at the thought that one of her sons had such a close encounter with what could have been very serious or fatal.

Although we had never heard of the term *skiing*, back then we would fabricate our own equipment from scrap wood. We would strap the wood to our feet with hemp string, and it served the same purpose as skis. We would attempt to go down the low mountains and hills until the wood of the makeshift skis would come apart. The real fun was inventing the idea and the challenge of making it work, at least for a little while.

At times we would also sled down the steep slopes and hills with no sense of fear or danger. We were always thinking of the next adventure and how we could make it more challenging and exciting. We had so little and lived in such a rural environment, yet we felt that we were on top of the world. We felt that we had everything at our command, with a level of enthusiasm that drives every young boy's and girl's curiosity and excitement to the maximum. In life, if we believe everything is good, then more than likely it is, and that is what keeps us going. In my way of thinking, this was a child's life at its best: enjoying everything that nature has to offer and creating your own adventure that fuels the creative childhood memories for a lifetime that we can share with our children and grandchildren. In those carefree days, every Irish child living in these poor rural areas was part of a lifestyle with great memories of fun and adventure. Although every child was different, no child was left behind; there was always a strong instinct to bring along the less adventurous and make everyone feel that they were part of that adventure that was so much fun. Our parents were always very involved and made sure every child was included in sports and play.

My mother would never want to see a neighbor's child going home sad because they were left out of whatever was going on. She would always want to make sure that no child was feeling left behind. She loved children and was always on the lookout for every child. She had little tolerance for selfishness and would say we had to share whatever we had, including what we ate. I think her teaching to be kind and share played a part in my years of volunteering, which I always enjoyed, and I thank her for that.

CHAPTER 13

Grade School

Uragh Boys' National School was a primary all-boys grade school consisting of an old-style two-room schoolhouse that started with kindergarten (infant class) through second grade, which was held in one room; third to eighth grade was held in the larger classroom. There were approximately sixty to seventy students between the two rooms, and there were two teachers, a husband and wife, of which one was the headmaster. The lower-grade teacher was a mild middle-aged woman who took things in stride and was good to her very young students.

The schoolmaster who taught the higher grades was a very competent, much younger teacher with great command of all the five subjects that he taught, but he was very moody and had a temper. He would take out his frustration on the students, in particular the ones who were in his bad books. I was one of the students who was always in his bad books, for the most part with good reason. He was a very strict disciplinarian and did not spare the stick. His typical punishment was where he would make the student put out their hands, and he would give six heavy slaps, three on each hand, with a heavy rod, and when his right foot came off the floor while he was exerting the heaviest slap he could deliver, you knew he meant business, and you also knew that no matter how tough the student was, he was going to be in pain.

In cases of particularly bad behavior, he could give six slaps on each hand and at times draw blood. In most cases, his punishment was less severe. But for more serious issues, he would dish out what I would consider cruel and unnecessary punishment. His bad temper and dispensing cruel and unusual punishment made parents very angry. When parents found out their child had been the victim of his bad temper and abuse, they would come to the school.

They would come to take out their vengeance on him and in some cases carry a stick or a hurling stick, which somewhat looks like a hockey stick. The schoolmaster had played hurling in his younger days, a unique Irish sport that uses a hurling stick to hit the ball mostly in the air. There was one particular incident where the father of a young lad of about twelve years of age came to the school to have it out with the schoolmaster. This boy was small for his age, a good student and a well-mannered young fella. However, the boy did something the teacher did not like and as a result became the victim of the headmaster's insane abuse. When the boy went home and told his parents, who were lovely people, the father became very angry. The father was a small man, whereas the schoolmaster was much bigger and well built, so when the boy's father came to the school, he had a small battle-ax in hand and literally wanted the schoolmaster's head. The schoolmaster was very clever, and since the boy did not come to school the next day, he anticipated that the father would be responding in kind to the severe punishment of his son.

The schoolmaster locked down the school doors and windows and ordered the students not to open any doors. When the father got to the school, he started banging on the door with his axe and screaming. The schoolmaster was shaking with fear and did not know what to do, since the school during those times did not have a telephone where he could call the police. Fortunately for the schoolmaster, after a long display of anger and outrage, the boy's father left, yelling all kinds of scary threats. There was no justification for beating the boy, and the father was irate and wanted revenge. This went on for more than an hour before the father finally left. The schoolmaster stayed inside the school for many hours after the students left for home. He was afraid the boy's father might be waiting for him outside the school and attack him with the battle-ax. Many of the students in the classroom were to some degree enjoying the excitement.

However, some of the younger and more timid boys were also scared. The schoolmaster was a nervous wreck, and he never lifted a hand to that boy again. All this made for great community gossip—the local people would pry for more information as they could not get enough of this story. This was what the schoolmaster deserved, and it was a shame that no one ever took him to task and taught him a lesson so that other children would not become victims of his wrath. Teachers who beat children more than likely come from abusive homes themselves and do not realize the damage and suffering that they are inflicting on the children in their care as teachers.

One bright sunny day at lunchtime, while playing in the schoolyard, I saw an opportunity to take out some of my revenge on a classmate bully. The bully would pick on me and call me names and would threaten to beat me up. I despised the bully, who was bigger and older than I was, and desperately wanted to defame him. He was standing on top of a ditch where below there was standing water in a deep, swampy, muddy hole. When the opportunity presented itself, I very quietly and unassumingly launched an attack and quietly pushed him off the ditch and into the deep, muddy swamp hole, where he started to sink so fast that within seconds only his head and flailing arms were above the muddy water. The swampy mudhole was like quicksand, and the more he tried to get out, the more he sank deeper; he was terrified and screaming for his life. Although he was not well liked, after some time the bigger boys tried to get him out, while others were shouting "Let him sink," since no one likes a bully.

The rescue team of older boys had little success getting him out and had to call the schoolmaster in desperation to pull him out. The schoolmaster, who was big into river fishing, had to get a rope from his car trunk, which he threw to the sinking bully, and after a long hard effort, the teacher and a few of the bigger boys finally got him pulled out.

When he got out, I was in some ways relieved, and in some ways wished he had suffered a little longer. No one likes a bully, especially those who were the victims of his bullying. After he got pulled out, the schoolmaster took him home in his car in order for him to take off the wet muddy clothes and shoes. He was crying like a baby from the fear of drowning in the deep, swampy, muddy water and maybe now realizing how vulnerable he'd become where even a much smaller boy could inflict pain and humiliate him.

There was no one coming to his defense; everyone had only disdain for how he treated his younger and smaller fellow students, and I felt the same way—it was sweet revenge. When the schoolmaster dropped the boy off at his house, he skedaddled as fast as he could before the boy's mother saw him, since he did not want to have to explain to her what had happened; as big and mean as he was, he was scared of her. When the boy got home and told his parents what had happened, his mom, who was a very mean, small little woman, waged all-out war on me where she stalked my path to school for weeks with a big blackthorn stick in hand, such that I had to take a completely different route—I had to wade across a river and travel an additional two miles to get to school. From that day on, the boy never picked a fight with me and considered me evil and bad, which to some extent was true, and I wanted him to know that if you messed with me, you would get the horns. I also wanted all other bullies in the school to know that if you messed with me, you'd better be on guard all the time, because sooner or later I would spring a surprise attack. This earned me the nickname Kevin the Terror, a badge I proudly wore.

As a result of this deed, I now had to face my punishment. I was severely punished: the schoolmaster beat me with a stick until blood came from my two hands, and he slapped me around until blood came from my nose. I literally thought he was going to kill me, and the anger in his face and eyes was so scary.

When the blood from my nose ran down my face, I guess for me it was a sense of fight or flight—I launched at him with a great fury, swinging with an intensity that I never knew I was capable of. My launching at him took him by surprise, and it was then he realized he went too far, and he stepped back, and the only thing that he could say to save face was "I will report you to the police," but instead he sat down at his desk with his hands on his head and, I am sure, began thinking "What have I done" and "Have I created a monster?"

From this point on, he treated me with skepticism and with a subdued presence, and he did not dish out any more punishment. It is my opinion that he felt that if he were to apply the same type of punishment again, he might end up in a duel with me, and that would not be good, or worse yet, he did not know what I might be capable of doing that would forever embarrass him. When the priest came to the school the next morning, he and the schoolmaster went outside and had a very long talk.

When they came back in, the priest said nothing but stared at me for a long time. I am not sure if it was meant to be a form of intimidation, or maybe he was afraid that if he said something at this point, he did not know how I would react, but he knew I was very capable of defending myself. Then when the bully came back to school, the schoolmaster called him and me up in front of his desk and told him if it was not for what he'd gone through he would have given him the same punishment for his bullying and picking on younger boys. For me there was a little stardom for my act, and many of my friends and others who were the victims of his bullying were proud of me for taking on such a daring act and launching at the schoolmaster. They thought it was heroic, but little did they know it came out of fear and desperation, and there was no one to come to my rescue—a little scary for a thirteen-year-old.

When I got home from school, my father knew right away, as soon as he saw me, without anyone telling him, that I had been through the mill.

My father was very intuitive and could see instantly if something bad had happened to any one of his children. I could not tell him what had happened, since I knew he would not be too pleased with what I had done, in particular launching at the schoolmaster. I did not tell him what had happened, but need-less to say, this story, like every other story, was all around the village in great detail within hours. My mother was horrified and could not believe that one of her children could be caught up in such a quagmire and was concerned about my reputation as the bad boy.

When my father found out the next day what had hap-pened from a neighbor whose son was a friend of mine, he met me with a big smile and said, "I heard you took care of the bully." Not another word was said other than "I want to know about the schoolmaster's punishment and if he hurt you," but all I would say was that it was my fault. My father was a very calm person and hard to rattle, but when it came to protecting his children, there was no limit to how far he would go. I said I should not have pushed the bully into the mudhole, and he replied in a soft tone, "Sometimes, son, you have to stand up for yourself in this world." It was not considered macho for a thirteen-year-old to have parents come to the school to protect him or to yell at the teacher for a beating. A young macho lad was expected to take his punishment and wear his scars proud-ly. This type of cruelty among schoolmasters during those times in Ireland was widespread and not uncommon.

Unfortunately, many a young student suffered at the hands of a bad-tempered teacher.

The schoolmaster knew the student code that the macho lads would never tell their parents about severe punishment from the teacher. It would be much worse to be considered a "mama's boy" than to take your beating and move on. School bullying was very prevalent, and there would be usually one or two bullies in all the higher grades. There would always be those, including me, who would challenge the school bullies and take them to task. These challenges would result in after-school fights, usually on the way home from school. These fights would be nasty and bloody, and there could be some serious injuries, like a broken nose and black eyes or worse. When the school-master would find out or walk in on one of these fights on his way home, there was hell to pay. He would ground all who were involved and keep them back in school for hours after closing.

The school curfew would last for weeks and sometimes months. The curfew would stop the fighting for a period, but it would always start up again. When things seemed to have settled down, it would start up again at a more remote location. The fighting would again be brutal, and there was always some young lad who suffered as a result. Fighting was also a form of entertainment and excitement for several reasons, as follows.

The local police and the schoolmaster outlawed it, and of course the clergy did too, which only made it more challenging and exciting. Knowing that there could be a bust from any of the above authorities added a level of excitement to each event, and fights would include an escape plan in case any of those authorities should come on the scene. When the schoolmaster or the police would find out, they would go through their ritual of scolding and threats.

They would threaten reformatory school by putting the fear of God into all who were involved, in particular the instigators. The police would monitor the school route for months. The police would warn that anyone involved in a fight where some-one got seriously hurt could end up in a reformatory school until they reached the age of eighteen, and that was a scary thought and something of a deterrent, at least for a while.

The reformatory school was like a US juvenile detention center. This threat would scare the wits out of most of the students for a period of time. However, no one from the local village school ever went to the reformatory school for fighting.

However, there were two young lads who burned down a hay barn while hanging out and smoking cigarettes who both got one full year in in a detention center. However, the odds of ending up in the detention center for fighting were remote, so the cycle of fighting would continue and start all over again. The closest that I came to reformatory school was when one evening after school, on my way home, one of my classmates picked a fight in the center of the village. Never one to run away from a fight, I stood up to him and got the upper hand over the boy. In retaliation for him picking the fight with me, I was beating him severely when the local cop (garda) showed up and pulled me off my opponent. The officer gave me a major scolding and slapped me around, saying, "You did not have to hurt your schoolmate." The next day he came to the field where my father and I were working to talk to him, which was scary. Although my father always told us to stand up for ourselves and not let the bullies walk all over us, he was very annoyed at me for beating this young lad so badly. He told me how he had to talk to the officer in order to keep me out of reformatory school. This was a major scare and stayed with me for a long time. In retrospect, I am sure this was just a threat where the police officer told my father to keep me out of trouble, since he was friendly with my dad.

When I was about twelve, my mother would send me into the village to pick up groceries and the necessary household items. One nice sunny day around noontime, as I was on my way home with the items that I had picked up at the village grocery store, a group of young lads around my age were hanging out in the center of the village, at Burns Corner. When I came close, one of the bullies walked up to me and challenged me to a fight.

All his friends were cheering him on. In those days I would never back down from a fight, since I had to maintain my reputation as a fierce scrapper who was not afraid of anyone. I put my groceries in a safe spot along the wall and went at it with great venom.

After a while I got the better of my opponent. I ended up giving him two black eyes and a bloody nose. This boy, John, was almost a year older than I was; he was average in size for his age and was one of a large family. He lived on the corner of the old cobblestone boreen that went from the main road into my hood. John, who was a bully and fancied himself a scrapper, went home bloody, battered, and crying, with two big black eyes and a bloody nose that covered all his clothes with blood and mucus. He was a very poor loser and cried like a baby when I got the better of him and won the fight. To his chagrin, none of his friends came to his assistance. Instead, his friends called him out for being a coward and a bad fighter and a big crybaby.

When his father saw him, he was outraged and wanted to know who the villain was that had beaten his son so badly. John told his father that it was that bad boy Kevin who lived up the old boreen, at which time his father vowed revenge on me for hurting John. The father was very angry with me, and the next time my mother sent me to pick up some goods from the village store, John's father was working in his garden and waiting for me. I had the good luck of anticipating that he might want revenge, since he was known to be very protective of his children. I knew he would go after anyone who would hurt his children with a vengeance. In anticipation of what might happen, I brought my dog Diver with me for protection. Diver was a crossbred mutt, and as far as we knew, he was part German shepherd and part collie, a very handsome dog. He was very smart, and I was so proud of him. He was my pal, and everywhere I went he came with me, and I knew he would always protect me. Well, when I came to the corner of the boreen and the main road where John lived, sure enough, out came his father screaming and roaring at the top of his voice, "You villain! You hurt my John," and then the old man came running after me with a furor.

Clitter-clattering down the road as fast as I could run, he chased me with a big stick in hand, down the main road toward the village, screaming at me with a vengeance. I was pretty sure that I could outrun him, but I was taking no chances while he was in pursuit. I gave my dog Diver the signal to go after him, and sure enough Diver took off like a bullet with his head down and his tail down between his back legs, so I knew he meant business. When the father saw Diver in pursuit, he turned back and ran for his life, but he was not fast enough. Diver ripped the backside out of his pants with his teeth, and you could hear the father screaming for help; he was frantic and terrorized. Fortunately for him Diver did not draw blood, just ripped off his baggy pants.

Although Diver was a very friendly dog that loved people, he would have eaten him alive if I had not stopped him and called him back. This was a big embarrassment for the father, and of course the story went around the community and the village like wildfire. The bad boy Kevin had commanded his killer dog in pursuit of poor old Murphy, and it had nearly eaten him alive. The local gossipers had a field day with the wild story and were saying, "That lad will stop at nothing—he is a terror." I hardly ever saw the father after that experience, but I was taking no chances. I was convinced that he was not going to let me get away with hurting his son and making my dog chase him and tear his clothes off. This was a major embarrassment, and one way or the other he would want me punished. For months after this episode, I would take a different route to and from the village, which was by my Aunt Sissy's house. My aunt Sissy was a wonderful lady, so kind and gentle. She was my father's youngest sister. She loved kids, and the ones that were always in trouble she had a real soft spot in her heart for. She loved to hear the wild stories of how I got in trouble again. When she heard the story about Murphy and the dog, I thought she would never stop laughing.

She was a great listener who would never lecture but would give kind and gentle advice.

She was very much like my father and had a very big, big heart. She would always tell my father that I was her favorite. Now, looking back, I can see that she knew I was always in a little trouble and she was softening the way for me. When my parents heard this story, they were horrified, and I was not allowed to bring Diver to the village anymore. My father got a great kick out of the whole event but did not say anything other than "You and that dog are a terror." It was my mother who had the biggest problem with this issue; she felt that I had gotten out of hand. My mother was very proud of the family name, and protecting it was very important to her, and she had a real problem with any member of the family that was going to blacken the family name. She felt that I was out of control and was also concerned about what I was capable of doing, no matter how outlandish it might be, to get the upper hand over the bullies or anyone who crossed my path with a vengeance, and that she did not like. My mother in many ways was very much passive and did not like fighting or troublemaking and was very determined to put a stop to such behavior when it came to her children. My father always supported my mother, but I think deep down he got a kick out of the whole episode, which became a circus. When my aunt Sissy knew that I was in trouble, she would always ask me if I wanted her to speak to my father. I would always say no and take my chances that he would not find out what happened until it became old news. I knew that Aunt Sissy would eventually tell him but always in a way that she knew would not get him worried or upset. My aunt Sissy and my dad were very close and always took care of each other. When she would see me, she would always have a big smile on her face as if to say, "What trouble are you in now?" She would always have candy and cake; she was over-and-above generous, and all the children in the community loved her. Every child should have an Aunt Sissy—she was like a guardian angel.

CHAPTER 14

Dogs

Dogs were an intrinsic part of my childhood. If I close my eyes and conjure up any memory from my childhood, a dog is guaranteed to be a main character, or at a minimum would make a cameo appearance. I recall the various dogs that entered and departed my life as if they were members of the family. They were always there—loyal, empathetic, and coconspirators in my daily adventures. There was nothing I would not do for my dogs, and it always seemed mutual. Since we needed our dogs to be utilitarian and not just pets, we usually went with the hardworking sheepdog. These sheepdogs were not fancy purebreds; they were rough-and-tumble working farm dogs and, for the most part, mutts. Their days were not the cushy nine-to-five of the factory workers in town. These dogs started their days at dawn and ended as the sun set behind the Crathy mountain range.

Despite all the hard work, our dogs always made time for us. With six boys and two girls, they were always ready for some adventure—they had their paws full. The countryside that was our playground was also their playground. They played games, hunted, and fished with us. When we played football, the dogs would sit on the sideline watching for a ball to come over so they could chase it. They would join us in climbing up the mountains and down the quarries and caves. When we would climb up trees, they would stay at the bottom of the tree barking as if they were cursing God for their inability to join us.

One of my favorite dogs was the dog named Diver. Diver was a big, beautiful, dark brown with a coat of glossy, shiny hair that made him look so rich. He had big glassy brown eyes with a black spot on the white of his right eye that made him so distinguished. When he looked at you with his deep, genteel eyes, your heart would melt, and you would want to hug him. He had a big bushy tail always in the up position, with a full curl that made him so adorable.

His big furry tail looked like a big furry wheel sitting on his back that made him look so proud. He had short ears that were always in the vertical position above his head when he was looking at you. Diver was very macho and was not afraid of any other animals; he would take them on and fight to the bitter end. The dog we had before Diver was named Caption. He was an old sheepdog—part terrier, very loyal, and a great dog for herding cattle and sheep. He was a tan-and-white color, very loyal and a great farm dog. He did not have an outgoing personality and was very low key. Caption lived until he was thirteen, which was a good age for a sheepdog/terrier, and he died of old age. When Caption died, we got a new pup right away from a neighbor. The pup was Diver, a crossbred, and it appeared that he was part sheepdog and part German shepherd, a beautiful dog. From the beginning Diver had a sparkle in his eye and, unlike Caption, was anything but boring. You could tell he had that little bit of bad about him that made him different and special. You knew that he was always up to something—chewing on furniture or a pair of shoes and so on. My father was a very neat, handsome man who took great pride in himself, and when he went out to the market or church, he would always dress in his best suit, white shirt with a starched collar, hat, and black laced boots so shiny you could see yourself in the glare. Although his suit was twenty-five years old, it looked brand new, with every crease like the day he bought it. My mother always made sure his clothes and shirts were ironed so that he always looked his best and well cared for, which made my mother so proud of him. His shirt was the detached-collar type, and the starched collar was always so white and clean; he looked more like a banker than a farmer with his dress spit-shined boots. Local people would say that when my dad and mom got married, they were the best-looking couple that ever entered the church. As soon as my dad got home, off came all his Sunday best, and everything was hung up in place.

He was especially proud of my mother, who was very attractive and always looked great and was considered very smart within the farm community that she loved. This was his life that he loved, and he liked to tell people how lucky he was. When it came to dress, this was a trait that none of his six boys took real seriously—all of us are much more causal. On Sunday morning my father always went to early Mass, which was at 8:00 a.m. There was one morning when my father was getting ready for early Sunday Mass, but when he went to get his shoes, there was one missing. He looked all around but could not find it anywhere. When my father encountered any type of a problem, he would always yell for my mother. "Mary Ellen," he yelled, "did you see my shoes? There is one missing." We were all in bed, and Diver was in my bed, hidden under the clothes, since it was a big no-no to bring the dog to bed so we would try to hide him underneath the blankets. We were warned that farm dogs can have fleas, but we were willing to take that little risk because he was so cute and a big part of the family. My mother, who was always working—cleaning, knitting, mending, or making clothes—rarely got to bed before midnight; however, she got out of bed that early morning to help my father look for the missing shoe, but to no avail. Then she called all of us to get up and look for the missing shoe. My father was very annoyed about his missing shoe and was scolding to himself and wanted to know if I had played a trick on him. I knew better, since this kind of trick would result in serious punishment, since church was one of the most important things in my father's life. My father was very devout and would say his prayers every morning and night out loud so we would hear him. He was big on leading by example.

Every night after supper, we had to kneel and join him in saying the rosary and a whole litany of other payers. Diver would lie down next to me during the rosary, and I would try to get Diver to pray, which would get my father very angry.

He felt it was sacrilegious and mocked the church teachings to try to have the dog pray. He would say, "You will go to hell for making a mockery of the holy rosary."

He would not say much until after he was done with the rosary. Then he would put Diver outside and yell at me. I would get a big lecture about how unlucky it was to make a mockery of God's prayers, and then he would say to my mother, "Where did this pagan streak come from?" By now everyone in the house was on a mission, trying to locate my father's missing shoe. I walk down into one of the big fields that we called the calves' field, where all the newborn calves would learn to graze on the very nice fine green grass and where we and Diver played as children; it was one of Diver's favorite spots, where he would lie down in the sun for hours behind the very large boulder in the center of the field, and sure enough there it was, all mangled, with Diver's incriminating saliva all over the shoelaces and upper part of the shoe. The shoe had about twelve lace holes, and the upper three rows on one side were all chewed and gnawed. This was a terrible quagmire, and I was having a tough time knowing what to do. Should I throw the shoe away or bring it home? With Diver's incriminating evidence all over the shoe, what would happen to Diver? I knew that my father had a soft spot for dogs, but on the other hand my mother did not. My mother would put the dog outside in the coldest weather, and she was also somewhat concerned about my influence on Diver. I think she felt that Diver and I were inseparable, and I would encourage him to do bad things, which was partly true.

After a great deal of thinking, I decided to bring the shoe home, and of course the first thing my mother said was "I knew it was that damn dog."

My father looked a little sheepish. He looked at the shoe and said, "Mary Ellen, well, these shoes are twenty-five years old, and I've had at least one set of new soles and heels installed, and it may be time to get new shoes."

He went on to say, "I can clean this shoe up, and my trousers will go over the damaged part so no one will see how bad the shoe really is, and that will do until I get a new pair." It was obvious that my father was trying to lessen the impact of the crime. He too wanted to protect Diver from the wrath of my mother, who wanted to ban Diver from ever entering the house again. After this episode Diver and I kept a low profile for a few weeks, knowing how angry Mom was. After this episode

I built a nice fieldstone thatched mud-wall house for Diver. I was about twelve at that time. It was about eight feet by six feet in size, and we hung out there with the dogs and loved it. My dad was so proud of the stonework structure, and he would show it to his friends and tell them "Kevin built it."

The next-door neighbor had a big red white-headed bull that did not like Diver. As soon as the bull would see Diver, he would come running toward him with his head and big, long horns down close to the ground, which meant he was out for the kill.

Diver was very clever, and when the bull would come close to him, he would make a quick turn and go behind the bull and nip him on the heel of his back foot.

The bull would kick violently and go around in circles, trying to get Diver with his horns or a kick. A kick could kill Diver, or if the bull caught him with his horns, which were long and sharp, he could also rip Diver's body apart, which could be fatal. This would go on until the bull would finally get tired and walk away. By the time the bull got tired, Diver was also tired and would be glad that the duel was over. I loved to watch these fights, knowing that Diver was very smart and would not get caught by the angry bull, and when the bull walked away, I considered that another win for Diver. While Diver was performing his act, he would back up and look at me, looking for my approval while knowing that I was enjoying the duel or otherwise I would have called him off. Sometimes it is the little things in life that give us the most enjoyment.

CHAPTER 15

Fishing Dog

Fishing was one of our favorite hobbies. For the most part, we fished in the mountain streams and rivers. The local farmers, including my father, leased the gaming rights of streams and rivers running through their land, including their mountain moorland, to the angling, hunting, and gaming clubs, which were part of the aristocratic society that was very prominent in those days when many were very wealthy.

As children we would go where most anglers would not go, and the farm owners' immediate family members were allowed to fish and hunt on the property where there were gaming rights. When we went fishing, we had very limited fishing gear and no fancy equipment. Our fishing equipment consisted of a fishing rod that we would cut from a hedge; we would tie a piece of nylon fishing line or a piece of hemp string to the rod and attach a primitive fishing hook to the fishing line or string. We would dig up some worms at the large farm manure pit, where there would be plenty of big fat worms that made great fishing bait. We would fill up a small bucket with worms and some moist dirt that kept them alive until we were ready to start fishing. The live worm dangling on the fishhook was a great attraction for the fish to bite.

One beautiful, bright summer's day, we were fishing in one of our favorite mountain streams located at the foothill of the mountain when along came a young angler from the gaming club with all his fancy fishing gear and fishing garb. He really looked the part. He had a real fancy fiberglass fishing rod and reel that was so impressive it glowed and glittered in the bright sunshine. He was a real Brit, with a real British accident that we could barely understand, and I am sure he had trouble understanding us. We had our colloquial peasant slang he had to decipher. However, he was a very nice lad and asked how we were getting on with the fishing. We had just gotten there and had not caught any fish at that time. He asked us if he could join us, and of course we were delighted and immediately said yes. He introduced himself as Paul, at which time we told him our names and our dog's name, Diver. He loved dogs, and when he saw that Diver was friendly, he patted him and then gave him a big hug, which forever endeared him to us. Diver was a big part of our fishing gang, and he fit in like he was almost human. This stream had mostly trout except that during spawning season some salmon would swim up the stream, but they were rather small and few in number.

After many hours we caught about five or six fish each. However, our English friend with all the fancy gear had caught none, and he could not figure out why he was not catching any fish and asked what he was doing wrong. I told him his fancy glittering gear was too fancy for mountain stream fishing and was scaring away the fish. He got a great big laugh out of that. The real reason he was not catching any fish was probably the type of bait he was using, which was flies, whereas we were using big, live, fresh squirrely worms.

He decided to change his bait and use some of our worms, and finally he caught a nice sixteen-inch trout, which is a pretty good size for a mountain stream, and he was so happy. After he caught his first big trout, he started rattling off words that we'd never heard before, but the big smile on his face told the whole story. This gentle young angler enjoyed fishing and socializing with the local peasant boys, and particularly their dogs. He was a very intelligent young lad and wanted to learn from the locals their simple fishing techniques that seemed to work so well, which had been handed down from generation to generation with no fancy equipment. Diver would sit on the bank of the river next to me with his eyes focused on the river, looking for any sign of trout moving in the water. When some trout would move out from underneath a big rock and pop up from the bed of the river into the open waterway, Diver would watch every move. When the time was right, he would make a big pounce into the stream, grab the fish with his mouth, and bring the fish to me. He would be as proud as can be with his tail wagging, knowing that I would have a treat in my pocket. When he would let me have the fish and I would give him his treat, my younger brother, whom I was very close with and inseparable from, would accuse me of bribing the dog.

Diver caught three trout that day, which really amazed the angler, who caught only a total of four. He had never seen a fishing dog before. He wanted to know if we would sell the dog, and he would give us whatever price we wanted. We would not part with Diver for all the money in the whole world. He was our pride and joy and was one of us, which made him so precious. Everyone that got to know Diver coveted him; it was like having a pretty young girlfriend that all your friends would like to be with. Again, the young angler was amazed at how loyal we were to our dog and would not sell him for any money. He loved dogs and appreciated how loyal we were and how much we loved our dog. Every time Diver would dive into the stream to catch a fish, the angler would pull out his camera and start taking pictures, at which time he would ask all of us to sit down and hug the dog while the fish was still in his mouth, and again he would take a picture. He too loved animals and had a dog of his own, who was more of a hunting dog but not a fishing dog. He said he would love to be able to impress his mates by having a dog that could catch fish. He said his friends were always telling big fishing stories that he would love to top. He wanted to know if Diver was a male or a female, and when we told him he was a male, he was disappointed because he was hoping if it was a female he might be able to get a pup. Then he asked us if we could get him a pup from Diver's mother.

He said he would pay the owner and us good money. He wanted a dog like Diver so badly that he was willing to pay any amount of money, which apparently was no problem for him. I told him I would talk to the family that gave us Diver and ask them to keep a pup from the next litter, for our new English friend Paul as he was willing to pay good money. That made him very happy, and he said he would be back in two weeks to see if there was any luck. Diver's mother at this time was very old and might not have any more pups, but we did not want to disappoint Paul by telling him that Diver's mother might not have any more pups. We also told him that Diver's father more than likely was a stray dog and might not be around anymore. However, he was so enthused with Diver he went on to say a fishing dog would be so great and it would be the talk of his hometown. He asked if he could meet up with us again in two weeks, and we were delighted that someone so grand and posh would even think of meeting up with us peasant boys again. He saw that we were fun loving and having so much fun—it almost seemed he wanted to be like us, not a care in the world, seeking adventure in its simplest form. We agreed on a time and a location to meet at the mountain stream, and we were there on time, but he did not show up, and of course we were disappointed. We were so amused by his accent, the funny words that he spoke, and he was just so much fun and great to be around. It seemed after a few hours like we had known him all our lives; he would call each of us and the dog by our name with his posh English accent. Because we lived in a very poor rural area not far from the foothills of the mountains, there was not a lot of opportunity to meet up with strangers, especially foreigners. This fact made Paul so special, and when our parents heard the story, they were disappointed that they did not have an opportunity to meet him, and my mother told us, "The next time you fish with Paul, invite him home for tea. Although the Irish nationalists were no fans of England and its occupational tyranny.

They knew that the average Englishman had nothing to do or say when it came to colonization or the political agenda, and that for the most part, the English were lovely people.

In particular, they had no problem with the anglers, who were very welcomed visitors that brought money and prestige to this very poor, very rural area. The anglers were not afraid to spend money in an environment where there was little to spend.

They were also very generous and mingled homogeneously with the locals in the pubs and on the street. My mom said he must come from a lovely family. My parents used to say that if young people were nice that was an indication of good upbringing, and you knew the parents were also lovely people.

We had a great time telling all our friends and family about the angler we met and the great time we had with him fishing. It was just so great.

For months after, we would be taking off his British accent for fun. Every time we went fishing, we always hoped we would run into Paul, but it seemed that was not going to happen. He was a very handsome young man with a very charming personality, and I am sure some pretty young girl got ahold of him and he fell in love, and that put an end to his fishing.

During the fishing season, our little village would have several anglers staying at the village inn. The anglers had money to spend when the natives had very little to none, and therefore the merchants loved to see them come. They brought a sense of pride and celebrity to this area that was very poor and rural, which the anglers enjoyed. They loved to go into the pubs, have a pint and talk to the locals. They were very generous and would treat everyone at the bar to a drink. Meeting and talking to the locals were a great experience for them. Some of the local people thought there might be British spies among the anglers, since this rural border village was an IRA hotbed of activists and sympathizers, including all of us.

However, there was never any indication that there was any type of covert angler involvement, and many of the anglers were very sympathetic with the Irish cause, but for the most part they avoided such discussions and would only elaborate on how much they loved Ireland and the people, in particular in the gaming communities. Many of the Anglers loved to brag about their Irish roots or where someone in their family came from. They loved to name the village or place that someone in their family came from, which endeared them to the local village's people. We loved to tell our friends at school about the angler and how he loved Diver and how he was amazed that Diver would jump into the stream and catch fish. The following summer my two brothers and I were back again at our favorite fishing stream with Diver when guess who appeared coming across the heathery moor with its beautiful scent and purple blossoms? It was Paul with a gorgeous young woman so eloquent and beautiful, with a big smile, and it just seemed they were made for each other.

Paul introduced her to us, and her name was Amy. He went on to tell us with great pride that Amy's grandmother came from the foothill of the mountain about a mile and a half across the moorland, where the old fieldstone ruins of her grandmother's house still stood. Paul and his girlfriend loved this spot and told us that he had met with the farmer that now owned the small rural farm and was in the process of buying the old homestead ruins; he would build a Swiss chalet in their place and use it as a summer place for Amy and him to spend time hunting and fishing. Amy loved Ireland and would have loved to move and live there full time, which he too would have loved, but they had to stay home and take care of the family business and all their farm animals that they loved.

We were too young to understand romance, but their love for each other was so in bloom that the beauty of the purple mountain heather and the whin bush's yellow blossom with its beautiful aroma seemed to welcome these young lovers to be part of the mountain's beauty. Paul loved Diver almost as much as we did, and that endeared him to us. His girlfriend, Amy, a huge dog lover, could not stop hugging Diver, and that quickly endeared her to us peasant boys. Diver was one of my favorite dogs. He would lick people, run around in circles, and then run up to me, jump up, put his paws on my shoulders, and look for approval. Diver was so much a part of my life that my mother, a religious and somewhat superstitious woman, was always afraid that I would bring Diver to church.

If sweeping the floor out the door swept away all our good luck, she couldn't even begin to fathom the plague that would befall a family who allowed a dog into church.

She would warn me not ever to think about such a thing and that it would be sacrilegious. "Kevin!" she would howl in a voice that escalated the more resolute she got. "By Jesus, if you're bringing that dog to church, Father O'Riley will ban you forever." This of course had the opposite effect she intended and just served to make the temptation greater.

Every day I went to school, Diver would be waiting at the door for me to come home.

He would run around in hoops with excitement when he would see me. All the schoolboys loved Diver and would hug him and pet him, including the schoolmaster.

The schoolmaster was a person whom for some reason Diver never warmed up to like he would with other people. Maybe he gave off a mean psycho vibe, and Diver also did not like anyone in uniform, including priests. No matter where I would go, including church, Diver would be waiting for me to come out, and of course my mother was always afraid, since the church entrance door was always open during service, so Diver could wander into the church looking for me, or worse yet, I might encourage him to come in.

Diver had great intuition and could round up large numbers of cattle and sheep as if he were reading the ID tags that were fastened to the sheep's and cattle's ears. He could pick out his sheep or cattle even when they were mixed in with large neighboring herds.

In some situations, there could be hundreds of sheep that to the human eye all looked the identical same, other than the owner's stenciled marking that the dog could not read, at least as far as we knew. He would quickly separate his sheep from the neighboring herds, round them up, bring them home, and then line them up in a row to be counted and put into pens.

One lovely, cloudy, warm spring morning when the skies were low and appeared to be touching the mountaintops, Diver and I went checking out our sheep herd on the side of the mountain terrain. Being only eleven years old, I usually preferred playing to doing the chores of the day, but with Diver, I felt as if he and I were on a special mission. Diver, in his typical efficient manner, ran ahead of me and rounded up all our sheep so I could count them. When I was done counting the sheep, he came up to me and was ready for the next assignment. However, I quickly realized that something was wrong with Diver. My brave best friend looked up at me. His deep, dark chocolate eyes emoted a sadness that ran through my body like an electric current. I knew right away that Diver had eaten poisonous bait.

The neighboring farmer would scatter poisonous bait on the mountains to kill the wild dogs and coyotes that attacked and killed his sheep and cattle at night.

I was overwrought with fear, sadness, and panic, but Diver, always the strong one, knew he was wounded and accepted the inevitable with grace. I, on the other hand, stood there talking to him and telling him he could not die. He was my dog and best friend. As Diver took his last breath and collapsed right at my feet, I wanted to scream and cry, but Irish culture did not allow boys my age to show emotion or cry; that was only for girls. But the loss of an animal that you loved as dearly as a sibling was a bitter pill to swallow, and not being able to cry and let the tears flow made it that much worse.

This was literally very painful and heart-wrenching and so hard to bear. I felt I was to blame, since my father always told us to make sure that Diver had his muzzle on when we were checking our sheep in the mountain terrain. He knew the danger. Diver hated the muzzle, and it affected his ability to round up his sheep. Now I had to head home with a very broken heart to tell my father the horrible news. I could tell that my dad was ripped apart on the inside and was very sad about losing Diver. While he himself was trying to stay strong for me, he knew only too well how devastated I was, knowing how much I adored Diver and the sad effect it would have on the rest of our family as well. He turned to me and said, "Son, we will get another dog right away." Within a few days we got a new dog, a beautiful shepherd mix pup, and although he was adorable, no dog could take the place of Diver. He was a very special dog and was put on this earth to be my dog. This was the very first time in my life that I ever suffered a loss that had such a devastating impact on me. Although I had no idea how to deal with the loss, I knew that life had to go on despite the deep sadness and emptiness left by Diver's passing. After I got my composure back, my brothers and I went to where Diver died and buried him with great honors and placed a big rock and planted flowers on his grave.

For months after, we would go to his grave and talk to him and tell him how much we missed him. When the word got around that we had lost Diver, the neighbors would come to our house to sympathize and say what a great dog he was. If I were around, they would be looking for that tear in my eye, but I knew I had to stay strong. Everyone loved Diver. He was the envy of every dog lover. Each one of the neighbors would sing praises of how wonderful and gorgeous he was and how much they'd admired him. They would then tell their lengthy stories about dogs they'd lost for a variety of reasons. Some of them would be very emotional talking about the wonderful dogs they'd lost.

Many would have tears in their eyes that they would try to hide when in public. Some of the stories would get a little far-fetched and had a bit of exaggeration. I loved those stories, and just to know that there were others who felt the same pain as I did was reassuring for an eleven-year-old boy. When they would leave, my father would laugh and fill me in on the ones that had a bit of exaggeration, but of course I did not care. I could not get enough of these dog stories. I loved the stories and wanted every dog to be a big hero and the one that made their boy or girl proud. My mother, who always felt dogs should be outside and never in the house, was also very sad and would say how great a dog he was but that I'd spoiled him. One of my favorite dog stories was the one my father loved to tell me as a very young boy, the one about a great dog, a coursing greyhound that became very famous. The dog's name was Old Master McGrath, and he started out as a small weak pup but went on to be the most celebrated and successful greyhound of his time. He was born in 1866 at Colligan Lodge in County Waterford, Ireland, the home of James Galwey, a well-known Irish trainer and owner of greyhounds. Master McGrath was one of a litter of seven pups, and although small, he was powerfully built and won the Waterloo Championship Cup three times, in 1868, 1869, and 1871. He became such a celebrity that his owner at that time, Lord Lurgan, was requested to take his famous greyhound to be seen by Queen Victoria and the royal family.

There is also an Irish ballad that I love that celebrates Master McGrath. To this day there is a bronze sculpture of Master McGrath in Lurgan, County Armagh, Northern Ireland. His pet name was Dicksy. The lyrics end with the words "Old Ireland had many fames in the days that are gone, but the best and the greatest the world ever saw was the champion of champions, old Master McGraw."

CHAPTER 16

Oscar

Tara, our youngest daughter, was always a big dog lover, and my wife and I promised her a dog for her ninth birthday. Our oldest daughter, Colleen, had gone away to college and we thought a dog would help with the transition. We went to a place where they sold puppies, and she immediately fell in love with a little cairn terrier. As soon as she saw him, she knew he was her dog. We took the pup home, and our daughter named him Oscar, but I thought she should call him Oscar Patrick to make him sound a little Irish, so we settled for Oscar P. (*P* for Paddy.)

A number of the family members were not too keen on the *P*, partly since a number of the extended family members had the first or middle name Patrick, but they soon got used to the name, and when they got to know Oscar, they quickly overlooked the middle name.

Oscar was a very special dog. He was very handsome and had a personality that was so outgoing and larger than life. The children in our neighborhood loved Oscar and would refer to our house as Oscar's house. They would come to see him and play every chance they would get. The small children in the neighborhood would call me Oscar's daddy. When I would get home in the evenings from work, he would literally go through hoops with excitement. My daughter would remind me now and then that he was her dog and not mine, and of course I would just laugh and tell her to ask Oscar whose dog he really was.

Although she wanted Oscar to be hers and hers only, she appreciated how much the rest of the family loved her dog. Oscar had great intuition and could tell when there was something wrong within the family. When my younger brother fell to a fatal accident and the word came to our house, needless to say, I was very upset. In those types of situations, I like to be alone and deal with the loss in private. I moved from the family room to the living room to be alone, but my friend Oscar did not want to see me alone.

He followed me into the living room, and instinctively he knew that there was something disturbingly wrong. He lay down at my feet and would look up at me as if to say, "I am here for you." Oscar was extremely playful and would continually beg family members to play with him, and as a result he got a lot of attention from all of us. The more attention he got, the more he wanted. Oscar loved to tackle and play rough, which required putting on a heavy coat so he would not nip through when playing. His intent was never to nip, but in the act of playing he would sink his sharp teeth in to grab on. When the playtime was over, or as we called it, "the big fight", he would come up to me and lick me all over. This was his way of letting you know he was only playing. When family and friends with small children would come over to visit, Oscar would be primed to do his big fight attack, and the little ones would look on with astonishment. They would be partly scared and partly amused by this wild dog going for the jugular. When playtime was over and Oscar would settle down and start licking me, the children would see that he was just playing rough. After he was done playing and making up, he would go to sleep like a baby.

The children loved to play with and pet Oscar, but after the big fight attack, they would be a little timid and hesitant for a while. Then they would realize that Oscar was only playing and that he was to some extent trained by family members to put on this big show, which he loved and performed so well. When Oscar performed his attack act and children saw him in action for the first time, all the family members would be looking for the reaction of the children. They would be taking pictures and probing the children to see what they taught of Oscar. When Tara went off to college, Oscar was sad, and although she was not there, he would continue to sleep in her bed, and that she loved. Tara brought him to her dorm a few times, and that was an experience. Oscar, although neutered, liked to get on people's knees and do what some dogs do.

Tara had a tough time defending this behavior to her roommates, but Oscar was so lovable her friends overlooked his bad behavior. The boys loved him, and his bad behavior only endeared him to them, and they enjoyed having him around. My wife and I went on vacation for a couple of weeks, and Tara volunteered to take care of Oscar for the two weeks after getting approval from her college roommates, not realizing that the more familiar Oscar became with his surroundings, the more he showed off some of his bad behavior, which was somewhat funny but embarrassing, except to the boys who would come around and loved Oscar. The more embarrassing he became, the better the boys liked it. Oscar became a boy magnet for the girls, and that covered a multitude of sins. Toward the end of Tara's college years, Oscar at fourteen years old started to slip into bad health, and she was heartbroken. After she graduated from college, she went abroad on vacation with her older sister, and while she was away, he passed. My wife and I nursed him as long as we could. Now we had the difficult task of telling Tara. So, my wife and I decided to pick her and her sister up at the airport, and on the way home I gently broke the sad news, and needless to say, she was devastated that she was not home to take care of him during his final days.

We buried him in a nice quaint spot with a headstone and flowers. Tara could never bring herself to go to Oscar's grave and cried for weeks if Oscar's name came up. We were all devastated at Oscar's passing, and all his memorabilia are still all over the house twenty-some years later, and Tara still holds on to her favorite picture. Oscar was a star in the eyes of the family and always the center of attention. His pictures are still all over the house close to twenty years later, and the family talks about him like he is still alive.

Oscar lived until he was fourteen years old, at which time he developed what appeared to be an inner ear infection, which he was treated for. Over time his condition got worse to the point where he could not stand up.

The veterinarian who was taking care of Oscar was not sure if it was an ear infection or a brain tumor. The veterinarian wanted to do exploratory surgery, but my wife and I said no, and we also convinced Tara that surgery might only prolong his suffering.

Prolonging Oscar's suffering and subjecting him to exploratory surgery just did not make good sense. Tara had a very tough time with that reasoning, but being a very pragmatic young woman, she soon saw the reasoning as the better choice.

Since there was no assurance that the surgery would make him better, she also agreed that it probably did not make sense. A few months before Oscar died, my wife and I went to Florida for a week's vacation, and Tara, who lived in Hoboken at this time, came home to stay with Oscar since he was really her dog. Two days after we left on a seven-day vacation, we got a panicked call from our daughter. Oscar had taken a bad turn, and of course we had to cut our vacation short and come home to help our daughter take care of him. When we left on vacation, he would get very down and sad, so when we got back, I talked to him, and he started to perk up a little. We got him special food that was high in protein, and he lived for about another month.

That was a sad day in our house. My wife cried, and I cried on the inside, and we both felt so bad for Tara, knowing she would be devastated. After Oscar's passing there was such a void when we would come home and not see him in his cozy little bed; it left a very empty feeling. When Tara got back to Hoboken, she and her fiancé got another dog, a beautiful Italian greyhound–Lab mix she named Laddie. Now, years later, her husband and two young children love Laddie. He is a very sweet dog, but he too is getting old, and another sad day is on the horizon. Five years after losing Oscar, my wife and I are thinking of getting another dog, but the big question is what type of dog, and it cannot be a dog that will compete with Oscar.

We would not want to erase the wonderful memories by getting another dog like Oscar.

That would not be fair, since no other dog could ever vie with Oscar. Our friends tell us that when the new dog comes along, we will get attached, and very soon the new dog will take over as the new pet. Dogs are the closest things to people, and only true dog lovers can understand these stories. Oscar brought so much fun, entertainment and pure joy to our family that again only dog lovers can understand.

His presence was always there in a very big way and was much bigger than life. Sometimes a child was crying on the street because a friend was not sharing a toy, or the child fell and scratched their knee. As soon as the child saw Oscar, they would run over to hug him. Instead of tears, there would be smiles from ear to ear. Oscar would walk away with his tail wagging. He would have what looked like a big smile on his face, knowing that he'd made a little boy or girl feel happy again. Oscar had a very special way of connecting with little children and was in his glory when there were children around. He would immediately put on some type of a show for them by running in circles, standing on his back legs, and so on. It was fun to watch him connect with children, and seemingly that is why all Tara's male college friends were so intrigued by Oscar.

Then there was Oscar's friend the squirrel. In the backyard, where there were very high oak trees, the squirrel would run up and down the trees playing a game with Oscar, who would chase the squirrel for hours. When the squirrel thought that Oscar was losing interest, he would chase Oscar back to the house. The squirrel would play tag up and down the trees for hours until Oscar would finally get so tired and had to give up the chase. He would enter the house through his own little private push-open doggy door and lie down in his cozy little bed and go to sleep for hours.

CHAPTER 17

Paddy

After we had gone a number of years without a dog, Tara wanted her parents to get another dog, almost like the parents that want a grandchild. She would keep asking when we were going to get another dog. One day I was volunteering at our downtown Rotary festival when our daughter and her mother showed up and insisted that I come and see this gorgeous dog at the Eleventh Hour Recue. Tara insisted we had to adopt this dog. The dog's name was Larry. He was a yellow Lab and what seemed to be part pit bull with a huge personality. He was so adorable when he got up on his two back legs and put on a show. Although I was still not ready to get another dog, I could not disappoint my daughter, and I could see my wife was also sold on Larry, but she left the convincing to Tara. Well, with little choice I said yes, at which point Tara, a huge dog lover, was ecstatic, and her mother had an ear-to-ear smile on her face, and with that all said, how could I say no? In particular, the way Larry sold himself big time, just like a pro, made him an easy sell. When Tara and her mother brought Larry home, Tara invited the rest of the immediate family to come by and meet Larry, an eight-month-old big puppy that knew how to win people over as if he were trained to do so. As soon as Larry was home and comfortable, which came easily to Larry, no one felt that the name Larry matched his big personality, and although I liked the name Larry, I had a very close family friend with the same name. However, the question was whether we should give him a traditional Irish name, one that would match the big personality, so we had to come up with a new name, and since we are for the most part an Irish family, a number of Irish-sounding names came into play. After a great deal of discussion and quibbling, the name Paddy was agreed to, which was great until my brother Joe came to visit.

My Brother Joe's birth name is Patrick Joseph, but since our dad's name was also Patrick, our parents always called him Joe, and when he was serving in the U.S. Army, his friends all called him Paddy. So, he particularly did not like the dog's being named Paddy, since his birth name was Patrick and he was Paddy for short among his friends. Since Patrick is a very common Irish name, there were also nephews and relatives with the name Patrick, so that took a little explaining, and since we could not change Paddy's name again, my brother begrudgingly accepted and became a big Paddy fan. When he calls on the phone, the first one he asks for is Paddy, and when he comes to visit, he loves to give Paddy a lot of attention and take him for a walk.

When all the family heard, including our three grandchildren, who were very young—twins who were three and a half and a younger sister who was two—they were so ecstatic, and all came to visit Paddy. The grandchildren all immediately fell in love with Paddy and could not get enough of him and had the time of their life with him; they played for hours. At one point Paddy, a big dog for eight months, at sixty pounds back then and now eighty pounds, jumped right over my grandson, Connor's, head while both were running around the backyard.

Needless to say, Connor was scared, and it took him a few minutes to regain his composure. When all the family members went home and Paddy cooled down, we noticed he was limping. At first, we did not think much of it, thinking he had strained a leg or something minor with all the excitement of playing with the grandchildren, and we decided to wait for a few days, hoping it would go away, but it did not and if anything got worse.

When we took Paddy to the vet, we quickly found out that our new puppy had a condition very common in yellow Labs: a dislocated hip, medical term *dysplasia*. The vet informed us there was no choice other than major surgery. We were devastated as if it were a child, and then the cost was a number that we were not ready for.

The vet broke down the cost. There were two options, one costing $1,800 and the other costing $2,500. Our daughter insisted on the one that was most likely to render the best results and of course was the more expensive one, which we agreed to. The operation was a big worry for the family; we were wondering if he would be OK.

Then postsurgical care was another concern, since Paddy was a very active eight-month-old puppy, so how we would keep him quiet for three weeks? And indeed, that turned out to be a major challenge. Our daughter Tara, who lived in Hoboken, would come by after work every evening to check on him until the vet gave him a clean bill of health.

The surgery was very successful, though the vet warned us that as he got older the joint might become arthritic. However, with all that said, there was one episode where I put a stake in the backyard with a nice long swivel leash where he could not run around and prolong or impair the healing process. As I walked into the house and checked on him out the back kitchen window, to my horror I saw him up on his two back legs, one where he'd had the surgery, jumping like crazy trying to get loose. I was sure that he had done serious damage to the hip that had been operated on only two days prior, but fortunately there was no issue, and he was back running around after his first two weeks. At the first postsurgical visit, the vet reported that he was doing great and did not have to come back. However, he informed us that as Paddy got older arthritis might affect the joint. Now that he is twelve-plus years old, the vet's warning has come to fruition, but with a little dog aspirin now and then and the herbal supplement XTEND, he is doing great. Paddy is a great dog in so many ways—so loyal, the best guard dog ever. We can go to bed with doors open and feel very secure. He likes to steal food off the counter and pillage the garbage can when we are out. But overall, he's a great dog and a great companion. He has a huge presence, a very intimidating bark with an aggressive demeanor, until he gets to know you.

As he gets to know you, he quickly becomes your best friend and will lick you all over. Yes, his bark is much worse than his bite—he welcomes everyone as long as my wife, Tara, or I am around. At twelve-plus years old, Paddy is in great shape, and he walks three miles most days with me or my wife. He loves his walks.

As soon as we get up in the morning, he is doing hoops by the front door to get out on his walk. I am not sure if it is the walk or the time together when it is just, he and I that he likes so much. There are many Paddy stories, some good and some not so good. We cannot leave him alone with strangers, because as soon as we leave, he becomes very protective and does not trust the strangers. In one situation I had to leave while a contractor was replacing an in-ground pool heater, and before leaving I asked the contractor if he was OK with Paddy. He laughed and said, "Can you see we are big buds?" Paddy seemed to like the contractor, who was a big dog lover and had a German shepherd of his own, and that was how it seemed; however, I had no sooner left when I got a panicked call. The contractor was asking me to come back immediately and saying that Paddy had turned into a monster. "He is trying to nip me," he moaned. As soon as I came back, Paddy put on his big smiley face and became an angel dog, while the contractor was white as snow and looked traumatized. The contractor, a real nice, low-key guy, was so embarrassed—he grew up with dogs and a big dog lover, so how could this happen to him? Then he said to me, "Can I try to pet him?" at which time I said, "Yes, of course." When the contractor approached Paddy, he jumped up on him and licked him as if to say, "I am sorry." Needless to say, after that experience we never left Paddy alone with strangers no matter how comfortable they felt. Paddy was not good with other dogs. If they in any way infringed on his privacy, he would become very aggressive and attack. There have been several situations when Paddy has embarrassed me big time.

One time I took him to a downtown outdoor park event where there were many people and a lot of dogs, and while I was mingling in the crowd, I ran into an old friend that I had not seen for a while, and he had a beautiful cockapoo. When suddenly, his dog went to smell Paddy, Paddy very viciously attacked to the point where I was horrified and very concerned that the other dog might have gotten bitten. I told my friend to thoroughly check his dog and if he had any concerns to take the dog to the vet and pass all associated costs on to me. It was fortunate that I had Paddy on a short leash and was able to restrain him. This was a very embarrassing situation, and my friend was so surprised, saying "He looks like such a sweet dog," and I could only say "I guess you cannot always trust a dog, no matter how friendly," and he agreed.

Then Paddy has a thievery streak where he will go to extraordinary efforts to confiscate food if it is not stored in a very safe place. My wife and I have fallen victim a number of times when we have put steaks, lamb chops, and other foods up high but not high enough, and he managed to reach them when we turned our backs. It seems that as soon as we leave, he goes on a rampage, looking for what he can find.

When we take him on a visit to my daughters' or son's house, I must warn them to put food away, but Tara is a trusting soul when it comes to dogs, and with a big soft spot for Paddy, she too has fallen victim. No matter what Paddy does, Tara will always have his back, and that unconditional love is always there, and I am painted with the same brush. My wife gets very mad at him and wants to kill him until Paddy waits for the right moment and noses up to her with an angel dog face, and she cannot help but to forgive him. Then there is the part where Paddy makes us proud because he is the best guard dog ever, and when there is any kind of activity in our very quiet neighborhood, not only do we feel safe, but all our surrounding neighbors also know that Paddy is always on the job, and if there is something he deems unusual in the surrounding area, he will circle the fence. He will circle the yard back and forth until what he deems a threat is gone. He loves his own private doggy door, which gives him the freedom to go in and out at will. Our backyard is fenced in, providing a level of security, but should any type of invader come around, that person would not want to take on a large, eighty-pound dog with what seems to be a pit bull head. Paddy also has a soft spot, and when I came home from the hospital after having major surgery, when I would convalesce on my very comfy easy chair, he would lie at my feet and look up periodically as if to say "Are you OK? He loves little children and is so gentle and loves to play with them, and the children compete for his attention. When my wife and I go on vacation, we have Tara and her husband Mike come twice a day to feed and walk Paddy, and when our daughter is not available, we bring in a dog sitter, but with all that he is so lost and very sad: he will not eat or drink for at least three or four days, and he walks around in a daze. When we get back home, it takes a day or two for him to get back to his old self. When my wife and I go out for the evening or for some event, he will not eat until we come back home.

We think he suffers from separation anxiety because he drags his bed all over the place and still, at twelve years old, tears stuff up. We also think he feels abandoned and becomes anxious, which always makes us feel bad. When we go on vacation, he is always on our minds, and my wife or I will check on him on a regular basis, and when Tara and Mike are taking care of him, they text us on a regular basis and send us pictures of a happy face, and we know he is in good hands. I have to admit he is very spoiled, and maybe to a fault. The more spoiled, the more they depend on their owners, and that is not always good, since we want our dog to be happy all the time rather than being sad when we are not around.

When they say a dog is man's best friend, that is for the most part an understatement—dogs become so much a part of the family you wonder how you could live without them.

CHAPTER 18

Horses

Horses, like dogs, are very special animals, and they too are very smart in their own way and have great animal instinct. Like dogs, they get very attached to their master and will follow him around, but to a lesser extent. They are beautiful animals and have an aura of great pride and strength. Growing up, I always wanted to have my own horse. The neighboring farmer had a beautiful mare that was about three years old and that I named Nelly. The neighbor tried to train her to be a working farm horse but ran into difficulty when the horse would rust (back up) rather than go forward and would not cooperate with him, so he gave up and just let her graze on the land.

When the neighbor would harness her to pull a cart or any load, she would rust and stand on her hind legs rather than pull the cart in a forward direction. This behavior is a severe form of rusting and is a major problem that poses a major issue for the owner because the mare might never become a working horse.

At this time, I was a young lad of about sixteen years old. I loved animals and was very good at working with them. I was young and intrepid and full of confidence that I could make this beautiful animal work for me. I spoke to the neighbor about the horse and asked if he had any interest in selling her. He said yes, he would sell her, but only to someone who would take good care of her. He too was a big animal lover, and maybe that was part of the problem—he was too easy on her when training. Then he asked me if I was interested in buying her. I told him yes, I was, but I would have to talk to my father. I asked the neighbor a lot of questions about the horse, and he was very candid. He told me all the good and bad in great detail.

He knew that I was very good with animals, and as a result he felt if anyone could make this horse work it would be me.

However, his main concern was that she would be treated well and not abused. Many of the professional horse trainers can be very tough and somewhat cruel to the animal in order to get the results they are looking for, and that the owner did not want for his horse.

I went home and talked to my father, who had heard all the stories about the neighbor.

There were many stories in the farm community about how the owner had failed in trying to train the horse to work (which is referred to as breaking in the horse).

My father, who grew up with horses, was very skeptical and doubted that anyone could break in this horse after the owner had failed and more than likely caused irreversible damage. He was also particularly concerned since I was not a big, robust lad like the people who normally broke in horses and could run the risk of getting hurt in the process. His main concern was for my safety; he felt there was the potential for me to get hurt breaking in a horse that was already spoiled by the owner and as a result might react badly when again attempting to train. However, with a great deal of persuasion and audacious young confidence, I was able to convince my father to let me buy the horse. There was an agreement that if breaking in failed, the neighbor would take back the horse and refund the payment. My father was very uncomfortable with this decision, but now that I was older, he wanted to show his confidence in my ability. He also felt that if I were not successful, I would learn from the experience.

I went back to our neighbor and explained to him my father's position. I told him that he would go along with the deal with the stipulation that if the horse could not be broken in the neighbor would have to take her back and also would have to refund all the money.

The neighbor, who was very much a gentleman, said in reply, "Here is the deal: I will give you the horse for forty pounds, and you do not have to give me any money unless you are satisfied with her training performance."

I was so elated (what a guy!), and my father went to the neighbor and personally thanked him for being so generous and putting so much trust in me. When I brought the horse home, I christened her and was determined to make her work.

My father, being an industrious farmer, always had an abundance of oats and feedstuff in storage. The first thing that I did was to start feeding Nelly a small amount of oats, which she loved and which made her stronger. After a month or so, her coat of hair started to shine so beautifully, and one day her previous owner, our neighbor, came by to see how she was doing and was amazed at how good she looked and asked me what I was feeding her. Horses, like dogs, bond with the person that feeds them. Although the previous owner had taken good care of her, she had never gotten this type of treatment, and she loved it. When I would visit her in the fields, as soon as she would see me, she would start to neigh and trot toward me. The neigh was her big hello. Now that spring was coming quickly, I had to come up with a program to start training Nelly. My first approach was to take Nelly for long walks and back her up gently, and she responded very well. The next step was to install her head harness with a grinding bit in her mouth in order to make the inside of her mouth more sensitive so that she would respond to directional requests, such as those for left and right turns, that I would make by pulling on the reins that were attached to the training bit. The reins were attached to the head harness holster that held the bit in place in her mouth. Selecting the right training bit was a major undertaking with so much for me to learn. The need to select the proper mouth-training bit was paramount to successfully breaking in the horse. Selecting the wrong type of training bit would end in disaster, causing the horse to violently rust and as a result ending the opportunity to successfully move forward with the training process. I knew this was an area in which I needed some good, experienced advice from someone who had many years working with and training horses.

As with many things in life, when breaking in a horse, you get only one shot at it. Keep in mind that a horse is one of the most intelligent animals and will detect the trainer's incompetence and will no longer do anything that the trainer demands. Worse yet, the horse might rust and stand on her back legs.

This is where the trainer could get seriously injured—or worse, killed with a wrong move.

Training a horse is very serious business and can be very dangerous for trainers if they do not know what they are doing. Although I was very young and inexperienced, I had enough instinct to know there was no room for error. My father had no experience breaking in horses, but as in everything he was full of great intuition, and when he would give me advice, it was always spot on. My father recommended that I go visit an old family friend who grew up with horses, including racehorses, and had oodles of years training all kinds of horses, again including racehorses. It is important to understand the overall strength of a horse. According to James Watt, a Scottish engineer, one horsepower can potentially move 550 pounds, versus the average man, who can move 110 to 150 pounds if in good physical shape. On my father's advice, I visited our neighbor Mr. O'Brien, the horse expert. He was a very nice man who loved to help neighbors, loved young people, and was very well respected in the community. He had a large family and some kids that were around my age and were neighborhood school friends; we were always together.

He was amazed that a young lad could be so enthusiastic about the monumental task of training a horse. So of course, he was delighted and honored to be able to help in every way he could, including helping me with some of the more difficult training tasks. The first thing he did was to advise me in a very nice way on how dangerous training a horse can be. Mr. O'Brien asked me to excuse him for a minute and ran into his house yelling for Mel. Mel was his wife, a wonderful neighbor and a friend of my mother.

He went on to say, "You will never guess who is here and what he is up to." Mr. O'Brien's wife insisted I come in, sit down, have a cup of tea, and tell her about my big adventure, and then she ran to the back door and yelled for her son Gregory, who was one of my close school friends, to come in.

She said to her son, "Guess who is here?" and of course Gregory was delighted to see me and wanted to help me break in the horse, and he too was a big-time great help, and the idea of breaking in a horse was right up his alley. My dad used to say breaking in and working with horses was in their blood, and I would have to agree. The son, just like the father, was a natural when it came to horses, and the two of us made a great team, and he too loved horses.

After I had a big warm cup of tea and one of Mrs. O'Brien's delicious scones, Mr. O'Brien sat down next to me, and with a big smile and one arm around my neck, he said, "Kevin, my boy, do you have any idea what you are getting into, and does your father know what you are going to be taking on?"

I said, "Yes, and he advised me to talk to you, since you know so much about horses." With that the big smile on his face went ear to ear, and again he put his arm around my shoulder and gave me a big hug. I greatly appreciated Mr. O'Brien's help. I wanted some guidance. I wanted to make sure that I was going in the right direction with this critical task that I knew so little about.

He was such a wonderful neighbor—he would come over with his son, my friend Gregory, and would always say, "Kevin, my boy, what are you up to now, and how are you doing with Nelly?" He took great interest in Nelly's progress and would say with a big smile, "Son, you have a big job here to do, but you are doing great." He was the most positive man ever who always made you feel that you were on top of the world, and if things were getting tougher, he would always say, "You are the one to do it, and Gregory will help you because he loves to work with you, and anything to do with horses he loves. I want you to know all Gregory wants to talk about when he is at home is you and Nelly. This is such a big story in our house, and we all cannot stop talking about you and Nelly." Mr. O'Brien would meet up with my father and have long talks with him. He was always so positive in talking about my progress and the great job I was doing breaking in Nelly. This was great for me and gave my father a great sense of pride.

My father was very nervous about the whole process and how well I was doing training Nelly but got some comfort from knowing that I had the best mentor ever. My mother did not like to talk about it because she was so scared that something could happen to me or Gregory. My dad would tell Mr. O'Brien how wonderful his son Gregory was to work with me day and night. My father also felt better that that I was not always alone with Nelly and would say, "You cannot always trust a horse." Gregory and I loved Nelly and trusted her to the end. She always made us feel like she was part of the team. Mr. O'Brien was a very interesting character and widely recognized for his broad intellect and knowledge in a very broad range of tasks. He was very well respected within the community and could always be counted on to step up and meet the many challenges that neighboring farmers would have to deal with, in particular when it came to animal illnesses and problems.

My father was a great fan of Mr. O'Brien and had great respect for his knowledge. He shared his wealth of knowledge so generously among the people that he considered his many friends. You could hear my father and Mr. O'Brien laughing a mile away; they enjoyed and appreciated each other's company. Mr. O'Brien was always good for a great story and his litany of great one-line jokes. My dad was a more serious type of man but loved spending time with Mr. O'Brien and would say with a big smile, "He lightens my heart."

He knew how to make my father feel good by assuring him of the great success that I was having with training Nelly.

My father got great encouragement from knowing that Mr. O'Brien was my training mentor and that his son was my best friend. The next step in the training process was to install the necessary pulling harness on the horse. I would walk her around for about two hours a day for a period of two weeks. It was important that she get used to wearing the harness before I attached a load. The next step was to attach small loads, such as logs of wood, for her to pull around the fields. I would have her walk slowly and gently while I would continually talk to her. While talking to Nelly, I would praise her and pat her on the neck to let her know that she was doing well. At the end of each session, I would get her a nice treat of fresh oats and fresh water to drink. The next big step was to hook up a two-wheeled cart and have her pull the cart. Back then the two-wheeled carts had big iron-shod wooden wheels with spokes. The iron-shod wheels made a lot of noise when we were riding on the old cobblestone lane, which Nelly had to get used to. No load was added to the cart for the first week, whereas on the second week small loads were progressively added until there was what was considered the maximum load. This was where the training became very challenging. For some reason, the noise of the iron-shod cartwheels made her very nervous. When the cart was attached to her harness and she had to start to pull it, she would start walking funny, kind of sideways. This was a time when my friend Gregory was great. He, like his dad, had all the natural instincts when it came to working with horses and he always had such a lovely, soothing personality that made him so perfect when it came to calming Nelly. Gregory had a gorgeous sister with a big personality who was a year younger than Gregory, and there was a little bit of a two-way puppy love crush where she and I would talk forever. Gregory knew that we liked each other, and he would always tease me; if I said or did something funny or maybe a little bit bad, he would say, "I will tell my sister," to embarrass me and see my face blush like a laden lamp. I was always hoping his dad was not around to hear Gregory's comment about his sister and me. After Gregory and I would pat Nelly and gently talk to her when she would start to walk sideways, she would lift her feet and put them down in almost the same spots until she would get her composure back. I would stop and talk to her and again give her a small amount of oats and a drink of water. I would keep talking to her in a soothing but firm voice in order to get her to pull the cart slowly. During this time, I could not show any sign of stress or emotion and just continued providing assurance and positive reinforcement until she got comfortable pulling the cart. All of a sudden, she started to move out with the cart like there was no problem.

When training a horse, the trainer has to be very careful and not show any type of negative emotion, since that would send a signal to the horse something was wrong and could have a very adverse effect on the training process. From that point forward, there was never a problem with her pulling the cart. Now it was time to start adding small loads to the cart on level ground. It was very important not to overload it, since that could cause her to rust, which would be a big problem, since once a horse starts to rust, it will probably never pull a cart forward again. Rusting is the ultimate indicator of a rebellious horse. Now again it was time to follow the same process by starting with a small load at the bottom of a small hill and repeating the process up the hill while adding to the load a little at a time. Going up a hill posed two concerns, as follows: the pull would be much harder, and when she stopped, she had to maintain a slight pull to prevent the cart from rolling backward. After going through all the cart exercises for about a month, it was time to do some real work. The next big step was to get into the cart and again have her pull the cart slowly while I guided her using the extended reins that went through the horse's collar harness spikes from inside the cart.

Then Gregory would walk in front of her to make sure she did not attempt to run away with me in the cart. He was my friend and partner, and we did everything together, knowing we were a team, like brothers. This was a very important part of the training, since many functions could only be performed using the extended reins, such as mowing a meadow.

This training task required two people: one to be by the horse's head, ready to grab the reins at the head halter, while the other person was in the cart, using the extended reins, and that was where Gregory was great. He was the best of the best. If the mare decided to bolt while I was in the cart, using the extended reins, he was there to grab the halter and hold her.

This process was followed for the first five or six times we used the extended reins. Then Gregory and I would alternate, he would ride in the cart, using the extended reins, while I would walk in front of her, monitoring the progress. Now it was time for the biggest training task of all, the mowing machine, which was the final training task and by far the most difficult and the most dangerous, since the mowing machine had very sharp moving blades that were used to cut hay. The mowing machine could be very dangerous for the horse as well as the trainer.

If the horse were to rust or run away while cutting hay, it could be catastrophic. Again, during the training process, this was a two-man job where one walked in front of the horse while the other sat on the machine, guiding the horse and operating the machine while cutting the hayfield. The training process required both people to be very knowledgeable and in sync while in the training mode. We also had another friend who mowed hay meadows as a business and was excellent with horses. His name was Terry. Terry was a friend of my father and Mr. O'Brien, and he helped me to put the mowing machine on Nelly and set up the harness properly. Terry had Nelly pull the idle machine around the hayfield a few times before activating the cutting blades.

The cutting blades made a loud cutting noise that the horse had to get used to.

After Terry mowed the first few laps arounds the meadow, he then let me get on the machine and cut the next few laps while he stayed on the sideline, giving instructions, and Gregory walked in front of the horse while offering Nelly verbal soothing encouragement. First, we used a meadow that was already cut and had Nelly pull the machine while the mowing blades were operating so she would get use to the noise of the mowing machine. The next day Gregory and I repeated the same task, except I put the mowing machine into operation where there was light grass. I repeated this task for about one hour each day with my friend Gregory for one week so Nelly would get comfortable with the noise. Now she was trained to start mowing regular meadows but in small quantities until she got the hang of it and used to the weight of the load. This process was repeated until Nelly was finally broken in to be a working horse.

Terry was also a great friend of my father and very good with horses and machinery. Like Mr. O'Brien, he too was extremely helpful in every way with his very low profile; he was a giant of a man with a lovely personality in every respect. For a few months I kept Nelly's workload light and increased the load by a little every day until I knew how much work she was capable of doing. As it turned out, she was a great workhorse and became very easy to handle. A big thanks to Mr. O'Brien, a teacher, a scholar, but most of all a mentor who knew exactly how to work with the youth and motivate them to be the best in what they did. As for me, I was a strong-willed, very independent adolescent, but because of Mr. O'Brien, not only did I learn how to train a horse, but I also learned the most important lessons in life: how to be a friend, how to be a good neighbor, how to be a teacher, and how to work with young and intrepid teenagers who already have minds of their own and in some ways want to do it their way when at times they may not have a clue.

Then there were Mr. O'Brien's son, my friend Gregory, a chip off the old block, and of course Terry, who was the best of the best. Terry was a master of the ins and outs when it came to machinery and horses. And with his low-key approach, he could move mountains. Looking back at those wonderful times and great people, I realize how fortunate I was at the tender age of sixteen to have people like the O'Briens and Terry in my very young life and to have a pal like Gregory, and of course my father, who was big enough to stand by and let his young son take on a task where often great men failed. It is only now that I can appreciate the extraordinary wisdom of my dad during those somewhat primitive times in rural Ireland to let me give it a try, despite all the danger and potential pitfalls. Not only were all these great men mentors on the workings of breaking in a horse while operating complicated farm machinery, but also, more important, I received a lesson in life on how to mentor young people in such a positive way, and that has stayed with me for the rest of my life.

To some degree that is the reason I became involved with teaching the trades as part of continuing education in our vocational school system in the United States and mentoring young people in the trades and the business world. There was only one minor problem with Nelly: she did not like working for anybody other than Gregory and me because we spoiled her, and as a result that required some additional training. I would have to be present while other members of the family worked her until she became comfortable with them, and I would insist that they treat her exactly the same way Gregory and I did if they wanted good results. She became a terrific working horse and was the envy of the community. Nobody could ever figure out how a sixteen-year-old boy and his friend could make a horse that had already been spoiled in training by a previous owner work when grown men had failed.

Nelly was fourteen hands high, which was approximately seven feet to the top of her shoulder. She was very sturdy and well built. To this day I am very grateful to our wonderful neighbors Mr. O'Brien, my friend Gregory, and Terry; they had a lot of horse-training experience and offered their help and advice. That was extremely valuable, and I could not have had the same results without their wealth of experience, knowledge, and assistance.

Although they have all passed away, they will always have a place in my heart as the kings of nobility. I loved to ride Nelly and go galloping all over the place, and it seemed that she liked it too. In those days we had no fancy riding harnesses or riding saddles and just rode bareback and would hold on to her mane. I would attempt to stand on her back while galloping; however, she did not like that too much. She would rebel by putting her head down, throwing up her hind legs, and throwing me off, which could be very dangerous. Horse-riding accidents where the rider falls off or gets thrown off can result in serious injuries. Some of the common injuries are broken limbs, head injuries, and the most serious of all, a broken neck. In some very serious but rare situations, there can be spinal damage where the victim becomes paralyzed. My father used to continually warn about the danger of horseback riding and falling off. Little did he know that I was standing on the horses back while she was galloping? He would have had a fit if he only knew.

My family had a second farm about two miles away from where we lived by road, which consisted of an old cobblestone boreen. The remote farm was where my father planted most of the crops. When the crops were harvested, we would take them home using the horse and cart. One day I was on my way home from the remote farm with a cartload of farm goods. While riding on top of the load, I saw another young man with his horse coming toward me. Nelly was in heat, and when she saw the other horse coming toward her, she suddenly bolted and took off while I was riding on top of the cartload of farm goods, and when I tried to pull on the reins to stop, her the reins got caught under the saddle.

I tried to break the reins loose, and they would not come loose, and when I reached out over the horse's back in an attempt to loosen the reins that had gotten stuck, I lost my balance and fell underneath the cartwheels and got dragged for some distance along the cobblestone boreen. If it were not for the young man, Freddy, a school friend with the oncoming horse who came running to my rescue, I would have been seriously injured or worse while under the large iron-shod cartwheel. When I got out from under the cartwheel, I got up and brushed myself off the best I could. I was in severe pain, and my right arm and right-side ribs were severely bruised to the point where I could hardly move or use my right arm for months after. When I regained some of my composure, I untangled the reins, checked Nelly out, and headed home with the cartload of farm goods. On my way home, I had to pass my favorite Aunt Sissy's house, and when she heard the cart noise coming, she knew it was me, and there she was, out with a treat of tea and cake. Just like my dad, she was smart and very intuitive, and she saw that something was wrong. She asked me whether I was all right. She said I looked very pale and did not look like my usual self. I told her the story but asked her not to tell my father. I was afraid if my father heard the story, he would not want me working alone with Nelly, and of course I did not want that. It was not until months later that my father found out, and he was annoyed that I had not told him. He was concerned that I might have internal injuries that had not been attended to and could have serious consequences. Although I had little knowledge of what to do, intuitively I had performed my own physical therapy, or what I thought was physical therapy, for months by lifting my arm up and down a little every day until I had full use of my arm.

In spite of all the trials and tribulations, Nelly was a wonderful animal, and I treated her like a pet. One day Nelly was not feeling good—she had some type of stomach cramps. She came up from the fields to our house and came around to the back door, which was usually open.

She put her head in the open door like she was looking for me. She was prancing her feet, and I knew there was something wrong or bothering her. I gave her a drink of tepid water and walked her around the road for about an hour until she stopped prancing with her feet. She was almost like a human and knew when to demand attention. My father always said I had her so spoiled, and I could only agree, but it was fun spoiling her— she was like a big baby. When Nelly started working, she had to get shoes on all four feet in order to protect her hooves. The iron shoes also gave her traction to pull heavy loads. I will never forget the first time I took Nelly to the blacksmith for shoes when she was almost four years old. The shoes were made from iron bars and were formed on an anvil after the iron was heated to where it was molten hot in the forge fire. The hot, molten iron was formed into horseshoes by the blacksmith using a hammer and other blacksmith tools on an anvil that was used to forge or repair metal objects. When the shoe was formed to be the perfect size for the horse's hoof, the blacksmith put the red-hot shoe on the horse's hoof. The red-hot iron shoe burned the outside surface of the hoof and allowed the shoe to properly seat without hurting the animal. The shoe was placed on to the horse's hoof, where special nails were used to fasten the shoe to the hoof. When the hot shoe went on Nelly's hoof for the first time, she almost went through the roof. Her reaction to the hot shoe was not from pain, since there is no pain, but the smoke, smell, and fumes scared her. The blacksmith in our village was one of the best in the business, and we would not take Nelly anywhere else. The blacksmith was taken by surprise when Nelly jumped up, but being extremely knowledgeable with horses, he knew exactly what to do to calm Nelly down. He put her to one side while he installed shoes on another horse while at the same time, he kept a conversation going with Nelly. Every so often he would rub her face, pat her on the neck, and talk to her until it was like she knew and understood him.

When it came time to install Nelly's shoes, she was as calm as could be. It was like a miracle how she became so calm, and the blacksmith said, "I told you she would be OK."

The blacksmith was a great judge of horses, and there was nothing he did not know about them. He said Nelly had the makings of a very fine horse, and he could tell she was well taken care of by her nice soft coat of hair and pleasant, easygoing demeanor. He went on to say, "You take very good care of this horse, don't you?" I was so amazed at the skill and knowhow he demonstrated in dealing with horses.

He just knew exactly how to calm their fears and put them at ease like he had known the horses forever. He went on to warn, "Horses are just like people, and if you treat them right, you will have a friend that will do your heavy work for a long time." It was just amazing how in such a short time Nelly and the blacksmith had bonded like they understood each other. This was another great experience where I learned so much about horses. I am convinced that animals, in particular horses and dogs, are much smarter and have much greater instinct than we give them credit for. In the mountains there were wild horses, and my brothers and I loved to chase them and try to corner them so we could jump on to their backs and go for a wild ride. Attempting to ride a wild horse was extremely dangerous from many points of view. Wild horses can kick, which could be fatal if a kick connected with one's head or other vulnerable parts of the body, and of course to try and ride a wild horse was even more dangerous because if the daredevil missed his foot, he could get trampled by the wild animal. This was so dangerous, but it was great fun, and we would spend hours upon hours chasing the wild horses, and when one of the wild horses would get cornered, the rider would jump on its back. Once the horse was mounted, the rider was off for a wild ride until thrown off, which was always inevitable.

These wild horses were beautiful animals, and they had so much grace, and for horse lovers they were a pleasure to look at and watch in their wild wilderness habitat where only heather and wild fescue grew. It is said that the Irish Gypsies used to capture the wild mountain horses and train them to pull their caravans. The Gypsies, who are also referred to as the Irish tinkers, were very skilled at training horses, and when their horses were trained, they became very valuable, and the Gypsies would also sell them in the marketplace, mostly to farmers, and get good money for them. But the more astute farmers would not buy the wild mountain horses because they felt the wild breed could not be trusted to work and was known to run away while attached to machinery while working. This posed a major safety issue for all involved, and there were many tragic stories that went around. Training Nelly to be a great workhorse was one of my most memorable and rewarding experiences growing up and is one I will always treasure, along with the wonderful neighbors and friends who played such a major role in in mentoring and assisting in the process. Now that I am older and have children and grandchildren of my own, I can reflect on how supportive and wonderful my father was, and in particular how brave he was; he knew the danger involved in breaking in a horse but still was there in full support. I have also reflected on all our wonderful neighbors and the friendships that he cultivated despite his, for the most part, shy demeanor. Parenthood, in my opinion, is the most challenging and yet the most rewarding aspect of life. You have only one chance to get it right, and if you do, the rewards can be great, and if you do not, there can be a lot of trials and tribulations along the way that can have an effect for generations to come.

After emigrating to the US, I had not seen my friend Gregory until one day in London, at my younger brother's funeral, who should show up but Gregory, who had traveled hundreds of miles with his beautiful, much younger sister to be there for me and our family. I was so touched.

CHAPTER 19

Irish Gypsies

The Irish Gypsies, also referred to as tinkers or travelers, are a nomadic people that travel all across Ireland in colorful caravans pulled by very high-spirited horses that are more than likely wild mountain breeds. The name *tinker* is mostly an old Irish term derived from their tinsmith trade: they made cans, pongee buckets, bathing tubs, and other tin products that they sold door to door, mostly to farm households. The products were custom-made items that farmers and households could use in a primitive environment.

In those days the Gypsies did not own any land or dwellings and lived year-round on the road in the horse-pulled caravans that they would park along the roadside. The Gypsies also would buy and sell horses. Their horses would feed along the roadside and ditches, where there was plenty of good, lush grass due to the nice, temperate, moist Irish climate. It is estimated that there were at one time approximately twenty-five thousand Gypsies that traveled the roads of Ireland. Their main source of income in those days came from tinsmithing pots and pans and selling them for farm household use all across the country and at town fairs, which were a monthly event in every town and little village throughout the country.

The Gypsies were also known for selling horses, which were for the most part wild mountain horses that they captured and trained and then sold at the market. They would also buy old horses and donkeys, and they would ginger them up and sell them at the market, where they had a reputation for being very creative and resourceful in ways that were less than creditable, and that is why most astute farmers would not buy horses or donkeys from the Gypsies, knowing their questionable history and somewhat shady reputation. When I was growing up in Ireland, every town and village would have a market day known as the fair day.

This was a perfect venue for Gypsies to sell their wares. They would set up stands and hawk their products by soliciting every passerby.

The Irish farmers in general were very kind to the travelers, and if they had a good day at the market, they would support them by buying a little of their merchandise and also buying them a drink if they met up in the local pub. During the fair there would also be all types of other market stalls where people would sell everything that you can imagine. The little village where I grew up was called Swad, a short name by the locals for Swanlinbar, a picturesque little village located in the northwest corner of the republic and in County Cavan, in the province of Ulster. This was one of Ulster's nine northern counties, a very rural but beautiful scenic area with mountains, glens, and glistening lakes.

On the north side of the town, there was a beautiful large lake called Lough Erne, and on the south side there was a smaller beautiful glistening blue lake, Brackley Lake, that could be seen from the elevated surrounding terrain. Swad was located in a valley at the foothill of two mountains. This was a very special place and will always have a place in my heart. The village was very spirited, and there was always something going on, often competitive local community sports, where we had our own big-time football hero, Owen Roe, who was one of the great County Cavan All-Ireland footballers and brought fame to the county and his little village, Swad, in 1947. This little village would have all kinds of stage plays, bazaars, bingo, and numerous other events at the village town hall, and then there was the annual village carnival, where people came from all over, and it was just great. Although there was very little money in those days, everyone was so happy and upbeat, and life seemed to be all about people, friendships, and true concern for everyone's well-being. Today Swad is surrounded by at least four nice golf courses, two of them five star, each with a beautiful hotel and great food.

There was a deep sense of loyalty and support for the less fortunate. People whistled and sang these melodious rebel songs as they went along their way like they did not have a care in the world. Everyone was greeted with a warmth that was nurturing and comforting. These were the days, and we were taught they would never end, but Ireland, too, in later days sold out to the fortunes of the modern industrial world, where today it is much more about the material things and there is less time for the comradery and warmth that were so much a part of the old times. I love the Scottish poet Robert Burns's old-time song "Auld Lang Syne," and that says it all in so many ways, but with that said, the future is always moving in a forward direction, and that is the way it is meant to be. In life there always has to be a balance, and each generation has to carve out what is best to make life more complete in this very competitive global environment that seems to engulf the free world, whether it be for better or worse.

CHAPTER 20

A Fair Day

The fair day was a very festive day when the farmers would meet, and when business was done, they would go to the pub for a drink. Every village and town had a fair day when the locals would sell livestock and farm products. When the farmers would sell livestock, the deal was always consummated with a good-luck drink in the pub, typically a pint of Guinness and a shot of Jameson or Scotch that would be on the seller. This custom is still to this day alive and well in rural Ireland, where it is common to treat the buyer when a deal is made, and if not, after the deal is made, there is usually a promise to buy a round of drinks the next time they meet in the local pub. The promise is always kept, even if it is a year later. The farmers would bring one of their sons or daughters to the fair to help watch over livestock that was bought or sold, and when it was sold, the youngster would join their dad for a drink. The child would be treated to minerals and cookies, and the selling farmer would always give the child a half crown (two shillings and sixpence), and if the farmer had a big day, the child might get five shillings sterling, which would be a big day for the child during those very poor times. Both way this was a big treat when money was very scarce, and the child in those days would feel very special.

This little village's surrounding area had a radius of about five to seven miles that ran up the sides of the two mountains.

One side overlooked Lough Erne's glistening shores and the northern mountain ridge with its heather-purple peak and glowing yellow whin bushes, which made the village and surrounding area very picturesque. On the south side there was Brackley Lake, which could be seen from Swad's higher elevations and was located outside another very quaint, picturesque little village called Bawnboy.

There was a population of approximately three hundred families at that time in Swad and the surrounding area. There were thirteen pubs in the village of Swad, and most of them also sold groceries and general food, including animal/farm supplies. Everyone, young and old, loved the fair day and would spend all day walking around from stall to stall. There were also many performances—musicians, artists, acrobats, and so forth, and all types of street performers that were just so splendid and entertaining.

The local people, including the children, loved the festivities and the spirit of all the events. This was a place where many a farmer met his wife. In the older days, the matchmakers were on the prowl, ready to make a match or casually talk to, and learn more about, potential candidates. In those days the father of the bride offered a dowry based on what he could afford, and that made for interesting conversation. In this regard there are many great stories where the farmer bargained with the father of the bride for a bigger dowry. The younger and prettier the girl, the lower the dowry, since there was plenty of demand for the young, pretty girls. The village would be so festive, with all kinds of market stalls selling everything from fish to all kinds of foods, tools, and toys; there was something for everyone to at least look at, although the wares were not affordable for many.

There would be all kinds of artists and actors riding unicycles while juggling balls; there were also musicians and crooners, and so on. Back in those days, Sunday was the most festive day in Ireland, where people met and greeted each other after church. Most people went to church, where there would be up to a dozen altar boys, and everyone loved the High Mass where all the great tenor voices would chime in and raise the roof of the church. Back then the church would be packed; people lined up outside to hear Mass and the choir and the melodious voices. What added to the festive atmosphere was that all the older people would come down from faraway mountains and dells in their beautiful horse-drawn traps and carriages.

This was like something you might see in some of today's old western movies.

During those long-ago days, people everywhere were so happy with their very simple lives and large families, and although there was little money, everyone would be dressed to the nines, smiling ear to ear like there was not a care in the world; this was a good indicator that you do not have to be rich to be happy. Not surprisingly, today Ireland still ranks as one of the happiest countries in the world; however, it too has its strife, as every country does, no matter how prosperous.

CHAPTER 21

Hunting

Hunting was also a big part of our young lives. We would hunt the moorlands for pheasant, and since we did not have firearms, we relied on our dog to raise and take down the pheasant as it was climbing from the heather. It was a rare occasion when the dog caught the pheasant, but when he did accomplish the catch, was a major triumph for the dog and young hunters. We hunted mostly rabbits, fox, and badgers, and again, since we did not have guns, the dog was the big attraction. Diver was a great hunting dog although something of a mutt; he was not like a full-bred hunting setter. Diver was great at chasing rabbits, and he would chase them into the boroughs and cairns, and then we would dig them out if they were not too deep in the caverns. Diver would also be in there digging for all he was worth, using his back paws like a little backhoe, throwing dirt in all directions. This was great fun and so exciting. When he would finally dig out a rabbit, Diver would be just as excited as we were.

We loved to chase fox but rarely caught any. There was a nice bounty for fox skin and fur, which made the fox a great catch. The anglers and hunters hunted everything from fox to badger and pheasant with their full-bred gorgeous setters and guns. When Diver would catch up to a fox, there would be a big fight, and it could get pretty bloody; we did not like to see the animals suffer or have Diver run the risk of rabies. We would help Diver kill the fox, but Diver did not want us involved. He would snarl at us and wanted to do it all himself. He would turn into a monster dog when he was going for the kill, and you had to stay back until he was done.

When it was all over, then he calmed down and became his old jolly self again and would run up to me or one of my brothers, hoping to get attention.

The badgers were almost impossible to catch, and they had very deep burrows, so it might take days to dig down to their habitat. The badger is a fierce animal and has very strong jaws that could seriously hurt a big dog, let alone a small one. We were very protective of Diver and restrained him when we saw danger. Since Diver had no fear, he could get himself in trouble. The badger could hurt the dog with his fierce, big strong jaws, and since we did not have guns, we would only hunt them down but did not let the dog catch up with them. The rabbits were always our big catch, and we would go out at night with large, powerful flashlights, and when we would see rabbits coming toward us, we would blind them with the big bright light until Diver would pounce on them and bring them back to us, usually alive. Rabbit has very nice, tender meat when cooked. The meat is like chicken, only much tenderer. Our parents loved when we brought home rabbits. They made a great meal, and we loved the soup and meat. The most difficult task was killing the rabbit, since they were so cute, and many times we would want to let them go. However, knowing that dinner meat was in short supply made the rabbit an attractive catch for a delicious meal. Hunting amid the comradery of family, friends, and Diver was such a wonderful experience. Most young children growing up in today's world will never have that wonderful, exciting experience. Every young boy and girl should have the opportunity to go out into the wild and hunt at least one time when growing up.

There was a mountain range within walking distance from where we grew up, a great area for hunting, where there was plenty of long green fescue grass that was great for rabbits and great breathing air. The highest mountain peak within the mountain range was Cuilcagh Mountain, which was about two miles from our house.

Cuilcagh Mountain was about twenty-two hundred feet high. The northwest side, with its very steep cliff, looked out over a beautiful blue glistening lake surrounded by a beautiful green pasture where all kinds of wildflowers blossomed.

All the beautiful colors were radiant in the magnificent sunset as it went down over the lake, where all kinds of wild birds and animals made their habitat. On a beautiful long summer evening when darkness did not come down until close to midnight, you could see groups of anglers who knew the area well congregate to watch the beautiful sunset over the lake with their cameras while taking in nature's beauty at its best.

The local folklore had many tales to tell about the lake at the foothill of the northwest slope, where it was said that there had been sightings of mermaids. It was told that many farmers, when herding sheep at the foot of the mountain in the very early hours of the morning, sighted these creatures in the clear blue glittering water, and as a result, in the summer months, there would be throngs of visitors hoping they would see a mermaid based on the many folklore tales.

Young tourists and hikers from all over who loved to explore the mountains, and had heard of these mythological creatures, would camp out by the beautiful green banks of the lake hoping for a mermaid sighting. The area around the lake was a beautiful shade of lush green grass that spread over many acres of land; sheep, wild cattle, and horses fed where the green pasture ran up to the mountain foothill. On the southeast side of the mountain foothill is where the Shannon Pot rises. The Shannon Pot rises out of the mountain foothill just like a typical mountain spring; it runs 224 miles across Ireland from northwest to south, where it flows into the estuary below Limerick. The Shannon River propels one of Ireland's largest hydroelectric power stations at Ardnacrusha on the River Shannon.

The Shannon Pot starts off as a mountain spring; it produces a medium-size stream that takes on many tributaries along the way down the mountain range to where it becomes the largest and longest river in Ireland.

The Cuilcagh Mountains are also very close to Benaughlin Mountain. Benaughlin Mountain is part of the Cuilcagh mountain range. It rises up to about twelve hundred feet high, but this is a relatively easy mountain to climb. The mountain base is steep, but there is a road that runs close to the base of the mountain, which makes this low mountain attractive for the novice climbers. Close by are the nearby Marble Arches and deep caves that attract tourists from all over Europe and the United States.

Benaughlin is a great attraction for young families who want to do a little mountain climbing but do not want to hike for miles to get to the base of the mountain. When we went mountain climbing, we would always bring Diver, who was the best climber of all. He always added a very special dimension to the trip, chasing all types of game that he would raise from the heathery cloak. He would disappear in the mountain caverns, chasing animals and barking as he went deeper into these dark caves. We would follow him into the caves, calling him to come back for fear of losing him inside the deep, winding caves where in some areas raving water flowed. All kinds of wild animals lived, and some hibernated, in the long, deep caves and these animals were fierce protectors of their territory. From the top peak of the Cuilcagh Mountains, on a clear day, you could see eight Irish counties and a number of beautiful lakes that glistened in the distant sunlight, and if you waited for the sunset, when the sun would drop down on each mountain range, it was so delightful and a spectacular scene. Those were the days, so much fun, so carefree, when it seemed that the world and all its beauty were at our command. Again, we thought it would never end.

We immersed ourselves in this simple lifestyle with so little yet so much of everything that nature had to offer, and money could not buy. The young and daring inquisitive mind has a great desire to climb high and to seek beyond the horizon where few minds wander and to take in the wonders and beauty of nature at its best. The beautiful mountain flora with its unique and fragrant aroma made you feel you were in wonderland as a child. The purple-headed blossoms and other beautiful wildflowers and delicious edible berries of all types that we would feast on were so great. This experience of exploring the mountains and their surroundings in their simplest form provided a wonderful enrichment for the young mind. To explore is to grow by looking far beyond what eyes can see or imagine.

Yes, we were so poor and yet so rich in everything that this simple life had to offer. How fortunate we were to be born into this type of lifestyle, which was like living a dream that fostered the fondest of memories, that forever has created an imprint that will always be cherished.

I would give the world to live my boyhood once more with friends and comrades all. This was a boyhood lifestyle that was full of simple fun and delight in an unadulterated world. The commercial and materialistic lifestyles that most people seem to gravitate toward in today's world can become emptier the more we consume. We have only one life to live, and I am glad that I have had the good fortune to experience a little bit of both worlds. As I look back on growing up in Ireland, I know it was poor but wonderful. It was that young, carefree, adventurous life that made me who I am. As a young man, I moved on to the great city of London and later to this great country, the United States, to pursue all this great country has to offer, and I have to say I made the best of it while on a different path to a new adventure. That too has been rewarding and life fulfilling, and now I can honestly say yes, I have had the best of all worlds.

CHAPTER 22

Mountain Climbing

After hearing all my stories of mountain climbing with the dogs, our youngest daughter, who loves dogs and loves the outdoors, had a great desire to climb Cuilcagh Mountain. I promised her that we would climb the next time we would visit Ireland. When she was about sixteen years old, we made a trip to Ireland for a visit with family. In order to keep my promise, one beautiful day my wife, sister, nephews, and niece took our daughter on a trudge to climb Cuilcagh Mountain.

She was so excited but did not realize that she had to hike a mile or more through very rough terrain to get to the foot of the mountain and then have the energy to climb the mountain. The terrain was covered with heather and foliage as high as one's knee in some areas, and there were bogholes, streams, and soggy terrain due to an earlier rainstorm that had to be navigated. This hike got us only to the base of the mountain, and it was getting late in the evening to make the big climb. My daughter was a very good athlete and played a number of competitive school sports but was not fully prepared for this hike, thinking it would be a cakewalk, so we collectively decided to put the big mountain climb off for another day, since it was getting a little late, and at the same time we knew that we had a two-mile hike back through the same rough terrain to where the main road was located. For her this was a great experience from which she learned a great deal about the basic preparation and time involved before taking on a big mountain climb. She loved the experience and was more determined than ever to make the hike to the summit. Now that she has her own young children, maybe one day she will take them and her husband, Mike, on a trip to the foothill of Cuilcagh Mountain and start on that climb that she once dreamed of.

The good news is that now the local county council has built a side road that runs all the way to the foothill of the mountain; this construction was initiated by the Irish tourist board since in today's world a lot of European tourists love to mountain climb but may not have the time to wade through the rough terrain to start their climb. Tara now has a greater appreciation for the wild and the preparation necessary to be ready for this type of terrain. She also realized that her father and his family were born into this type of lifestyle and that it was very much part of him. In in a similar way, her mother also grew up in a very rural farm community in the western part of Ireland. This was a beautiful scenic area with high fieldstone ditches and beautiful lakes and dells where nature lavished its bounty. Tara assured me that she was still determined to climb to the Cuilcagh Mountain summit one day but would have to do a little more mountain climbing preparation and she would need to do so when there would be less time restraints.

This was a wonderful experience for my daughter, one that she will always remember and draw from. She has a greater appreciation for mountain climbing and what is involved in making such a climb, although Cuilcagh Mountain would be considered somewhat low range when it comes to the big mountain climbers who take on heights that are ten or more times higher. I would not be surprised if she became more interested in mountain climbing, since she enjoys hiking. What seems very simple on the surface is not always that way once you have the opportunity to explore all that is involved. I do hope that one day our daughter will climb Cuilcagh and other mountains and have a great story to tell and share with her children, or better yet, do the climb with her children. When I reminisce and think of those childhood days, I appreciate how lucky we were to be born into such a poor, simple, yet extraordinary childhood lifestyle. I feel privileged, and that I would not trade for all the money or luxury in the world.

I also believe being poor growing up has advantages. The poor child has to expand his or her mind to go beyond the materialistic lifestyle of the rich and reach for what nature has to offer. The rich live a more protected and controlled lifestyle that can lack the real childhood experience where the poorer (often wild and hearty) have no limit to where they will go and fear no danger. The most important factors in the poor child's mind are adventure, camaraderie, and excitement, and they make the best out of every opportunity that their young, inquisitive minds can explore. The poor child at a very young age develops into a more confident specimen that can take on any venture or challenge that life puts in their path. The rich child does not always have the opportunity to use their wings that their creator provided to fly into the wild and seek out what nature and the world have to offer. The poor boy and girl have to cut a path through this big world that every young boy and girl sees as vast, daunting, unknown and challenging. If the poor boy or girl trips and falls down, there is no one there to help them to get up, and that develops an inner strength of independence and self-reliance;

they know life is theirs to win or lose. Intuitively they have to be a self-starter who will get up and move on to take on the next adventure. I always relished being a poor boy with nowhere to go but up. There is always some risk in adventure, but knowing if you fall, that you can get up and start all over, without losing confidence in yourself, is what will keep you going. Risk-taking builds character and self-reliance that will forever drive you to the next adventure. When young and uninhibited, we tend to enjoy living on the edge while waiting for the next opportunity in a world where we yearn to expand beyond yesterday's dreams. During those early days, the essentials of life were in very short supply, and in the area where I grew up, everyone was struggling from day to day, but the interesting thing was that no one complained, and everyone was happy.

Everyone went on with their lives as if they were doing just fine. I guess you could say for the most part they were doing fine, since people did not need much to survive, and for the most part they lived off the land, and as long as they were happy and willing to work, their basic needs were provided for. They believed in the old adage the farmers knew: "The precious sea can feed them all."

Ireland had a caste system, which was a carryover from the old British influence where two pennies looked down at one. This was part of the reason you never heard people complain about money or complain about being poor. No one wanted their neighbors or friends to know how poor they really were because that could put them in a class that they did not want to be in. These people were so proud they never asked for anything.

However, in today's world, the more people get, the more they want, and little if any is appreciated. The interesting thing about growing up in Ireland was that one of the most important factors was taking care of the poor. Schools and churches and so forth were always collecting for the foreign missions, and as poor as people were, they would always contribute some of whatever they had to those less fortunate, which I think was a very noble quality.

CHAPTER 23

A Salesman

One of the farm products among many we used to sell at the market was cabbage plants. We would go from town to town within a radius of twenty miles on market days and sell cabbage plants to the area locals for their gardens. Cabbage was a very popular vegetable, known for its many nutrients to keep the body healthy. In Ireland, every household grew cabbage in its garden and crop fields. The young cabbage plants grew into big heads of cabbage that were harvested and could provide cabbage until the following year's crop was ready for use. The cabbage plants were one of the farm products that would be smuggled across the border and sold in Northern Ireland's local town markets. In Northern Ireland, there was a little more money in circulation due to British farm subsidies and a higher children's allowance. My father always raised a large field of cabbage plants for the early spring markets, since this was a very lean time of the year when there was very little other income. From about the age of twelve, I sold cabbage plants in all the surrounding town markets and fairs. I was gifted with natural sales ability and loved to sell. All the cabbage plant dealers would line up outside the town market entrance gates or on a streetcorner during open market days to sell their goods. Most of the cabbage plant dealers were much older than I was and were very seasoned salespeople, and some of them could be a bit sleazy. They would undercut their competition with very elaborate tactics and hackneyed sales lines, some of which could sound slick and disingenuous. All this usually worked to my advantage because I was a very young lad and looked very young for my age. I had a pretty good sales line of my own, and many of the prospective buyers got a kick out of listing to my sales pitch since I was not much more than just a child of about thirteen.

Crowds would gather around, and before I knew it, I would be sold out. Many of the big cabbage plant dealers could not wait for me to sell out and go away. The public cattle market would open about 10:00 a.m. and I would always be sold out by noon or before.

When business was slow, some of the big dealers who would have a lot of product to sell would ask me to sell some of their supply. They would offer me a commission, and if the commission was acceptable, I would sell for them. This allowed me to make some money that I could put in my pocket. My father did not like the idea too much, since he did not know what the quality of their product was. He also knew many of the big dealers were slippery, but on the other hand he did not want to stop me from making a few coins for myself. One year, I sold a number of bundles of what they said was regular green cabbage for one of the big dealers and later found out it was wild cow kale that grows wild and bushy. The following year some of the customers complained that the plants were not regular green cabbage and that they looked more like cow kale. One customer, a lovely, very friendly man, laughed and thought it was funny and said it grew ten feet high and he had enough kale to feed the whole community. Of course, I had to talk my way out of this quandary and must have done a pretty good job because all of the customers came back and bought from me again that year. I was so happy that my reputation did not get tarnished, and that was the last time I sold for the big dealers. It was not until then I realized that my father was again right about not knowing the big dealers' product quality. Many years later, I told my father the story about the cow kale, and he got a great a kick out of it and said, "My boy, what did I tell you?"

All I could say was "I know, Dad, but it was pretty funny," and he smiled with a big grin from ear to ear with pride that this was one of the many lessons in life that I was about to learn. My father always preached that honesty was the best policy. I am convinced that in the long term, honesty always pays off.

This was a wonderful experience and taught me to be competitive and self-confident. There were a number of boys a few years older than I was at that time who tried to sell their cabbage plants but were somewhat shy and had little confidence in their sales ability.

Most of them had a tough time, and at the end of the day, they were lucky if they'd sold five of the fifty bundles they'd brought to the market. The main reason that they were having so much trouble selling was that they were afraid, not sure of themselves or what to say.

They would laugh at my lines but did not have the confidence to deliver any type of line.

They were scared to walk up to prospective customers and explain their product, including its cost and value. That is what sales is all about: knowing your product, identifying your prospective customer, and closing the deal. In a very competitive environment, if you are boring and allow your prospective customers to wander around, you will lose them to the fast-talking competitor. It is important to make your best introduction, since you will never get a second chance to introduce your product to the same person. Sales is all about making an impression, selling yourself, closing the deal, and moving on to the next customer. If you let a customer, go without closing the deal, for the most part you will never see that person again. That becomes another missed opportunity for the sale of your product. I used to feel bad for some of my friends who were so nice and great people but not good when it came to selling, and they hated it. I always enjoyed selling, and needless to say, life is all about selling yourself in everything we do. No matter how good your product is, if you cannot sell it, it has little value. To a great degree, the same goes for the business world. From the lowest level to the top, it is always those who can sell themselves that move up the corporate ladder, and also the same goes for the U.S. military. In many situations one could be doing great work, but if no one knows that one is doing it, one may not get the recognition one deserves.

CHAPTER 24

Irish Culture

A big part of Irish culture was built around the church, both Catholic and Protestant, over the years, and in particular after the Reformation. Nowhere was this true more than Northern Ireland, where the firebrand Protestant evangelical ministers spouted hate and destruction to the Catholic minority. The clergy were on a pedestal, and whatever they said was the law. Just about everyone from all dominations went to church on Sunday during those days and holy days of obligation. In most households people had to recite morning and night prayers after rising and every night before going to bed, and failure to do so was considered a mortal sin by the church. At night all family members knelt down and participated in reciting the mysteries of the holy rosary. The rosary is made up of fifteen mysteries broken into three sets, and at least one set was recited before bed, which was a long, drawn-out process where everyone had to participate in following the mysteries. The mysteries of the rosary are based on the holy seasons, which consist of Christmas, Easter, Advent, and Lent.

Every Irish mother's dream was to have at least one of her sons become a priest or a daughter become a nun, and from the time a child was born, the virtues of a religious life were instilled in the young. The sacraments of the church were taken very seriously, starting with baptism, Holy Communion, and confirmation. The sacraments are the foundation on which the Catholic faith is built. From there it is up to every young man and woman to practice. "Be a good Catholic and lead by example" was the credo.

Missionary priests would come to every Catholic parish church throughout the country at least once a year. They would put the fear of God into the hearts and souls of the people, especially the young.

The missionary priests would preach mostly fire and brimstone in order to make sure that they would scare anyone who was slipping a little in their faith. The objective of the missionary priests was to instill a level of fear in order to get the skeptics back on track again. There was confession every day and night during the mission, and the congregation was told that failure to attend a monthly confession was a mortal sin that required forgiveness. The missionary service usually lasted seven days; a service would be held each evening with a different theme, one more intense than the other.

The church would be overflowing to the point where everyone in attendance could not get into the church. Young and old came from all over the parish, and some from other parishes.

When the word got out that the missionary priest was very charismatic and knew how to work the audience, the crowds would become immense. The larger the crowds, the better the missionary priests liked it, and most of them really knew how to attract the crowd.

There were always those who would like to stand around the door, and some on the outside of the door. I remember when one missionary priest got so mad at those hanging around the entrance door that he shouted from the pulpit that they were a poor example for their children. He went on to yell that true followers of Christ would come into his house and join in the sacraments of Mass.

For a short while after the missionary priest made this big scene, the stragglers came inside the door but would only stand up and not go into a seat where they had to kneel and pray.

The church would be full every night, and the bigger the audience, the more firepower the missionary priests delivered. They wanted to make sure that they got to the hearts and souls of everyone in the congregation. Those that were not overly religious also found the oratory and delivery of the charismatic missionary priest very entertaining at a time when there was not a lot of outside entertainment in the small rural villages.

The missionary priests' measurement of success was based on the number of people in attendance. As with any good show, if the audience got bigger every night, that meant a successful program, and they would promise to be back. For the following few months, our parents would keep reminding us of the words of the missionary priests. They would work hard to instill those ideals and principles in order to pave the way for our salvation.

At a young age, all this religious teaching has an impact, but in many cases, it is short- lived in the minds of the youth. It is very common for the youth to challenge everything, including many aspects of church teachings. Religious teaching requires faith, and the Catholic Church teaches that without faith there is no redemption and that to question what is considered to be the teaching of Christ and the Gospel is a mortal sin. The church considered questioning religious teaching sacrilegious, and it was very much condemned and off limits for a meaningful discussion. The Bible warns those who challenge such teachings, in Matthew 10:33, "Whosoever shall deny me before men, I will also deny him before my Father which is in heaven." In today's world, those kinds of warnings are not taken as seriously by the youth; many are questioning religion and if there is a God.

My two older brothers were altar boys, and they were exemplary in their duties and in carrying out their roles. So now it was my turn to be next in line, and I had to go through a very rigorous altar boy training program. Since Mass was in Latin, the altar boys' response had to be also in Latin, and that too was part of the overall training. My parents bought me the altar boy robes, which they could ill afford, but having three sons serving Mass as altar boys was a very proud moment for my mother. Then came the first Sunday for me to perform my altar boy duties. There were about eight to ten altar boys serving that Mass, and most if not, all were my school friends.

When you get a large number of young boys who are all friends together, there is always going to be trouble because boys will be boys. One can always more than likely predict there will be at least one who will be an instigator and will try to get the rest of them going in some way that may not be pleasing. Sure, enough the giggling and bursts of laughter started, and then it just got a little worse until the priest saying Mass saw what was going on. He was livid. He was a very cantankerous, bad-tempered priest who had little tolerance, especially when it came to altar boys' bad behavior. In many ways he was something of a psychopath who had no patience or understanding when it came to children's behavior. He should have separated each altar boy with some distance between them while signaling some signs of discipline. Instead, he immediately ordered four of us off the altar and scolded us using the pulpit in the presence of my mother and the congregation. For an altar boy to get thrown off and not allowed to serve Mass again was the biggest shame ever for the boy, his family, and the school he attended. It was almost worse than a criminal offense because all the family, friends, and neighbors, many of whom were in church, knew about the scene. There would be all kinds of gossip and exaggeration that would make things much worse than it really was. My parents were horrified, angry, and humiliated beyond any imagination. This was an appalling deed, and my mother was literally crying with anger. She told me that I had disgraced the family. She went on to say that I must be possessed by the devil to be part of such a sacrilegious act. For my mother in particular, this was the worst possible level of humiliation—that one of her children could be so disrespectful and sacrilegious and bring shame to the family. She screamed at me that even a pagan boy would not disrespect Mass and the house of God. Then I was scolded and scolded for what seemed to be an eternity and then punished: I was grounded for weeks.

My father left all the punishment up to my mom, and I think to a great extent he understood that this is what children do and felt that to some extent you can expect some silly, innocent immature behavior from young children when they get together.

When I went to school the next day, the schoolmaster was in a horrific rage at the four of us. He had us circle his desk while he called each one of us out, yelled and screamed, and deemed me the ringleader that must be inspired by the devil.

I was in the doghouse so bad that I thought I was going to be there for the rest of my time at home and in school. In the afternoon the local parish priest came to the school. He was like a monster with rage. He roared and did everything he could to terrorize the four of us and in particular directed most of his anger at me and did so with a real vengeance.

He threatened to send the four of us to a reformatory school. He yelled that we were sacrilegious and a disgrace to the school, our families, and the church. Then he called me up to the teacher's desk and asked me if I was possessed by the devil, but I was too scared to open my mouth while the horrors of this episode lasted. All four of us were punished by having to stay in school an hour after everyone else went home for the following month. This punishment continued for at least a month. The four of us got yelled at, punished, and humiliated in every possible way, and they wanted to make an example of us in order to scare others from acting up on the altar in a similar way. We had to recite twelve rosaries as penance, and if we were caught laughing during the rosary, the teacher would beat us with his stick until he would see blood and keep us in class yet another hour after school. Some of the Irish priests had no mercy and were very brutal. They were also very biased and treated the rich children much better than the poor peasant children. The rich kids' parents put more money in the basket than the poor kids' parents, and they did not want to do anything that would have a potential negative effect on cash flow.

As a young boy, I became very disillusioned with the clergy and questioned how men of God could favor the rich children over the poorer peasant ones. It always seemed that rich kids could do nothing wrong. However, there was a very low tolerance for the poor kid. I was no saint and liked to challenge the system in many ways, in particular when things got boring.

I always had to start something that would create a little excitement and enjoyed living on the edge regardless of the pending punishment that lay ahead. For the most part, I always knew that there would be a price to pay for starting any kind of trouble, but at least subconsciously I was willing to take that risk. In Irish culture back then, to question the motives or the actions of a priest was sacrilegious and unacceptable. Some people believed that a priest's curse could haunt you for the rest of your life and that bad luck would follow.

The priest was considered God's disciple who could do whatever was necessary for their word to be done. The priest imposed a huge level of authority over the people and dictated not just what was wright and wrong, per church teaching, but also every aspect of family life. In many situations it was their own dissolute view of wright and wrong and not part of the Catholic Church's teaching. The clergy lived very well when the average citizen had very little. They always seemed to do OK, and it used to be said in Ireland that if there was a priest in the family, that family would never go hungry. There was a Sunday collection, the quarterly collections, and Christmas and Easter dues. The amount of money that each family contributed was read out from the pulpit by the priest, which was a way of shaming people to give more. In my opinion this was a form of extortion, in which many poor people were forced to give more than they could afford. The poor peasants had to fork over the hard-scraped pennies that were so necessary to provide the very basic essentials of life for their large families during those very tough times.

This type of extortion flies in the face of what the church is supposed to be about: taking care of the poor rather than humiliating them to give more than they can afford.

In many situations poor families sacrificed the bare necessities of life, such as food and clothing, in order to give to the church. The clergy were the first to get cars and televisions in rural areas and lived a life that was luxurious in comparison to most of their flock. Some priests were political and used the pulpit to express their own political philosophies and, in some cases used religious scare tactics to further their personal agendas. If there was an issue that they did not support, they would make strong statements from the pulpit denouncing the issue under the name of God and the church. In those days there was no separation between the church and the state in Ireland. It is my belief that the church held the people of Ireland back from pursuing their potential by dictating so-called church doctrine that in some ways was oppressive and self-serving and not for the better good. I am an avid believer in the true separation of church and state. No democratic country should allow church influence to be part of public policymaking. The freedom of religion is a very precious part of the constitution in most democratic societies, and that is where it should rest. The Irish people fought for their religion for centuries at the hands of an evil empire. As a result, they relish that freedom, and it should not be compromised in any way by the church. In earlier days the church had a very heavy hand in policymaking in the Irish Republic, where the bishops of Ireland had a large say in the affairs of the state. During the period from 1960 to 1970, the Irish government started to move away politically from the church influence and staged the beginning of a separation between church and state in the Republic of Ireland. As the state became more independent and started to move away from the church influence, a much more prosperous and professional image started to emerge.

This new image of openness and objectivity without ties to the church has led to the prosperity of the Republic of Ireland in recent years.

The church has its place in society, but it is never good when the church takes a dominant role in politics and the policymaking of a democratic country. With all that said, the vast majority of priests and nuns are holy, honorable people that do great work all over the world, including the great work they do attending to the sick, poor, and desolate.

My family and my wife's family, like many Irish families, have priests and nuns who are part of the family, all wonderful, hardworking shepherds who diligently and selfishly give their life to a higher calling, doing what they believe is God's work and spreading the word of God. My wife and I also have many wonderful priest and nun friends whom we consider part of our family and whom we admire and support. Although I am not very religious, I have great respect for the commitment and self-sacrifice of all dedicated religious people who put aside personal desires and ambitions to lead the faithful and do God's work, all for the betterment of all mankind. It is a great calling, and all clergy denominations deserve our support and respect for their great work making the world a better place.

CHAPTER 25

Education

I never liked school as a young boy and did not excel as a result. I did not want to be there. But, I had to and could not wait to get out. At the time, the average young boy left school at fourteen years of age, as I did. School was not an environment that was conducive to learning because there was little positive reinforcement for the young student. The teacher was brutal and used his power over the students by beating and intimidating them. In those days many of the teachers in rural Ireland had substandard qualifications and were not well prepared to teach the young student the fundamentals that would be necessary to propel them in the business world. In many cases they did not have the necessary training to understand the child. Positive reinforcement is necessary to encourage children in their development and early education. Many of the teachers got their jobs through influence rather than academic merit. Back in those days, being well connected with the local parish priest and local politicians was a good way to get a teaching or a government job. The schools had large classrooms where there could be thirty to thirty-five children with one teacher that taught six grades. The older and brighter students had to help the teacher with the younger ones and in some ways acted as the teacher's aides. Our parents tried very hard to encourage education and were very involved in helping all of us with our home studies and pushed us as much as they could. In rural areas the educational system and culture were not conducive to higher learning. In those years about 5 percent of the students who were the brightest went on from grade school to secondary school, and the remainder worked on the farms or hung around until old enough to emigrate. When they emigrated, they realized that they were missing the very basic and fundamental education that is required to make a good living in the world.

They found themselves working in manual labor types of jobs, and they stayed in that capacity for the rest of their lives. Some went back to school, as I did, to get the necessary education to be competitive in a competitive world. Some became entrepreneurs and bought pubs and other types of business where advanced education would help but was not necessary, and many of those who were willing to go back to school and work hard did very well. Today the Republic of Ireland's educational system ranks among one of the best in Europe; the emphasis on education has become the cornerstone of success for the island's booming economy. As a result of a world-class educational system, this small island has become the mecca of high-tech research and manufacturing companies providing good, high-paying jobs. Most of the industry consists of biotech, pharmaceuticals, electronics, software, medical devices, and other sectors that provide good jobs. Now people from Eastern Europe and other parts of the world want to immigrate to Ireland. Ireland's GDP per capita has a world-class ranking and is almost $556 billion, compared to $21.75 billion in 1980.

Under the British Penal Laws in the eighteenth and early nineteenth centuries, schools and schooling were illegal for some groups. There were schools where only those of the Anglican faith were allowed to attend; Catholic and Presbyterian schools were illegal and forbidden by penalty of the law. This era was referred to as the hedge school period, when schools were hidden and held in places such as behind hedges, in ditches, and in other hideouts. This very long, very dark period in Irish history set back generations of young Irish people, and it created a new culture of uneducated people that became a way of life. This was what the oppressor intended by depriving nationalists of the necessary education: it would prevent educated leaders from rising up to fight for what was theirs.

The main objective of the tyrant was to force a culture of illiteracy on nationalists.

By creating a culture of illiteracy, they would be able to prevent uprisings and revolutions led by educated leaders. The Irish revolutionaries have risen up in every generation for the past eight hundred years and will continue until Ireland is free, from Malin Head in County Donegal to Mizen Head in County Cork. Despite all these very brutal and oppressive tactics, the Irish people never fail to rise up again and again and fight, as they will until every sod of Irish ground and its people are free from the yoke of a dying empire's might.

CHAPTER 26

Farm Life

As a young lad, I loved working on the farm, where there was so much to do and such a variety of work where I had a great interest. Since I was very good with using my hands, there was all kinds of challenging work that I enjoyed. There was farm machinery to service and repair, and there were home repairs and farm building repairs, in addition to the work of building new farm structures, installing the crops, harvesting, and taking care of livestock. In those days farmers provided their own heating fuel—wood and peat/turf. The turf had to be cut from large peat bogs and harvested in great quantities to last for a whole year. The peat and firewood were oftentimes burned in an open fire or a wood- or peat-burning stove, which was referred to as a cooking range. Although there was no central-type heating system as we know it today, the homes were always very comfortable due to the mild climate that did not require a lot of heat from the open fire or wood- or peat-burning stove. Many of the stoves had a small heat exchanger that provided hot water that rose throughout the house where there were radiators, mostly in large clothes-drying closets where bedclothes and other garments were put to dry after spending time on extensive outside clotheslines. Most houses would have a big open-hearth fire where they would burn turf and wood on a cold winter's night. The open fire was warm and had an allure of comfort and a heartiness that made everyone feel good when the whole family gathered around the blazing fire. At our house, my father would smoke his pipe, while my mother was always busy cooking, baking, and mending or making clothes. The heat from the big burning fire would rise and warm the whole house. All the rooms throughout the old farmhouse had fireplaces, but the only time a bedroom fireplace was used was if an older person was confined to bed or not feeling well.

The big fire or stove was in the big country kitchen, where everyone assembled. The kitchen table was where children did their school homework, and later on, in the long winter nights, neighbors would come by for a visit, which we loved. The visitors would play cards or at times play music using a harmonica, accordion, or fiddle, and once in a while there would be a guitar player.

There was no end to farm work—there was always more work to be done by a number of people. This was the reason why farm children had to help out at a young age. It was a team effort, and during the harvesting season everyone had to chip in. My mother would take time away from her very busy household duties to offer a helping hand. The household work was enormous, since there was no electricity or household appliances. Everything was done by hand using washboards and handwashing; however, she would pitch in and help out during the harvesting rush. Due to the wet climate, there was a small window of time to successfully complete all the harvesting requirements.

After a big day's work where a lot got done, there was a great sense of accomplishment, and my father would be very happy and always make sure that everyone got recognition for their contribution. By showing appreciation for a well-done job, he would give everyone a good, upbeat feeling. At the end of the day, my mother would cook a big meal so the whole family could celebrate a good day's accomplishment.

In addition to the spring planting and harvesting, there was a lot of additional work, which included looking after the livestock and making sure that the herd was accounted for and healthy. There was also the preparation and feeding of the housed livestock such as pigs, hens, turkeys, and geese, collecting the eggs, and cleaning them for the market.

All the cows had to be milked, which is a very tedious job and requires as many hands as possible on deck to lighten the burden.

The small farmers cannot afford the mechanical milking machines. They have to do it all by hand, and that requires a skill level that takes a lot of training and practice.

Most farm children know how to milk a cow by age twelve, so they can help to share the workload. Farming is like any other business: it requires a lot of dedicated attention and the necessary skills. If you do not properly manage and take care of all the farm responsibilities, you will not be successful as a farmer. Not only are the farmer and his family required to be hardworking, but they also have to be intuitive. Farming requires a high level of smarts with a very high level of knowledge and a keen eye when it comes to taking care of livestock. If a farmer has ten cows and loses one, he has lost 10 percent of his business and potential income; therefore, he has to be very diligent and cognizant when it comes to the health and well-being of the livestock, including cattle, sheep, horses, donkeys, pigs, poultry, and so on. Livestock are to a great degree like people and require a great deal of medical care, including inoculation and preventative health treatment programs, to ensure limited losses from disease and plagues. There are all kinds of diseases that can befall each type of livestock and can literally bankrupt the farmer. Dedicated care and attention are required when cows are having calves and sheep are having lambs; an in-depth knowledge is required should an animal have difficulty in delivering its offspring, and knowing when professional medical help may be required to save the animal's and offspring's lives is essential. Livestock preventative health is very expensive and adds greatly to the cost of doing business in a market where the profit margins are so minuscule. In many cases the poorer farmers cannot afford the animal health-care costs and go without, which can be devastating when cattle get sick and die because they did not have the necessary inoculations and preventative health care, in particular when there is a disease of any kind that is spreading throughout the farm herd.

My big dream as a young man was to go out into the world and make enough money that one day I would be able to go back and buy my own farm. However, as with many other farm boys, when I got a taste of the good life and the big city lights and great friends, the desire to go back to the farm started to dwindle. When young people go out into the world and get a taste of big city life and meet new friends, everything changes. The farm boys become enamored with their new lives, and only a very small percentage ever go back to the farm. There is a saying that the boy will not go back to the farm after he sees Paris. Then the farm boy has a little more money in his pocket, which is hard to find working on a farm, and as a result the odds of the boy going back to the farm become more remote. There is also a saying that you can take the boy out of the farm, but you can never take the farm out of the boy. This is all very true. There is always a great veneration for the farm that was so much a part of our young lives, and there are the fond, long-lasting memories. On the farm every word spoken was farm talk, and the farm lifestyle is so ingrained that it is part of the farm boy's life until his dying day. It is not uncommon that when old people who grew up on farms start to get a little senile, their minds wander back to those precious days that they loved so well, and they start to relive the memories of the past. When I used to go back to visit family with my wife and kids, it was wonderful, and we would have a great time, but after a couple of weeks I was ready to come back home. As the saying goes, there is no place like home, no matter where or what it may be. When I go back for a visit, there is so much farm talk among the locals, and I now have a very limited interest. It gets old fast, and the desire to move on always seems to prevail. We have a wonderful lifelong friend who is going through the early stages of senility—she talks about her childhood days and sometimes thinks she is back on the farm in County Kerry and starts talking as if she were still there, as in her childhood days.

Although it is sad to see a loved one in this state of mind, there is a certain level of peace and tranquility in knowing that she is getting some level of stimulation from the memories of her beloved childhood. In this stage of a person's life, as the clouds of darkness come down, maybe it is not a bad way to fade into the sunset. The farm is especially a wonderful place for those of us who love animals, since there are so many different types of animals that are so much a part of our lives growing up.

The farm boy or girl who loves animals has a very special fondness for the farm animals and talks to them like they are almost human. The animals all know and connect with them in a way that only animal lovers understand. When I was growing up, to say you were an animal lover would have been considered silly, so it was a hidden, inward love that was always there but never talked about—but you can always tell a true animal lover. City folks, in particular the young, may laugh at the farm boy and his love for animals, but it is like any other love—unless you had the opportunity to experience it, you will never know what you missed. How we connect with the animals is how they connect with us in their own way. I am very grateful and feel privileged that I had the opportunity to grow up on a farm. Although it was a poor living, it was a wonderful life, where there was warmth and a sense of being connected on all levels and part of something that was larger than life itself. The sense of being connected gave one the security growing up that fostered the courage to go out into the world with great confidence and self-reliance.

This high level of confidence helps to establish a level of independence that allows us to succeed in life beyond our wildest dreams. I am very grateful. Like most young people growing up in Ireland during this period, I knew that one day I would go out into the world to make my fortune. This was something that young people yearned for, to see the big world, where there were adventures, big cities, and a whole new world to explore.

Exploring the big world has its challenges, but there is a level of excitement that propels the young. I could not wait for the time to come when I would start on a journey of exploration. The farm boy would see those who had emigrated before him coming back home in great style, with elegance and an appearance of great success. The Irish emigrants had a high level of success all over the world due to the commitment to hard work they had learned while growing up on the farms. Hard work manifests a sense of loyalty and desire to get things done and to make a difference. In most cases, due to their lack of a formal education, they took up the low-paying, laboring-type jobs that others did not want and moved up the ladder of success inch by inch, at least in relative terms.

The greatest incentive for success is the ability to see the rewards of one's hard work.

For the most part, the emigrants never complained and were happy to have the opportunity to make a living, no matter how menial or rough the work might be. There was always the incentive that if one works hard enough, one will make a better living to support one's family. We grew up in a time when one could advance with limited education, unlike today, when a higher education or a good trade or skill is a necessity to get a basic job. In those days gone by, if one advanced one's education, there were significant rewards available, and doors opened. In today's world advanced education is a must to survive in a highly competitive environment. Today the less educated have an uphill battle to stay out of the poverty roles unless they are fortunate enough to have family support.

Rural Ireland, late '40s

Farm Work: Me on Cock of Hay

Riding Nelly bareback

My brother and I in London

My Mom and Dad, early '60s

Our two Moms

Dating

My wife when we met

Basic Training, 1967

Wedding, 1970

Wedding, 1970

Honeymoon

First House

Our three kids

Oscar

Paddy

My Sister and I

Grandchildren

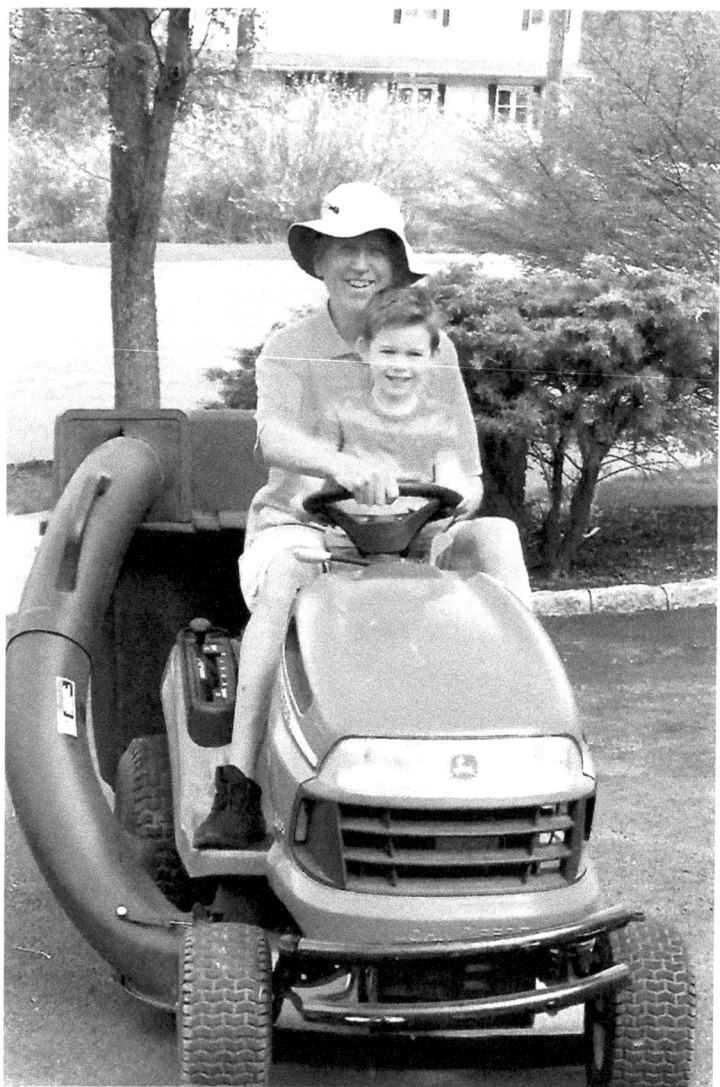

Jack and Grandpa

CHAPTER 27

Big-City Life

I immigrated to London in 1961 as a very young lad—wide eyed, wild, and hearty, ready to take on the challenges of the big world. In London I had two older brothers living in the Northwest part of the city, and I lived with one of them while living there. Sharing living expenses worked out well. My two brothers were wonderful, and we all got along very well and, in many cases, we had friends in common. They were very serious and hardworking and would have liked to see me be the same. During the early 1960s, London was booming, and there were help ads at every factory and construction entrance gate or site; jobs were very easy to come by. Immigrants were pouring into the United Kingdom from all over the world— the West Indies, Jamaica, Pakistan, and so forth. The Irish were accepted and treated as part of the British Isles with no restrictions, which was wonderful but hardly appreciated by the young Irish immigrants at that time. I was able to get a job right away working on a building site for a few months, but with winter arriving, I decided to get an inside job in a dairy, where I worked for the remainder of my time in the United Kingdom. Living in the United Kingdom was a wonderful experience, especially for someone who grew up in a very anti-British environment. I thought that the Brits were not to be trusted and that they hated the Irish nationalists and would like to see them all annihilated. There might have been a very small segment of the British population that was bitter due to the Troubles in Northern Ireland, which spread to some of England's mainland cities; however, fortunately, I never experienced any resentment. In some areas of England, there was a very anti-IRA environment due to the bombings and guerilla war tactics. This was true in London and other parts of the United Kingdom's large cities.

This guerilla war being carried out by the IRA was due to the British occupation of Northern Ireland.

However, again, my experience living in London was in complete contrast with any anti-Irish sentiment—at least on the surface, I did not see any. Living in London, I found the average cockney Londoner and Brits in general to be very friendly and very likable. I saw a great deal of hospitality and warmth from the average Brit; there was no indication of resentment whatsoever. I found everyone to be very open, very friendly and cordial on every level. It was the British political system and global colonization that gave the British a reputation of being heartless and rootless, whereas the average working Brit was anything but, and in general they were very nice people. Like many of my comrades, I was young and adventurous, away from home, and wanted to live life to its fullest every day. Many of us liked to live on the edge; there was always excitement and fun that kept the adrenaline flowing. The Brits enjoyed the very spirited aspect of the young Irish and enjoyed the associated stories and excitement that we brought to the workplace. I saw no resentment of any kind but did see a great deal of extended hospitality and outreach. The Brits were always ready to help young people in every way possible, and this was a nice quality.

I found the working people to be caring, with a great desire to do well and to contribute to the betterment of mankind, which is very noble and seemed to be part of the British common-man culture. I had one very heartwarming experience that I will always remember. I had a serious motorcycle accident where I came into contact with a car at an intersection and was thrown into the air and landed on the grassy shoulder along the side of the road. I was badly scratched and suffered a serious concussion. The police who came to the scene of the accident apparently took me home and gave me a summons notice that I found attached to my bike registration tag in my breast pocket the next morning but had no idea how it got there, which was puzzling.

However, the notice had instructions about where to appear in court, where I was charged with reckless driving. To this day I don't remember any part of the accident details, how it happened or who came on the scene; therefore, I was in no position to defend myself in court. The police did not take me to the hospital to get checked out, and to this day I do not understand why, possibly poor judgment by the police officer. However, I do not know when amnesia set in, whether it was right away or sometime later, which I assume might have contributed to the police officers' decision to take me home. Knowing what I know now, I think it is obvious the police should have taken me to the hospital regardless.

In today's world, when there is an accident where there is evidence of cuts, bruises, and a possible concussion, the police would be held responsible for such poor judgment.

If there was the slightest sign of impaired memory, there should have been a medical evaluation performed by a qualified medical team. It was not until I woke up at home in the middle of the night, sick and vomiting, and when I looked in the mirror and saw that one side of my face and head was completely black, swollen and scratched, and when my stomach felt sore where part of the motorcycle may have come into contact with it and caused an internal injury, that I realized there was something seriously wrong, and when I went to check my leather bike jacket, I saw that it was torn and dirty. I started to look for clues, and it was not until I found a police notice and a summons inside the jacket pocket that was attached to my bike registration tag that I realized to some degree what had happened. The police notice had some of the particulars of the accident, which gave me the first real inkling that I had been in a motorcycle accident. I was very confused and could not understand how I could have been in a serious accident where I got hurt yet did not remember anything about the accident, but that is what amnesia will do. This was a scary thought, and in some ways a morbid one. I knew that I was very fortunate to be alive.

I went back to bed and woke up in the morning not feeling well. I was very sore, had a bad headache, and was feeling sick and somewhat bewildered. I dragged myself out to work, and as I walked up the steps to the dairy dispatch platform where I worked, and standing there was big Reggie, a cockney.

Reggie was a foreman in the area where I worked. He was like a big teddy bear that was loved by everyone and had a heart that was just as big as he was. As soon as he saw me come up the stairs onto the dispatch bank, he saw that my face was black, swollen, and scratched. He yelled out, "What happened, Kevin? You are a mess." I explained to Reggie the gory details of the accident as best I knew, which for the most part was very little other than the police note in my jacket's breast pocket. He said, "How the police could let you go home? You could have a fractured skull or internal injuries." Big Reggie immediately got me into his car and rushed me to Hammersmith Hospital, which was about two miles down the road from where I worked. He treated me like a son, and for that I will be always grateful, and he will always have a special place in my heart.

This was the first time in my life that I found myself on the inside of a hospital, which to me was a scary place. I ended up in a very large open ward where there appeared to be hundreds of beds separated only by pull curtains. Reggie asked me if I wanted him to stay for a while, and I said no and thanked him. He warned me to do whatever they told me to do and said he would be back to see me in the evening after work. In the United Kingdom, the national health system bureaucracy was horrendous for working-class people. There was a big open ward with what appeared to be hundreds of beds lined up like in an army barracks, only much larger. This to me was even scarier. The rich, who had personal insurance, got private or semiprivate rooms and better all-around treatment. After Reggie helped me to get through all the hospital bureaucracy, a nurse took me to my bed.

The bed was part of a large open ward with hundreds of beds separated by pull curtains only, and she told me to get into bed and there would be a doctor within the next twenty-four hours that would check me out and decide what type of treatment was needed. She was a very nice middle-aged Londoner with a real cockney accent.

The nurse also said she would come back and check on me, and she said she would bring me something to eat if I was hungry. Well, I did not like this scene at all. The bed next to me had a very old man making weird noises, and another very old patient was yelling what seemed to be "Get me out of here." I did not fully understand what he was saying, so I looked around, and as soon as the nurse disappeared and went on to another patient, I re-dressed and took off.

I went back to work, but when I showed up back at work, Reggie yelled, "What are you doing back here? You should be in the hospital." I told Reggie that they said I was OK, but Reggie, being very astute, with teenagers of his own, looked at me and asked me why I was not hospitalized. He went on to say, "I hope you did not just leave without getting checked" and then said, "I knew I should have stayed with you." Reggie put me on light duty and kept checking on me every few hours to make sure that I was all right. He worried about me just like I was his own son, just a wonderful man. (One of God's noble men.) Reggie used to say to me, "Kevin, you have never been the same after that accident—it took that spark out of you, and I want to see that come back." Reggie was right—I did not feel right for at least six months after the accident and to some extent was never completely the same. After the accident I started to have some stomach problems that I'd never had before, which I attributed to internal injury of some kind, but I was very grateful that I'd gotten away so lightly, since it was a miracle that I was not killed.

The people who came from Newcastle, which is in the north of England, were called Geordies. "Geordie" was a nickname like the Irish had—we were called Paddies, Scottish jocks, and Welsh Taffies. Old Geordie was a very special person. He was in his sixties, and his wife was a lovely lady who had been in poor health for years, and Geordie had to take care of all her needs. He was very good to her and used to watch out for me like he was my godfather. Where I worked, many of my older coworker friends who could see the relationship would tease me and refer to Geordie as my godfather, and he loved that. When I would take a trip back to Ireland to see my family, old Geordie would offer me money in case I did not have enough, but of course I would thank him and tell him I had enough money, and he would tell me, "The next time you go to Ireland, I want to go with you because I have heard so many good things and how beautiful the countryside is." When I was growing up, my parents would never allow their children to take money from anyone. You were not supposed to ever accept what seemed to be charity. He would invite me to his house for tea and would tell me his wife would be upset if I did not come to visit. I would go once in a while, but most of the time I would have a good excuse and not go because I would be off with friends partying, doing a little boxing, or doing other fun stuff. I never wanted him to think that I did not want to visit, so it was important to always have a good excuse. Geordie and his wife were just wonderful people who loved young people, and since they had no children of their own, they fussed over young people and cared about them as if they were their own children. They always wanted to have close relationships with young people where you were almost adopted without knowing. (Just wonderful, very special people.) It was people like Reggie and Old Geordie that convinced me that the world is full of wonderful people who are always looking for the opportunity to do well and reach out to young people in a way that makes them feel special. I loved living in London and the lifestyle. There was a gang of us that hung out together and had some wonderful wild times. London, a large city, had great nightlife, and there was always plenty to do.

The city entertainment was great—there were nice beaches where the shore was about forty miles from the inner city, and there were beautiful parks with great entertainment from April to October. The south of England's weather was mild all year round, never too hot or too cold, and when snow came, it lasted at most only a few days or less before it was all melted. London's biggest weather problem was fog that could get really bad, to the point where you literally could not see your hand in front of you, and it could last for weeks or more. During very bad fog periods, there were situations where people got crushed between vehicles and in particular the double-decker buses that were moving at a crawling pace. The London parks were beautiful in the spring; parks like Primrose Hill and so many others were so beautiful with all kinds of flowers, and there would be all kinds of outdoor entertainment, including the circus with bumper cars and all kind of rides and events, including outdoor boxing, which was always a very big attraction for the younger people. Many of them attended the local boxing clubs that were located all over the city.

Many of the young people attending boxing clubs were training and hoping they would be the next Sugar Ray Robinson until they found out that was not going to happen. Sugar Ray was considered one of the world's best welterweight/middleweight boxers; he held the world middleweight title from 1946 to 1951. Boxing is like most other sports: no matter how good you think you are in your weight class, there is always someone better. During bank holidays, starting in the early spring and into late fall, there would be boxing and all kinds of other outdoor entertainment in the city parks, where crowds of people would attend. The outdoor boxing rings would have challenge fights by weight class for anyone who was willing to take on the ring champion. This was great fun, especially when one of your friends would take on the ring champion. For the first few rounds, the ring champion would let the challenger have some fun winning.

It was then that things would change. By the third or fourth round, things got serious, and the ring champion would come on strong, throwing some of his best punches until it hurt and there was no place to hide. From there on, the challenger would lose every round and usually got knocked out, or the fight was stopped in about the fifth or sixth round. Looking back, I am sure the park entertainment organizers did not want amateur contenders to get seriously hurt and always knew when to stop the fight. For those of us who loved boxing, it was an awesome experience to watch our friends and people we knew take on the ring champ. I came close but never challenged the ring champion, although there would be strong encouragement from my friends. Some from the boxing club, members and friends, knew who a worthy challenger would be and would cheer you on to take on the champ. They would chant "You can take him out," but I would measure up the ring champion and knew that these guys were not put in that position to lose the fight. When they did lose a round, you know it was a setup to create more excitement for the viewing crowds. Then there were the nightclubs, Irish dances, and Irish pubs all over London, where the young Irish boys and girls met up and hung out. The young Irish farm boys had very little in common with the young Londoners and as a result rarely hung out in the same circles. In some cases, the young London Irish would come together at weddings and other events where they would mingle. In rare cases the young English boys and girls would date their Irish counterparts and, in some cases get married, but that was more the exception than the rule. In the rooming house where I lived with a group of other young Irish, mostly in their late teens and early twenties, there was a group of young, pretty teenage girls who had grown up around the corner who used to come around. Some of us would meet up, and we enjoyed talking and hanging out, but rarely did any longtime relationships develop. Many of the girls had Irish parents or ancestry, but they all had real cockney accents.

The young Irish for the most part did not mix with other immigrant groups except in very rare cases, and for the most part, they kept to their own ethnic group. There were so many Irish immigrants in London it was like home away from home. Only there was more of everything; money and a lifestyle that was so different. We loved it, and everyone was having a great time. Everyone was so nice and congenial, which made life in London a wonderful and memorable experience. As part of the Irish Free State independence treaty, England still allowed a free flow of travel back and forth to Ireland, so there were no immigration requirements between the two countries. This served the Irish well, in particular after the First and Second World Wars, when there was a shortage of laborers to rebuild, creating an abundance of construction jobs. The Irish played a big part in rebuilding London and many other British cities that were bombed during the war. During this period many young Irish started their own building businesses and became very successful. As a result, after World Wars I and II, there was an abundance of work-related opportunity during the 1950s and 1960s. This great work environment went on for many years because there was so much demand and not enough labor or tradespeople to keep up with the workload. It was said that the Irish population in London north of the Thames was 26 percent. Other industrial cities like Liverpool, Manchester, Birmingham, Leads, Coventry, and so on had a similar large influx of young Irish that played a major role in rebuilding the bombed-out cities and towns after the war. After living in London for three years, I had grown up from a boy to a young man with a very full life and was very happy with my lot. I loved London but always had a yearning to see more of the world.

After the motorcycle accident, I was charged with careless driving and lost my driving license. The magistrate was a nice man and said, "You are a young lad, and the fine I am imposing will be the minimum." He went on to lecture me on how my poor parents back in Ireland would deal with me getting seriously hurt or killed. He went on to say, "Therefore, I am going to ground you for twelve months. This penalty is for your own good, and there will be an endorsement on your license for twelve months, which will forbid you to drive for one year from today."

He went on to warn me, "If you come back before this court within the next twelve months or during your driving probation for another driving violation, you will be in big trouble and could go to prison." Although the judge was very nice, he was an advocate of no-nonsense justice and had a reputation for being a big enforcer of the law. I loved my bike, and being able to scoot around carefree, meeting up with my bike friends, picking up girls, and taking them for wild rides, was so much fun. This situation slowed down my ability to get around as freely as in the past. The revoked license where I was somewhat grounded probably spurred my enthusiasm to move on my ambition to see more of the world. That led me to move to the United States, and the rest is history. My dad always said, "You cannot put a wise head on young shoulders," and now I realize how true and profound those words were. London at that time had one of the best transportation systems in the world—the underground rail service, the city double-decker buses, and the black taxicabs; there was none finer. However, being grounded, as the magistrate put it, made me feel that my wings were clipped. It was during this period that I started to consider actively moving on and seeing more of the world, which was a yearning that was always there. I started to look beyond the boundaries of the United Kingdom for new adventure and travel. During this period, I was not sure if I wanted to go to the United States, Canada, New Zealand, or Australia—there was also South Africa—which all seemed so exciting. These were vast countries where there was great weather, and since I loved the outdoor life and plenty of sunshine, any of these destinations seemed exciting.

CHAPTER 28

Time to Move On

Although I loved London—great friends, great city with so much to do—I developed the itch to travel and see more of the world. When I started to look into traveling, I met up with a number of travel agents, and one in particular on London's Oxford Street, which is in the center of London, was very helpful. This travel agent had a great deal of information on the United States immigration requirements and was American born. While serving in the U.S. military, he had met a lovely young English girl and gotten married, and they had decided to make their home in London. He informed me of a program where I could apply for immigration papers without a sponsor in the United States. This program required that the applicants have enough money to take care of themselves for a number of months after they would land in the United States. The amount of money required at that time was about $1,000, and the exchange rate fluctuated between $2.80 and $3.00 to one pound sterling. This sounded great, since I had no immediate family in the United States and did not want to impose on more distant relatives outside my immediate family or friends. So, I asked the travel agent to start the process, and I would follow up with whatever was required for implementation. He gave me a list of things that I had to do and to have ready the next time we were scheduled to meet. He was very accessible and would meet on weekends, so I did not have to take time off from work, which made the process very convenient since I worked six rotating days a week. I was very excited and wanted to move the process forward as quickly as possible and did not want to miss out on this great window of opportunity. No one thought that I was serious about going to America. We were such a close-knit gang of friends and two brothers that I saw every day. We did everything together and moved around in a pack.

It was inconceivable that any one of us would think of breaking up and going our separate ways. They all thought that I would change my mind when it came to make the big move, which they all felt was scary. My oldest brother went as far as to say, "By going to America, you are breaking up a happy family," and that hit hard.

I had made up my mind to move on, and nothing was going to stop me in this quest for adventure and a new life three thousand miles westward. Some of my friends felt a little disappointed that I was going to abandon them to wander into a land thousands of miles away. This was a country where I would have no friends and not know anyone. A land that I knew nothing about other than the stories told by other emigrants when they would make a trip back to their homeland. Then there was a young Irish guy around my age where I worked, and he had a brother in New York who had also moved to try out the big Yankee city but did not like it at all and ended up back in London at his old job, but that did not deter me. I was determined to find out for myself.

It is never easy leaving your family, friends, and comrades, never to return except to visit family. Most of these wonderful friends I never saw or heard from again, as all of them settled down and became occupied with families of their own.

In those days there were no cell phones and only one land line in the average house that was only used as a last resort to communicate, since back in those days it was very costly to make a transatlantic call and young lads do not like writing letters.

I was not good at communicating and got so caught up in my new life and new friends it was not until later in life that my mind started to wander back to those wonderful times that we shared as friends. I would love the opportunity to renew those friendships.

The hardest thing to do is to renew old friendships, since time changes and everything, including people, also moves on.

With a significant lapse in time, the best you can hope for is to have an opportunity to meet up with some of them. I started thinking it would be so nice to meet up with old friends and reminisce a little about the past. When we have the time to reminisce with old friends, we have to realize that they may have also moved on to lives they have chosen, which in many cases may be completely different from when we knew them in days gone by. Now there may be spouses and children, and a lot may have changed; some may not be around after all those years. As the years go onward, we must realize that the time may have come when we have to say a final goodbye and realize that there may be little room in their busy lives for old friends from the past who would like to renew that old friendship. With that said, I was very happy with the decisions made and would not want to change anything. Life is meant to revolve and move on to new adventures and places where there is new excitement and work on the dreams that make our lives whole and unabridged. During the early 1960s, immigration into the United States was a very rigorous process. I was fortunate to have a travel agent that was able to give me some good advice on how the US immigration process worked. The good news was that at that time the Irish had a large immigration quota into the United States, which allowed the application process to move along swiftly. The first step was that I had to apply to the American embassy for an immigration application, which had to be filled out in great detail and accuracy to be considered in the process. In my situation the travel agent reviewed and critiqued the application, which made the process go smoothly for me. Once the application approval was complete, I was notified of the dates, location, and what to bring to the embassy interview, which went well, and I would move on to the next step in the process. The interview was very in-depth, with a lot of questions as to why I wanted to immigrate to the United States.

There were a lot of questions about political affiliations, and at that time they wanted to make sure that there were no communist connections. Although this time period was long after the Joe McCarthy era, there were those who thought communism was everywhere, and to some extent it was and still is.

The US immigration department performed a very detailed background check: they checked out every place I had lived, including the village in Ireland where I grew up. The US officials met with a number of people in the area, asking a lot of questions as part of a background check.

The immigration department wanted to make sure that there was no criminal record.

Back in those days, any kind of criminal record would be a disqualification. There was a very major emphasis that all information must be accurate and properly vetted. After the investigator left the area, one of the local ladies met up with my mother and asked if I was in trouble, at which point my mother did not have a clue what she was talking about. When the background check was satisfactorily complete, I got a letter from the US embassy notifying me of a date for a physical. The physical consisted of a battery of tests, which were very rigorous and included chest X-rays, blood tests, cardiovascular testing, a flat-feet check, examinations of body scars (which I have plenty of), and so forth.

After I had satisfactorily passed the physical, there was a Q&A part, which I think was a basic competence evaluation. When all the testing and interviewing were completed, I was told that I would have to come back to get all the required inoculations. About two weeks after all the vaccinations were successfully complete, I received a US visa in the mail.

The US visa packet included a long list of *do*s and *don't*s, which also included all the immigration regulations for new immigrants. Failure to comply with the strict immigration regulations in those days would result in immediate deportation.

Some of the regulations were as follows: I had to register with the American embassy once a year to maintain an up-to-date green card. I could not apply for any type of government assistance for five years, and I had to register for the U.S. military draft and serve in the military when called upon. With a clean record and compliance with all immigration requirements, you could apply for citizenship after five years. Meeting all the visa requirements, which included all the medical testing and background checks, was a great sense of accomplishment.

I was pretty confident that the background check would come up clean. There had been a few minor brushes with the law, which would be considered misdemeanors. I was on cloud nine when I got my visa and told all my friends and family the good news. The news again was met with mixed emotions and some trepidation because my brothers and friends did not want to see me go and tried to persuade me to change my mind, but now that I had gone this far in the process, there was no turning back. I promised them if I did not like my new abode I would come back, and my two brothers told me if I ever needed money to come home, not to hesitate to contact them. This was a nice crutch to have, knowing that I could always return and be welcomed.

Upon receipt of my visa, I was eligible to travel to the United States, at which time I went back to the friendly travel agent to discuss travel options and preferred destinations. I told the travel agent I wanted to go to Manhattan, and then there was the question of my preferred mode of transportation: to fly or travel by boat. To travel by boat was much more expensive than by air at that time, but I wanted to travel by boat, although the cost was much greater. I thought it would be once-in-a-lifetime experience to cross the Atlantic Ocean by boat. As for traveling by air, I had plenty of trips going back and forth to Ireland from the United Kingdom, but to sail on a big ship sounded exiting.

There were many stories when I was growing up about emigrants who would be sick for the complete voyage, when the voyage back then would take six weeks or more to complete from Cove, County Cork, Ireland, to New York Harbor.

In those days most of the emigrants who left Ireland for America never returned. Many of the young people leaving were barely sixteen years of age when they emigrated to America and in many cases were never able to go back home for a visit. They got married, had families, and could not afford trips back to their homeland.

Since the probability of never seeing their homeland again was so real, the local community would have what was called the American wake for emigrants traveling to the United States. After the young emigrant had departed, family and friends got together to grieve the loss of a son or daughter. They made the assumption that they might never see that young boy or girl again. This was extremely sad and very painful, especially for the parents, and as a result there are many sad stories and songs that reflect those difficult times. In today's world it is hard to imagine your son or daughter, barely sixteen, leaving home never to return.

The travel agent told me he could get me on the S.S. *United States*, which at that time was one of the fastest and most luxurious passenger ships on the ocean. This was wonderful and very exciting, so I went ahead and booked a voyage to New York City for mid-July 1964. The travel agent also booked my lodgings at the YMCA in Manhattan, which was on the Upper West Side. The YMCA was the closest thing to a European travel hostel that was inexpensive and used by young people with little funds to travel. The night before I left London, my brothers and friends threw a big going-away party at a friend's house where my brothers were boarding and where I had lived for a short time, when I first arrived in London.

The owners of the boardinghouse were a husband and wife who were wonderful people, both from County Kerry. They always treated us like family, and Mrs. O., as we called her, the wife and owner of the boardinghouse, had lived in Manhattan for six years and worked as a registered nurse before returning to England to marry her Irish sweetheart.

As a nurse she had worked in a number of the New York City hospitals and as a result was very familiar with the neighborhood where the YMCA was located. Toward the end of the night, she came and talked to me and asked where I was going to in Manhattan and where I was going to stay. I explained to her that I was going to stay at the YMCA on the Upper West Side. Upon hearing where I was going to stay, she warned, "Oh, Kevin, this was a very bad area with a lot of crime when I was there seven years ago and may be even worse now." She went on to say, "I am sure it has gotten worse since I left the city seven years ago." I could see by her reaction that she was very concerned for my safety. Mrs. O. did not like the area and felt it was not a good choice. That did not bother me in the least. I thought I was a pretty tough guy—I did a little boxing at the local boxing club and could defend myself. Living in London back in those days, where the streets were safe and crime was almost unheard of, did not prepare one for New York City, where drugs, shootings, muggings, and robbery were commonplace in tough areas. The next morning, I headed for Southampton to embark on the SS *United States* and sailed for New York City. It was so exciting, a world away that I knew nothing about other than pure adventure. The ship made one stop at Le Havre in France for a short time and then sailed on to the port of New York City. The ship was magnificent and took about five days to complete the voyage. The seas were relatively calm, with only a few mild ocean storms, which made for pleasant sailing. It was one of the best times of my life. The food was wonderful. Most of the passengers were rich Americans.

There was one young lad that I met and befriended on the ship who was from Scotland.

There were a number of beautiful young American girls between the ages of seventeen and twenty-one that hung around with my Scottish friend and me. We had the time of our lives, not a care in the world, just fun and more fun. The rich Americans were extremely generous and wonderful people.

Some of them had some Irish ancestors, and when I would walk up to the bar to get drinks, they just wanted to talk and would not let me pay for anything. They were very interested in my adventure to America, and when they heard my story, some of them offered me jobs and all kinds of helpful assistance if I was interested. They gave me their addresses and phone numbers and so on. One of the passengers was a congressman from upstate New York who was very nice and gave me his telephone number to call him if I needed a job or anything else. He told me he had a big house, a wife, and four children but that there was plenty of extra room where I would be welcome to stay, and he would give me a job. I was amazed by the generosity and outreach of these people who to me were total strangers, but once they got to know you, they were like family. I am sure many of these people had children of their own around my age and just wanted to help in every way possible. Most of these people were very rich Americans who were very unlike the rich Europeans, who were much stuffier and would never mingle with the common folks, which was one of the many qualities that I was impressed by. I often wondered what my life might have been if I had taken up the rich Americans' generous job and living offers. The ship had all kinds of entertainment, and passengers used to come down from the first-class quarters to the tourist-class quarters to have fun and good entertainment, and some, especially women, let down their hair, having a great time, which was fabulous.

There was one very nice woman who knew I enjoyed dancing, and she would pull me out to dance, and then her husband, a very nice guy, would tease me and tell me not to steal his wife, and that used to get a big laugh.

The older Americans loved the party animal spirit and got a great kick out of our antics.

The ship entertainment people had competition dancing and gave out medals; I got some of the medals and had a ball. One of the young girls that hung around with us was about eighteen or nineteen years of age. She was a beautiful girl in every way. She was from Pittsburgh, and her father had an oil business. She wanted me to go to Pittsburgh with her and meet her father, who would give me a job, and they had a carriage house where I could stay, but I was not ready for any type of commitment of any kind. I wanted to see New York City. That was my dream, although I had no idea what to expect or what lay in store for me.

I was a little wild, hearty, and carefree, full of confidence, and I felt that I had the world at my fingertips, with all these wonderful people offering me jobs—and more, what seemed to be romance. What could be better? When the ship pulled into New York Harbor, I was in many ways disappointed that this wonderful voyage with so many wonderful people and new friends had come to an abrupt end. This voyage was almost like a fairy tale.

Although it was not very realistic, I was having such a great time I wanted the good times to go on forever. The wonderful memories of this voyage and the wonderful people that I met and partied with have stayed with me and will continue to for the rest of my life. I still reminisce about those wonderful times on that ship and how wonderful all those people were sixty years ago. This voyage was a great introduction to the United States of America. I knew right then that I had made the right decision in coming to America.

I was convinced the people that I had come to know on this voyage were my type of people.

They were upbeat, very positive, very self-confident, and full of fun, and they loved to party and let their hair down—what could be better? As I started to make my way off the ship toward the dock with no idea where I was going, I heard my name called over the intercom system: "Scollans, Scollans, Kevin, and report to the ship captain's desk. Please report to the ship captain's desk." This announcement caused me great concern. Who could be calling me? I did not know a soul, and nobody knew me other than the people I had just met and partied with on the ship. All kinds of thoughts ran through my mind.

Was it my aged father, my mother? Was there some type of emergency? With great hesitation I walked up to the captain's desk, and there standing by the desk was a very tall, affable-looking man with an FBI badge hanging from his lapel, which made him look very official when he spoke to me. "Kevin, you are Kevin," he repeated with a genial smile. I was somewhat relieved by the smile. He introduced himself as a friend of the Hartnett family and a cousin of Mrs. Hartnett, who was waiting for me in Morristown, New Jersey, with their two daughters.

I never heard of the name Hartnett or the Hartnett family, which was about to become very much part of my life. Then he told me that the woman I was about to visit in Morristown was a sister of Mrs. O'Connell in London who owned the boardinghouse where my going-away party was held. He went on to say that the woman in Morristown wanted me to visit them and that her sister in London had contacted her and told her all about me.

He went on to tell me that Mrs. Hartnett was a sister of Mrs. O., and then he also told me that he was married to Mrs. Hartnett's cousin. I was a little confused about how this all came about and said thank you, but that I had booked a room with the YMCA in upper Manhattan, and I would go there first and drop off my luggage and then go out to visit the Hartnett family on the weekend.

He saw that I was not too keen on going to Morristown, at least right away, and then he turned to me again with a big, very warm smile.

This time he flashed his FBI badge and said, "I work in law enforcement, and I can tell you where you want to go in Manhattan is not a safe area. This part of the Upper West Side is a high-crime area, and you are new to the big city. Like Mrs. O'Connell in London, we too are concerned about your safety." He went on to say, "I got you a bus ticket to Morristown, and these people would be very disappointed if you did not go out to visit them. I am going to put you on the Morristown, New Jersey, bus, and the people you are going to visit will be waiting for you at the bus stop. They are wonderful people. You will like them."

At this point I did not know what to do other than to go along with the program. When he took me to the bus, he told the bus driver to let me know when I got to the proper Morristown stop by the green.

When I landed in Morristown and got off the bus, the husband, wife, and two daughters were there to meet me. The young daughters were lovely girls, one about eight years old and the other about ten. They had heard so much about the London visitor from their parents, and they were so excited. As I was stepping down from the bus onto the sidewalk, the eight-year-old jumped up with her arms around my neck and gave me a big hug and kiss.

I was astounded. How could this be happening? These wonderful people that I did not know and had never met before acted like I had known them all my life. It was almost too good to be true in real life.

CHAPTER 29

Morristown

Morristown, New Jersey, was a beautiful suburban town. As the little girl hung from my shoulders, she was kissing me on both cheeks, and her mother with a big smile ear to ear said, "Oh, Kevin, do not mind her. She is just so excited to see you, and she has been talking about your arrival all week." The hospitality was so overwhelming I had to pinch myself. This was just too good to be true. The parents, just like my new FBI friend had told me, were the nicest and friendliest people you could ever hope to meet, and they welcomed me into their home like I was a visiting prince.

When I got to their house, the eight-year-old grabbed my hand and said she wanted to show me where I was going to sleep. Again, this took me by more surprise, that they had set up quarters for me to stay in. Now I was digesting all this kindness and their overwhelming hospitality, which was beyond comprehension for this young greenhorn who had just arrived not knowing what to expect, while going along with the program and still thinking about how I was going to leave here and live in Manhattan—after all, that was my dream. The evening that I landed, my new host family had invited a number of their close friends to meet and greet the new visitor. All their friends were wonderful, one nicer than the next. One of their friends, Pat, who was a supervisor in a local factory, said, "Kevin, I have a job for you if you are interested, and I will pick you up Monday on my way to work to meet the personnel manager." Pat went on to say, "I already spoke to the hiring manager about you, so this is just a matter of form." He told me that this was not a glamourous job but would get my foot in the door, and I could then look around for something I might like better. I went with Pat the next Monday morning and met the personnel manager, a very nice man who was a friend of Pat's.

The first question he asked was "Are you ready to start?" and as soon as I said yes, he took me to meet my new department supervisor. The HR manager then told me I was on the clock starting from 8:00 a.m. I could not believe that all this was happening so quickly, but I loved it and could not believe how quickly things happened in America. My host mom, Nora, told me that the owners of the house where they were renting the upstairs apartment were at their shore house and would be back on Sunday evening, and they would also want to meet me. It so happened that the landlord who owned the house was an Irishman and to my surprise grew up in Northern Ireland, approximately three miles or less from where I grew up—a wonderful man, and his wife, Mary, was from the west of Ireland. She too was a very nice woman with a very strong personality who held nothing back. She was a no-nonsense lady who loved young people and would make sure that they were on the right track. Everybody loved Mary. She was the Irish matriarch of this Morristown enclave known as Little Dublin, on the outskirts of the town's south side. The area was christened with the nickname Little Dublin because of the large number of Irish that had settled in this area as far back as the Revolutionary War. In recent years, the North

Jersey History and Genealogy Center, in conjunction with the Morris County Friendly Sons of St. Patrick, which I became part of, dedicated one area in a memorial service as Little Dublin Memorial Park. This was a historic and very personal moment for me, and I take family and visiting friends on a tour at every opportunity. That Sunday evening, when Mary the landlady got home, she too had another big party for me, where all her friends and a large number of the Morristown old Irish came to see the new arrival, whom they referred to as the greenhorn. We had a wonderful time, and she made sure that I was introduced to everyone. After all the introductions were made, she said, "Kevin what are your plans now that you are in America among so many nice friends?" She said, "You are very bright and should go to night school."

My answer was "Well, for now I plan to move to New York City, and then I may look at going back to school."

She did not like my answer and said in front of all who were there, "You are not going to New York City. Get that out of your head. You will have a great life here with all these wonderful people in one of the nicest areas in New Jersey. Now that Pat got you a job, what else would you want?"

Although I was known to never be short of an answer, I was dumbfounded and did not know what to say. My dad always preached that if you did not have the right answer, you should wait until you did before you opened your mouth. And then came his next words of wisdom: "Better to be thought a fool than to open your mouth and remove all doubt."

Mary went on to say, "You can go to New York City during the weekend if you like the city that much." No one argued with Mary. She always had the final word, and when she spoke, you could hear a pin drop. Morristown was a beautiful town, and I loved everything about it, and everyone I met was wonderful.

Everyone knew that Mary loved young people and would do anything she could to help them. Her only agenda was to see the young Irish, including her nephews and a niece who came over, do very well. She also loved to comment on the young Irish who had come over, gone to school, and done really well. When she would see them, she would tell them how proud she was of them. There was no one better than Mary, and she knew how to encourage and motivate young people in a very positive and direct, no-nonsense way where you knew whatever she said was only for your good.

Shortly after landing in Morristown, I bought my first car, an old English Ford Consul convertible, which had a great attraction for the girls—they all wanted to ride in it. Now I had to get my license and went to the Morristown Armory, where I asked what I had to do to get a license.

The guy behind the desk was very nice and probably part of the Little Dublin community. He asked if I had driven before. I said yes and handed in my UK motorcycle license. He looked over the UK license and said, "Give me a few minutes." When he came back, he handed me my new automobile driver's license. Needless to say, that would not happen today—now you have to meet the six-point requirement where the driver's license becomes your identification for domestic travel and so forth.

I was so surprised and so overjoyed with getting my license right away. When I told all my friends, they too were very surprised and thought that I fast-talked or pulled a fast one on the guy behind the counter. Since I had never driven a car before, I had to learn how to drive, which was much different from driving a motorcycle. I got behind the wheel on some of the back roads and drove around for a few hours with my friend Pat, who had just gotten his license, until I felt confident driving alone. My new friend Pat had gotten his license only about two months before I got mine, but he knew the rules of the road since he had to study to get his license and he had completed his high school driver's Ed program before graduating a few months earlier. I bought the car on a Tuesday evening, got temporary plates, which were good for fourteen days, and drove into New York City with my friend Pat that Saturday evening to attend an Irish social event at the City Center Ballroom on Fifth Street between Sixth and Seventh Avenues, where there was a very popular Irish show band playing. This was a real once-in-a-lifetime experience, driving into New York City for the first time while learning to drive and learning my way around. City driving was very challenging, and driving on the opposite side of the road made it more challenging. There were plenty of goofs and plenty of near misses and a lot of horns blowing, but we survived and made it back to Morristown without any major incident. My friend Pat loved it and thought it was so much fun.

The following weekend Pat and I headed to Boston. We went to an Irish ballroom on Massachusetts Avenue, where again there was one of the very popular big Irish show bands from Ireland playing. We had a great time and then visited my cousin, who was raised in Ireland and lived with her husband and family outside Boston in one of the suburbs. My cousin and her husband and family could not believe that we navigated all the way around the city and did not get lost. This was another wonderful experience and a great confidence builder.

I had a great time visiting my cousin, and since then I have become very close with the family; my wife and I attended their children's weddings over the years. Life in America was great, and I enjoyed every minute of it. I made some great friends, and some became lifetime friends. There was one in particular, my friend Pat, whom I hung out with and went to all the dances and parties with. We double-dated a lot and would always fix each other up with friends of the girls we would be going out with at that time. During my first winter in America, we had at least one heavy snowstorm, and the landlady, Mary, who owned the house where I lived lent me her snow shovel so my friend Pat and I could dig the car out of a big snow pile. My friend and I were in a hurry to meet two new girlfriends and forgot to bring the landlady's shovel back, which was a big mistake. My friend lived with his mother just up the street from where I was living, and he used to carpool with me to work until he got his own car. When we got home, the landlady was waiting on the doorstep for us, very angry about our not bringing back the snow shovel. She'd found the shovel lying on the sidewalk where we had dug out the car. She screamed at us and scolded us for being irresponsible and unappreciative, and rightfully so. My friend Pat, a big personality who was a big talker and could talk his way out of just about any situation, said to Mary, "Ah, this was my fault, not Kevin's," and with that she laid into him and read him the riot act.

My friend should have kept quiet and let her vent. This was a much-needed lesson in responsibility: we should have been showing gratitude rather than negligence and lack of accountability for her property. This story went all around the Irish community like wildfire, and people would come up to me and ask, "Did Mary ever forgive you for leaving her shovel on the side of the road?" and of course they were looking for a response that they would bring back to Mary. The wonderful thing about Mary was that after she reamed us out, it was over, and ten minutes later she would be inviting us in for tea and homemade scones, which were so delicious. She loved to see young people enjoy her cookies and scones. Mary had a big heart and always only meant well when it came to young people. She believed in keeping young people in their place and making sure that they were accountable for their actions and not shirking their responsibilities. Everyone in the neighborhood loved Mary, and again, she was the real matriarch of the enclave that no one questioned. She always had the final word. Mary had no children of her own, and what a shame. She would have been a great mother, and in some ways, she treated us like she was our mother. Morristown was a great, spirited town, and the people were so nice, not just the Irish. It seemed that everyone in the town was so warm that you always felt at home compared to London, where everyone kept to themselves until they got to know you. I had loved London and enjoyed the city life—it was a great town with so much to do and great people who, although somewhat private, were very nice and friendly.

These were the days when we were carefree and always having fun. Life was about having fun, good friends, and good times all the time. Some of the older people would warn us that the good times would not last forever and would remind us that when we would settle down and have families and responsibilities, things would change.

Having families and responsibilities was far from our minds at that time.

Mary would warn us that when we got married and had families things would change, but we would just laugh and pay little heed while thinking that was a long way off, if it ever happened.

I am sure many of the older folks wondered if we would ever grow up and settle down.

I liked to drive fast and loved to take wild chances, speeding and living on the edge.

The English Ford Consul became the victim of some of the wild stunts when I went over a humpbacked bridge so fast the car went airborne, and when it landed back on its wheels, the engine crossbar came loose, and the transmission dropped onto the road. This was a costly repair, and I had to call Bill, my host dad, to pick me and my friend up in the middle of the night. I gave him a different version of what had happened, and he felt sorry for us getting stuck on the road in the middle of the night. He was such a nice man and would always show up in these situations with a big smile and so glad that he could help.

The family I lived with was very Irish, and after a few episodes he realized that I was performing some stunts that were causing some of the car breakdowns. The word got around that I was a wild driver and liked to do crazy stuff. When the host family became aware of my crazy driving, Bill would say to me with a big smile, in his rich Kerry brogue, "Now, lad, you are going to have to slow down."

After I got the car fixed, it ran for about a year in spite of being put through a lot of gyrations that it was not designed to do. One lovely afternoon a crowd of us were on our way home from a ball game and traveling west on the main drag in Roselle Park, New Jersey, when I realized the gas tank was almost empty, at which time I had just passed a gas station, and with that I did a real quick U-turn and screeched into the gas station. When I pulled into the gas station, there was this big cop standing there who was watching the whole caper. The cop's name was Murphy. He was a huge man who walked up to my car and banged on the driver's side window.

When I rolled the window down, he let out a monstrous roar at me to get out of the car now. I was sure the handcuffs were going on and that I would be going off to the clink. Instead of putting me in handcuffs, he chose to scream at me for what seemed to be an eternity and threatened me that if he ever caught me in town again cutting up in this way, he would, "kick my f'ing ass". Then he went on to say, "I could have you locked up for reckless and dangerous driving."

After he finally left, I pulled up to the gas pump to get gas, where the attendant, who was a nice man in his forties, had seen the whole caper and got a great kick out of it. The gas attendant laughed and said, "You are a lucky boy. That is Big Murph, the "baddest" cop in town, and I am surprised he did not punch you in the head a few times, since he usually does, especially when it is kids like you guys acting up. All the kids in town fear Big Murph. They run when they see him coming, and he keeps them in line. You better never let him catch you again doing this type of stunt, or you will be in big trouble." After we got our gas and pulled away from the gas station, although I was pretty shaken up, we had a big laugh and thought this was the funniest episode ever and chalked it up to another great story that my friends loved to tell at parties, and I am sure it gets a little embellished.

On another occasion I was on my way home after a party in the early hours of the morning after dropping off a friend. When I was driving fast on a very windy, wet road, the car hydroplaned and went into a skid, hitting the curb, and then the car spun out of control up onto the front lawn and hit the corner of an old wooden church, causing some damage to the wooden church structure. The minster who lived in the rectory close to the church heard the crash and called the police. When the police came, there were two of them, both very nice, and when they started talking to me after answering some questions and exchanging the necessary particulars, it so happened they knew one of my friends.

My friend was part of the Little Dublin community, and I am sure the two cops had friends and maybe family there. The minster came on the scene, and I explained to him what had happened, and he was very sympathetic and very nice. I promised him I would repair the damage to the church, and he was pleased with that. The two cops took me home and dropped me off at my digs, and I was so happy they did not give me a ticket.

The next morning a local neighbor friend who was a carpenter came with me and repaired the damage to the corner of the wooden church and painted it to where the church minister was pretty pleased with the finished job.

I was so relieved that there were no tickets issued, and now I had another wild story to add to my repertoire. Mary used to say that the Blessed Virgin Mary had to have me in her arms, or otherwise I would be dead. There were a lot of old Irish around Morristown who loved to gossip, and I did a good job at fueling their fire. They used to say, "That Kevin lad—he is as wild as wild as can be, and the sooner he settles down before he gets killed, the better." Of course, I paid no heed to the gossip and just took everything in stride. I lived for the moment, loved the weekends, and let the good times roll. After I had lived in Morristown for about a year, my host parents, Nora and Bill, moved out of the upstairs rental apartment and bought a house up the line. At this time, I was like family, and they insisted that I move with them into their new house, which had an extra bedroom. I moved with them and stayed there until I was drafted into the army in 1967, which was during the height of the Vietnam War. Nora and Bill were more like an uncle and aunt, and they treated me like one of the family. I stayed with them for five years until finally I got married and settled down. When in the service, during my time off on weekends and on leave, I would come to their house, which I considered home. Nora, a wonderful lady, cooked and washed my clothes and was also so nice to my friends.

I would bring visitors from Ireland or London, and they too were welcome. When I went to work, she would pack a big lunch and all kinds of goodies to the point where my coworkers would tease me and ask me if her husband knew how she was taking such good care of me, and of course I would just laugh. Their two daughters were like younger sisters, and as the years went on, they babysat for our children when my wife and I attended weddings and all other family affairs. To this day I ask myself how I can be so fortunate as to have such wonderful, caring people like Nora, Bill, and their two daughters in my life. I have to say with humility that I was one of the luckiest ever to immigrate to the United States, where everything always seemed to be there for me because of the wonderful people who always seemed to come my way.

CHAPTER 30

The Yank

The summer before I went into the military service, I went back to Ireland for the first time to visit family. I rented a car and had to get used to driving on the opposite side of the road, which is always a challenge for the first few days. When I was on vacation in Ireland during those times, every day was party time, meeting old friends and family—it was just so much fun. Being a Yank during those times, you were treated like a celebrity. Back then most families in Ireland had a relative in America, which was considered the land of opportunity.

My parents were in great form back then, and everything was so wonderful. They were comfortable and loved to see their children come home, which was the highlight of their lives. One morning, my younger brother and I went to the nearest big town, Enniskillen, on the northern side of the border where I grew up, to do some shopping. We dropped into a local pub for a few beers, where we met up with some old friends and had a few too many. On the way home, after having a few drinks and driving on the opposite side of the road, we met a car coming toward us and sideswiped the car while trying to get back to the other side of the road. The oncoming car was a Volkswagen Beetle, and upon impact the front windshield popped out and there was significant damage to the car's front fender. Fortunately, there was no one hurt in either car. The owner of the oncoming car was a Royal Ulster Constabulary (RUC) Northern Ireland police officer, and he and his bride-to-be were on their way to their wedding service. This was an ugly scene: me, an Irish Yank who was Catholic and grew up across the border in an IRA stronghold—not a good mix. The Irish Protestants Unionist did not like Americans either since they felt that the Irish had a big voice in America.

I knew I was in big trouble and would have to put the best spin on what had just happened. The situation was very serious, and I had to show that I was mature and able to take responsibility for what had just happened. He called his police barracks for backup, and they were there in full force within minutes, and then I had a lot of explaining to do.

The lead officer who came on the scene was not nice to me, and after we exchanged particulars, the officer told me that I was responsible for the accident and that unless I was willing to sign an affidavit of guilt, he would have to take me back to the barracks, which of course was a place I did not want to go. The rented car was fully insured, so they knew there would be no problem collecting damages. In those days, being in Northern Ireland under British rule was like being in a communist country—there was no justice for nationalists/Catholics, and if I went to the police barracks, I might be there for a very long time. There were many situations where nationalists, including Irish Americans who were considered sympathetic to the nationalist cause, got brought in for no just reason and were locked up for many months or more. There was an Irish American attorney, Martin Galvin, a big supporter of the Irish resistance movement, who traveled back and forth from New York to Northern Ireland. He was the publicity director of the New

York–based Northern Ireland Aid (NORAID). He was arrested in 1989 in Londonderry, where he was bundled into a police jeep and driven away after taking a high-profile walk-through Northern Ireland's second-largest city. I knew how the British ruled Northern Ireland's justice system: you could get thrown in jail without a hearing or trial; this happened during a mass arrest that was known as Operation Demetrius, carried out in Northern Ireland 1971. With that in mind, I had little choice but to sign a release. It was imperative to get back across the border into the Republic of Ireland as fast as I could. Although I was fully insured, which was good, I could not rent another car in Dublin after admitting liability.

I knew the rental car company would contact all its affiliates in the Dublin area, informing them of the liability admission situation, which put the insurance company in a bad position legally. This incident made for a very exciting time and in some ways a vacation that I will always remember. Although the accident happened ten miles from the village where I grew up, when I went to church in my village the next day with family, which was on a Sunday morning, everyone knew about the accident. The gossipmongers were in full spin and had all the details of the accident as if there were private investigators on the scene. So needless to say, I had a lot of explaining to do to minimize the drama. That was what made rural Ireland's communities different: everyone knew everyone else's business, which could be good and bad. In those good old days, this was a way of life; the gossipers were everywhere and would make some of our present-day reporters look like amateurs. The good part was that everyone cared about their neighbors' well-being, but what was not so good was that it was difficult to maintain a level of privacy and not have the details of your private life spread across the community.

The Irish are also very good at making each story much more interesting and exciting than it really merits. In those days, every little town and village had an area or corner that was known for gossip, where all the older men hung out and chatted after church.

These men were just as good at gossiping as the old ladies, and if you wanted something to be told, you would give someone who you knew liked to gossip in the area a juicy story, and in particular, if you told that person in secrecy, it would spread even that much faster.

The culture in those days was the result of hundreds of years where the Irish people were robbed of everything they possessed by British tyranny and had no way of communicating except by word of mouth. They became so good at verbal communications that many developed very strong oratory skills over the years.

In the United States, many Irish immigrants became very successful in politics because of their verbal skills. Many were known to have great oratory that reverberated within their local communities. In spite of the accident issues, this was a great vacation, and had I a wonderful time.

I did not know that this would be the last time I would see my father alive. I am forever grateful that I spent much of that time with him, and I cherish those memories. He would be in his glory when any of his children returned for a visit. When I said to him that the accident incident was a spoiler, but I'd had a great time overall and promised to come home more often, he replied, "Son, it is these types of things that will make your trip memorable." He was always positive, always supportive.

My father was a very sensitive man who loved his family more than anything else in the world, and he was always there for us in every way. When any one of us would leave home, whether it was for the first time or after a vacation, he would be so sad that he would walk out into the fields to deal with the sad parting in his own way, with silent tears running from his eyes that he did not want others to see, and as a result he would not come back into the house until he got his composure back. He was a very private and a very proud man and always wanted to be strong for his family. It is only now that I am older and have children of my own that I can reflect on who my father really was. His faith, his dedication and love, and his loyalty to his family were boundless. His whole world was his children, and there was no load too heavy for him to bear for my mother and each one of us. Of the eight children, five immigrated to foreign lands to seek their fortunes, and he waited every day of his life to see each one of us come home, at least for a visit. His greatest wish would have been to see all of us come home for good, but of course that never happened.

There was only one of the five sons who returned home and settled down on a farm a few miles from the old homestead. My father did everything in his power to make sure my brother would be successful on his new farm, and my brother did not let him down.

He gave my brother some livestock from his own farm to get him started and was there at every turn to make sure he was successful. My brother was a great worker and very determined in everything he did. After a few years, the farm became very successful, so he bought up additional neighboring land. He got married to a great partner, built a new modern farmhouse where he and his family could live very comfortably, and has a very nice life. When I would make trips back to Ireland with my wife and children, we would all get together and have a great time. Life in the farm communities is very relaxing, with a great quality of life, but there is a lot of hard work that goes with maintaining a successful farm. Taking care of a farm herd requires great intuition and knowledge—knowing when some of the herd requires professional attention and many times nursing livestock back to health. Then there are the crops, which require a high level of knowledge in horticulture if the farmer is to be able to stave off disease. Just like in any other business, survival requires diligence and hard work, but at the end of the day, everyone seems so happy and content with their lot, and the quality of life is as good as it gets today when the necessary training and disease prevention are taught in local farm communities, including the proper fertilizer application based on the soil type.

CHAPTER 31

Military Service

In November 1967, I was drafted into the U.S. Army during the Vietnam War period. As I was getting ready to go into the army, my brother, who got drafted in 1965, was on his way out after completing a two-year active-duty commitment.

My brother spent a year in Vietnam with the 199th Light Infantry. His assignment was search-and-destroy missions in the jungles and rice paddies of Vietnam, and he was very fortunate to come home without a scratch, at least from a physical point of view.

I am sure war leaves unidentified scars that we will never know on every soldier who fights in battle. Like most war veterans of his time, he talks very little about the war or what they went through, except that once in a while, after a few drinks and in the right mood, he might give a little information. I do not pry or ask a lot of questions unless he is willing to freely discuss. War veterans who have fought in battle have to deal with the loss of close friends and comrades that died at their side, and you never know how they are dealing with those losses.

In the military you make very close friends, and you share the good times and bad. When one of those comrades falls in battle and nothing can be done to save them, it is like losing a close family member. This is why many soldiers in battle lose their own lives trying to save an injured comrade and bring them to a safe place.

When my brother was in Vietnam, this was a very difficult time for my parents back in Ireland, who were worrying about him every day and hoping that he would come home alive, like the tens of thousands of other parents who had to deal with similar situations. My brother came out of the service in August 1967, and I went in on November 7, 1967.

My entry into the military meant that my parents had to go through another two years of the same torture: worrying about me going to war. However, I was fortunate and did not end up in combat. I stayed stateside for two years.

Living in Ireland, my parents did not get the detailed daily news reports on the war like we would get in the United States, which made it more difficult for them, not knowing or understanding what was going on with the war and when it might end.

For me the army was another adventure, an opportunity to see more and learn what there is to know about military life. Being a soldier had a level of appeal, and while I was growing up in Ireland, there was a great regard for military heroes, warriors, and in particular those who fought and died to free their country, fighting the foreign occupier. Most Irish had some family member who fought in one of the many Irish rebellions down through the centuries in an attempt to drive out an oppressive occupier, and as a result some loved to speak of the warriors in their families. My family on my dad's side had a number of such stories, which I loved to hear about. My great-great-grandfather back in the late 1700s to early 1800s was a very young Irish freedom fighter who left his very well-to-do family in central County Fermanagh and went on the run. When being chased down by the Brits up in the mountains, close to where I grew up on the Northern Ireland border, he met a young woman, fell in love, and got married. The girl's dad gave him and his new bride half his land and livestock to get started; then along came their newborn son. Shortly after their son was born, the Brits got wind of his whereabouts, and he was captured and transported to Van Diemen's Land, which was a penal colony in southeastern Australia during the period from 1642 to 1855. Never again was he seen or heard from, according to family folklore, and many other Irish freedom fighters also ended up in the same exile. If it were not for that child being born, I would not be here today.

For me the army was a great experience, and once I adjusted to military life, I enjoyed all aspects of it. There was something about the military that brought out either the best or the worst in young people. If you decided to be a good soldier and go along with the program, it was a good life as long as you were not in combat. Military training for me was fun, since I was in good shape and enjoyed the long marches, exercises, and weapons training. For those who were not in good shape, the military training was torture.

There were two months of basic training and two months of advanced training in whatever specialty you were assigned as a draftee. By the time a soldier got finished with advanced training, he was in good shape and well prepared, ready for whatever came next. After advanced training, I came down on orders for Vietnam; however, about an hour after I was handed my military assignment, I got a call to report to the company headquarters to see the company commander. This was scary, and I knew there was something very serious, possibly

a death in the family. When I saw the company commander, a great guy, well respected by the trainees, who was always
very upbeat, I could tell there was bad news by the look on
his face. He had a very grim expression on his face not at all
like him—he was normally a very jolly man who always wore
a smile while reaching out to the troops. I thought it was my
dad, who was getting up in age, or maybe my mum. It had to
be something catastrophic in order for me to be called into
the company commander's office. The company commander
looked at me directly and said, "Private Scollans, I have not-
good news for you. Your brother was in a serious accident, and
the Red Cross contacted the post commander's office, which
contacted my office with a message that your presence is required at the hospital in Hackensack, New Jersey, where your
brother is in critical condition." This was a major shock to me.
My brother had survived all the horrors of the Vietnam War—
hand-to-hand combat and gun battles during search-and-destroy missions when many of his comrades did not survive. My
big concern was whether he was still alive and whether they
were just breaking the bad news to me easy. I am pretty sure the
company commander did not know exactly what his condition
was other than that when the Red Cross is involved, it has to be
very serious. This was an amazing twist of fate for a man who
spent a year in the jungles and rice paddies of Vietnam and
survived. He took part in many of the fiercest battles fought by
the 199th Light Infantry when on search-and-destroy missions
and never got a scratch. He came home and almost got killed
a couple of months later in a car accident while driving west
on Route 3 in the Secaucus, New Jersey, area. He was hit from
behind by another much larger car, and as a result of the impact

his car rolled over, and he was thrown out of the car onto the highway, and it was a miracle that he was still alive. The car rolled over a number of times on impact. When I got to see the wreck, the car looked like a sardine can—the roof was squashed down onto the dashboard. He had a fractured shoulder and a fractured skull, which was causing pressure on the brain and kept him in a semi-comatose condition until a spinal tap was performed by a neural surgeon to remove the pressure of the brain. The spinal tap could not be performed until a member of his immediate family or next of kin would sign off due to the risk associated with this life-or-death type of procedure. The reason the Red Cross contacted the post commander's office to have me come home was solely to sign off on this procedure. I was the only immediate family member in the United States, and as a result it took the Red Cross a few days to track me down in the military while my brother lay in the hospital in a semi-comatose state. Fortunately, he had the address of our cousin who lived in the Bronx in his wallet, and the police contacted her, and she was able to direct them in my direction, telling them I was finishing up military training at Fort Dix, New Jersey. She was able to give the police enough information that they turned to the Red Cross, and they were able to get in touch with my army unit.

When I arrived at the hospital, the neurosurgeon that would perform the spinal tap was waiting for me in his office. He brought me into his office and explained the severity of my brother's condition and the reason for the spinal tap. I asked him what the prognosis was, and he gave me a very grim report.

The neurosurgeon explained the procedure in great detail and said without the spinal tap the swelling in the brain would only get worse and eventually cause death, and with the spinal tap he had a 25 percent chance of coming out of it. Not good odds, but there was no choice other than proceeding with the procedure. After the spinal tap was performed, he appeared to be in worse condition than before. I did not expect him to make it, since he was in severe pain.

He looked completely out of it, and there was a serious groan; he appeared to be suffering greatly. My fiancée at that time, who is now my wife, was with me, and we went home with very little hope that he would be alive in the morning. The next morning was Sunday, and relatives and friends all over had masses and prayers said for him, including a special Mass by our cousin Monsignor Hugh, who was a pastor in Dobbs Ferry, New York, at that time. Early Sunday morning, with very grim expectations, my fiancée and I went to the hospital, and when we walked up to the door of his hospital room with great trepidation, to our greatest surprise, he was sitting on the side of his bed. He was shaved, had a big smile on his face, and was so glad to see us and was all ready for conversation. We were astounded and could not believe what we were seeing, and of course all my family and friends thought this was a miracle due to the number of masses and prayers said for him. The relatives were making all kinds of speculation as to who the priest with these great mystical powers might be. I was ecstatic and gained a new respect for medical science and the mystical power of priests and prayers.

It was a great relief to know that I did not have to break any bad news to my parents.

My parents were not made aware of the accident until years later, and my brother did not want them to know. He did not want them to have any unnecessary worry since our dad was up in age.

He was out of the hospital about a week after the spinal tap. I stayed home for another week in order to make sure that he got all his business matters taken care of, including looking into the details of the accident and handing the case over to a lawyer who would determine if there was liability involved. Once again, my wonderful host family we there; they took my brother in and cared for him back to health. Mrs. Hartnett was a nurse's aide. She was a wonderful caregiver and better than many of the top RNs. In the hospital where she worked, the patients wanted only her taking care of them since she was the best of the best in every way—so smart and so dedicated, a real people person, a lovely lady in every way, a real caregiver who loved her work, and it showed.

Knowing he was in good hands, I headed back to my army unit, and to my disappointment the company that I had trained with for four months had all shipped out to Vietnam, where I could not join them. These were my friends, young men that I had spent a number of months training with. Some of them were like brothers. We had shared great times playing sports, partying, doing a little drinking, and participating in all the typical GI fun stuff that becomes part of that military experience. Comradery and loyalty at their best, which is the real army way. When I got back to my army unit, I was put on a hold status, which meant hanging around performing miscellaneous duties that would come up. With all my close friends gone to battle, I felt that I had let them down, had not been with them, side by side, as I had been in the months of training. We always hoped that we would be assigned to the same units when sent overseas, and now I almost felt that I had reneged on that promise.

When least expected, a big break came for me. There was a new company commander who was mostly of Scottish background but who grew up in an Irish neighborhood in the North Bronx and was more Irish than the Irish themselves and treated me well. He would talk to me about some of his crazy Irish friends and the great times they used to have partying and raising hell. He was just a great guy and a great officer. While at early morning reveille, he came up to me with his big smile and told me after breakfast I should come to his office, where he told me he had an assignment that I was going to like. The brigade colonel, who needed an orderly/driver, would like to see me because I had been selected as one of the candidates. After meeting with all the candidates, the colonel picked me, and I am sure if my company commander put in a strong word for me. I was delighted and thanked the officer, my Scottish friend. The colonel was a very nice man and very personable. We hit it off really well. He was an older gentleman who had a wife and no children. The young army soldiers were his family. He was an Italian who had come to the United States as a very young child and had great respect for immigrants who were hardworking and good soldiers that could be counted on for their loyalty and integrity. He would talk about his parents when they immigrated and how they had to conquer so many obstacles, in particular the language and the anti-Italian sentiment among some of the people, just as with the other ethnic groups that came before them who had to deal with the same type of discrimination, such as "No Irish need apply," which was a statement frequently seen in the hiring announcements in newspapers throughout the United States and England throughout the 1800s. He was a man of high honor and had great respect and regard for all under his command, and although small in stature, he was a giant of a man. About three months after I started driving for the colonel, he came down on orders for Vietnam and asked if I would like to join him as a colonel's orderly, and he would promote me to PFC.

At this time, I was engaged to be married to my fiancée and had made a lot of wonderful friends on base. So, I told him that I would not volunteer due to other commitments, but if I came down on orders that would be OK. Being the gentleman he was, he understood, and he still put me in for PFC right on the spot. Now there was an opening for a message center courier/driver, which required a security clearance that I had to get. I applied for the security clearance and passed the simple test and went to work. Since the courier could be handling sensitive military documents, the position required a security clearance. This was a great assignment and an opportunity to meet all the post headquarters personnel, where I made many great friends.

Many of the post officers were very influential and decided on who got military orders.

Military orders typically came down from the Pentagon but could be influenced by the post command personnel. Military orders were what determined where a solider was going to be stationed and for how long. It was said that if someone fell out of favor within his unit, he could get shipped out, and many did for a number of reasons.

About three months after I got the message center courier/driver position, the SP4-grade E-4 in charge of the message center had completed his time on duty and was getting out of the service and going back into civilian life. The timing was good for me, and the brigade master sergeant offered me the position, which brought me up to an SP-4, which was great, and of course I welcomed the opportunity and was delighted.

The message center was a complete mess—you could not find anything, and there was a lack of organization. This was a great opportunity for me to straighten the place out and organize it in a way that meant we knew what documents were coming in and what was going out. After about a couple of months, the brigade message center was so organized that you would not recognize that it was the same place.

There were three privates working for me that I put in for PFC, and they were delighted. They were all wonderful people and very willing to follow direction, so we were a great team.

The brigade master sergeant and the brigade officers, including all four battalion officers, were singing our praises and could not believe how quickly the message center had changed. It had been a nightmare to deal with but was now a pleasure because everything was in order and the service was superb. The brigade publications SP5 in charge completed his time in service and also got out of the army and went back to civilian life. Once again, the sergeant major came to me and asked if I would be willing to take on this section also, since we had done such a great job in the message center, and he went on to say, "I know you can do the same with the publications section," and of course I said yes. He put me in for SP5, an E-5 pay grade, which was the same pay grade as a buck sergeant, and of course I was delighted. As with the message center, the publications department was poorly run, had no organization and no filing system, and was just a big mess.

The first thing I did was to pull out one of the best PFCs from the message center to work with me in cleaning up the publications center and put him in for SP4 and then took one of the publications PFCs and had him replace the message center PFC that I promoted. I also put my best message center PFC in for SP4. This meant that I had two lead SP4s to lead in each area of responsibility and to cover in my absence. The brigade colonel, sergeant major, and battalion officers all applauded the reorganization and said this should have been done a long time ago. Within a very short time, the new team cleaned up the publications center, and it too became a show place. When the field grade officers, mostly majors, from all the four battalions would walk in to collect the necessary forms, they could not believe it was the same place, and the word got around that the two groups were now organized and knew what they were doing for a change.

Instead of having to dig and search for documents and forms, the officers found that everything was now organized, labeled, and at your fingertips. The company and battalion commanders throughout the brigade loved the newly organized publications and message centers.

Now they could go and without delay pick up any document on file, and not only were the documents labeled, but there was also an alphabetical list of every document on file. If a company or battalion commander wanted a new document added to the file, there was a form to fill out and have signed by the brigade commander, and within two weeks the new document would be added to the file and available for military use. This approach raised the publications center to a new level, and as a result our team received all kinds of accolades and recognition.

I was very fortunate to have a wonderful team who were proud of their department and willing to do what had to be done. When the team saw that there was recognition, which I shared with them, including getting them promoted, when possible, that got everybody excited. No one was left behind. Everyone in the two sections got along together very well. We hung out together after work, where we ate and played together.

We all became great friends as well as great coworkers—we would go to the same parties, play the same sports, and so on. One day the sergeant major called me into his office and told me that our two sections were the finest in the brigade and on the whole post. He wanted me to know that he had put me in for the Certificate of Achievement. This is a very prestigious award within noncommissioned officer (NCO) ranks. I was elated, and to this day I proudly hang this award in my home office. Although this certificate means a lot to me, I felt that it should go to the team, since I could not have done what was accomplished without their hard work, support, and overall creativity.

When I told the sergeant major how I felt, he replied, "That is very worthy of you, but this is an individual NCO award. However, you can tell them one day they too will have the opportunity to work toward the same objective and also let them know that without all their good work this award would not be possible."

I liked the military, and when it came time to get discharged, it was a very hard decision whether to stay in or get out. I felt there was a very bright future for me in the military. I was in line for the next promotion, E-6, if I reenlisted, and my colonel friend wanted me to stay in and go to officers' school, and he would provide the necessary support and guidance. He kept telling me I would make a great officer. However, I was engaged and was planning to get married the next April after I got out. I had to see how my wife-to-be felt about a long military commitment and the possibility of long assignments where she might not be able to join me.

When I got home, I talked to my fiancée about the option to stay in the military or get out. Although she would not stand in the way if that was what I wanted, I could see that she was not too thrilled about the idea. Although we did not come to any decision, when I got back to base, I gave it more thought, and after wrestling with the idea, I felt it would not be fair to my future wife to be in a relationship where I could have to spend long periods away from home. This was the toughest decision of my life. I knew that I had the potential for great opportunities that would be good for me, since I liked the military, but it would not be so great for the person that I was planning to spend the rest of my life with. So, I had to make the hard decision to get out and go back to my old job that I had before I went into the military. When in the service, I had responsibility for a large crew and two departments that were well respected and admired all across the base, and now I was back to my old job, with no direct reports, where I would be responsible only for my own work. This was a big letdown from the military, where I had great accomplishments and recognition as a good soldier and a leader who knew how to get things done. When I told my fiancée of my decision to leave the military, she was delighted and elated.

However, all was not lost. In this wonderful experience, I had made great strides and now had the confidence that I could do anything that I put my mind to, and most of all I now had confidence and experience in organization and people skills. While in the service, I went to school and got a GED, and although I did not have a four-year high school education from Ireland, I did very well on all the exam subjects, which consisted of five high-school-level subjects: English comprehension, mathematics, social studies, history, and geography. The army GED instructor was excellent and did a great job covering all the material in a way that was easy to follow before it showed up on each test. He would warn that what he covered would be on the state GED test, and sure enough it was, and in great detail. I was surprised at some of my classmates with eleventh or twelfth grade education were having difficulty, and some failed the GED exams.

The GED accomplishment raised my confidence that I could do reasonably well in school if I worked hard at it, which gave me the impetus to go back to school when I got out of the military. While in the service, I also became a US citizen; this was another great experience, and when the brigade sergeant major heard that I was going for my citizenship, right away he volunteered to be one of my sponsors, and he asked one of the other young officers, a first lieutenant with an Irish name, to be the second sponsor. When the rest of the brigade officers and NCOs heard that I was going for my citizenship, they all wanted to be part of it. It was awesome walking up to the citizen board judge with two highly decorated military people as my sponsors, a sergeant major and a first lieutenant.

The two sponsors were great military men who inspired me in many ways and taught me what being a good soldier was all about. The sergeant major had some Irish roots that he was very proud of, and he kept saying he couldn't wait to tell his wife and children about this wonderful honor of being a sponsor.

In actual fact I think he was just as excited as I was. When a candidate normally went before the immigration judge for citizenship, the judge would ask a number of questions relating to current events and questions that related to who was running the country and how many senators or congressional representatives were from your state, but when I walked up in step with my two high-level, well-decorated military men, the judge had a big smile and said, "You came prepared." Then he asked my name and rank and issued my citizenship papers without any other question and then told the two military sponsors, "Make sure that you guys treat SPC5 Scollans well today." For me it was a great day indeed, and I had to ask myself how I could be so lucky.

The two officers sure did treat me well. They took me to a very nice restaurant for dinner and gave me a nice money gift from a collection that had been taken up back on post. All this was almost too wonderful to be real; I was treated like I was royalty for the day.

Everyone involved was unbelievably wonderful and treated me to a day that I would cherish for the rest of my life. I never expected this kind of treatment from my military superiors. The very next morning, I spoke to Mrs. Brown, a lovely African American woman who was the brigade civilian secretary, a woman loved by everyone and like a grandmother to everyone.

Mrs. Brown was overjoyed that I had become a citizen and called me into her office and told me they were having a big celebration for me at lunch the next day. She said the brigade major, who was also a wonderful African American female officer, wanted to celebrate my citizenship.

The brigade major was a very popular, wonderful lady who was always reaching out to young soldiers and loved celebrating their accomplishments. The party was at the brigade headquarters where I worked. The celebration was unbelievable. Everyone was singing Irish songs and just letting the good times roll. Mrs. Brown grew up in the Bronx in a mixed neighborhood where she had many Irish friends. She could relate to everything Irish and could sing all the Irish songs with her melodious voice and big personality. It was just great, and I was on cloud nine. Mrs. Brown whispered to me that I should say a few words, like thank you and anything else I wanted to say. I had no experience getting up before a crowd like this and didn't know any of the protocol but gave it my best shot. As I was finishing up my few words of appreciation, Mrs. Brown walked up to me and said in front of everybody "What a great job!" and gave me a big kiss right on the cheek; then everyone cheered and brought the house down. Mrs. Brown was so sincere and so wonderful. She only knew how to say things that made people feel good, and that was why she was a very special woman that was so loved by everyone. Although I was considered a good soldier and knew how to make the grade, I was not as squeaky clean as everyone thought. Growing up, I always had a bit of a bad-boy reputation and kind of enjoyed that role. During basic training I was many times the ringleader in carrying out pranks on other trainees and loved a good laugh.

When I worked for the post exchange (PX) part-time selling pizzas from a pizza truck on post, I charged more for the pizza than I was supposed to and rationalized what I was doing because we had to buy all the merchandise when we picked it up, and if we brought anything back, it came out of our pay, which I thought was not fair and as a result charged a little more to compensate at the end of the evening should there be any monetary losses. The pay was 10 percent in commission only.

So, I decided to up the price of the pizza an additional ten cents in case I did not sell all of them and to make up for any losses. I was the top salesperson and would sell twice as much as the next runner-up. After a few weeks selling the higher-price pizzas, I was on my way back after having a great night's sale when I met my coworker and friend Rebel, who informed me someone had called the PX supervisor about a pizza truck overcharging. The real story was that Rebel got greedy and got caught when charging a $1.25 for a one-dollar pizza that he sold to a very young officer. The young officer was wearing a T-shirt that made him look like a new recruit. The officer called the PX complaining about the overcharge. When Rebel returned to the PX, he was questioned by the supervisor, who said she had just gotten a call from an officer in one of the trainee-holding areas who complained that he was overcharged for a pizza. Rebel said it was not him and it must have been Irish, which was my nickname. Rebel said, "He has an accent."

The supervisor said, "No, it was a southern accident, not an Irish accent, and I know Irish would never cheat the customer." Rebel continued to blame me but did not want me to know and decided to warn me about the issue before I got back to the PX; he indicated that they were blaming both of us. This was a story he made up in order to save his skin because he knew if I found out that he was trying to pass the blame on to me there would be hell to pay, and he did not want to have to deal with me. I had the reputation of being pretty scrappy—I had done some boxing, and if you messed with me, you could be in trouble. At the PX gym, I had the reputation of having fast hands, and Rebel did not want to deal with what could be ugly. So, when I got back to the PX, the supervisor told me how Rebel was ripping off the troops, charging them more than the PX price for the pizzas, and how she had warned him that one more complaint and he would be out. She never mentioned at that time that he'd blamed me, but she told me later. I had all I could muster not to break out laughing, since I knew Rebel was a little sleazy.

He was considered a bit of a con artist that would steal the eye out of your head, and nobody back in the army barracks trusted him. Needless to say, that stopped the higher prices, and everybody working for the PX was warned that if they upped the prices on any product, they would be instantly dismissed. In the army everyone was looking for ways to make extra money, since the army pay for privates was ninety-six dollars a month when the lowest-paying job in civilian life was at least one hundred dollars per week. In order to make extra money, I would work on cars as well as working at the PX, and then when I became permanent party on post, I bought a car. It was a 1963 Ford Falcon with holes in the floorboards where you could see the road when driving. I covered the holes with a piece of sheet metal and kept the car for about five years. The car was great for going home on weekends, and I would pick up new recruits who wanted to see New York City and also take them back on Sunday night and charge each one of them a couple of dollars, which paid for my gas and car expenses and was a great deal for them because the bus fare would have been much more. Sometimes I would have five or six passengers crammed into the car. It was against army rules to pick up trainees on base, so they would walk off base, and there I would pick them up. They would be lined up along the roadside that headed toward the New Jersey Turnpike. You could still get in trouble for picking them up off base, but the risk was pretty low. One night I was on the turnpike, on my way back to the base with a full load of lads, when my friend Wojack came roaring down the turnpike at a very high speed in his 1957 Chevy. He had rebored the engine and had a real souped-up car. As he was passing me on the turnpike, he and his buddies were screaming out the window, "Scollans, you cannot park on the New Jersey Turnpike." About twenty miles farther down I saw a pall of smoke in front of me, and guess what it was—Wojack in his hot car. The engine just blew apart, and he was stranded on the turnpike.

He was devastated and could not believe what had just happened. I stopped and felt like laughing, but he was so distraught I told him that I would come back and pick him and his friends up after I dropped off my passengers. And then I came back again and towed his car back to base, for which he was very grateful.

Wojack worked in the motor pool as a mechanic and was one of the best mechanics in the motor pool. He was able to borrow a universal tow hitch so I could tow his car back to the base with my old Falcon. Wojack was forever busted by all of us about his hot car. He was a great sport, a great guy, a friend, and a super mechanic—there was none finer. He would just laugh and was loved by all.

During the 1960s, drugs were ramped up everywhere, and nowhere more than in the army. When I would get back to base on a late Sunday night, everyone was smoking pot. It was just the way it was. Fortunately, there were no hard drugs, at least that I knew about. Everyone was expected to take at least a few puffs, and if you did not, you could not be trusted, and that was the way it was.

The army is all about trust and honor, although everything that the GI does is not always honorable. The buddy code of honor was the way of the army, and if you could not be trusted, you better always be on the lookout. No one rats on their friends, and your friends are everything, just like a close family. If you do not have friends in the army, you cannot survive, and many new recruits who are loners find out only too soon that loners do not survive in the army. It is that unspoken code of honor that makes the U.S. Army what it is and so successful in battle and is the reason why so many soldiers are willing to die to save their comrades. When I got out of the service, one of my biggest regrets was not keeping in touch with my great army friends, who were like brothers.

Like many others, I had all the right excuses. I had just gotten married, children came along, I worked two jobs, and I went back to night school. We rebuilt our house and made it bigger for the growing family, and so we could entertain family and friends. Although life was wonderful, it was very full and hectic, with very little time for socializing other than with the extended family and very close friends. A number of my army friends wrote to me many times during the Christmas holidays, and they would always suggest getting together, and some would call, but unfortunately, I was always too busy. Now it is too late, and some may have passed on, and the others are all over the country and would be difficult to locate. I tried many times online to locate some of them, but to no avail. A lesson learned: one should always make time for old friends and family, since life is too short, and before we know it, time has passed us by, and we regret that we dropped the ball and did not keep in touch, and now there is a void that can never be filled, and how we only wish we could. With that said, we can only move on and work on the things we can.

Life is, at its best, a big learning experience where we learn every day, and in some ways, we are always trying to do better on all fronts, where continual improvement in everything we do is a positive process that makes the world a better place.

CHAPTER 32

The GI Bill

As a young lad in Ireland, I never took school seriously and would much rather have fun and stir things up a little than study. Although my parents were big on education and encouraged us to pursue schooling, growing up on a farm in a rural part of the country did not lend itself to the pursuit of higher education. When I got married and a family came along, I knew that I would need to go back to school and get a degree if I wanted to get ahead in the business world. I worked in the trades and was doing very well, loved my work, and had a wonderful boss; however, I knew that without further education my advancement would be limited.

I knew that going back to school and facing the academic challenges that lay ahead of me was not going to be easy, although I had achieved a GED while in the army and gotten an excellent GPA despite leaving school at fourteen years of age. However, I was soon to find out that a GED, although a great accomplishment, was a far cry from the academic requirements that were necessary to enter college. I started with Morris County College, an excellent school with high standards, where I met with a counselor who was wonderful and very helpful. I wanted to pursue applied engineering technology rather than engineering design, which was somewhat more rigorous. The counselor laid out both programs and the requirements in great detail and recommended which one was best for me, including all the prerequisite courses required in order to meet the minimum entrance requirements. The prerequisite courses that were required were daunting, but when one is young and ambitious, nothing seems to get in the way. I entered the program and worked very hard. What made this program so hard was that my limited basic secondary education had huge gaps that required attention for me to be successful.

Then there were also a number of gaps that were not included in the prerequisite program and required tutoring, which was expensive. I knew only too well that closing those gaps was not going to be easy. I would have to buckle down and work hard to meet all the prerequisite requirements. I had to work even harder, including getting some tutoring for issues not covered in the prerequisite program to fill in some of the voids that could not be passed over. Then I had to meet the matriculation requirements of twelve credits in humanities before I could enroll in the engineering technology program. For many years, I attended night school four nights a week and studied day and night, and often into the early hours of the morning and at work during my lunch break. In the end all the hard work paid off when I completed an associate's degree and continued to study for a bachelors. Now life was no longer all fun and play. I was starting to mature, although my wife would tell you I never grew up and still like to do some crazy stuff, if for no other reason than to see people's reaction.

For me the military was a great opportunity where I excelled in ways that I never thought were part of my DNA. The only wonderful thing about the Vietnam War period was that the GI Bill was great, and in addition to tuition, there was subsistence if one took the required credits, which resulted in a very heavy workload while one was working a full-time job. I worked for a large pharmaceutical company that also had a very generous tuition reimbursement program. I went to my supervisor (a great guy) and asked him if I was also entitled to the company tuition reimbursement since I was enrolled in the GI Bill educational program, and he said, "Yes, you are entitled to whatever is being offered, period." My boss was in the military during the end of World War II and then got called back during the Korean War because his MOS was in high demand, so he had great empathy for military people and would do anything he could to help.

Between the GI Bill and the company tuition reimbursement, I was getting paid to go to school. This was great because I had money left over for tutoring after paying tuition, which was nice again and was like having a part-time job. Going to school for many years' nights was not easy, especially for me with my spotty formal education, which meant I had to work that much harder to get passing grades. But the most difficult part for me was that I had two young children at home, a boy and a girl, both in diapers. My poor wife was home with them every day and night with no break, which was not easy, and she had very little relief. However, we considered ourselves very lucky—the million-dollar family—to have two wonderful, healthy children and another little girl that came much later. When I would come home from work in the evening, my wife would have dinner waiting on the table, I would gobble it down and run out to school for four hours, but the difficult part was that when I would be about to leave the house, each of our two children would grasp onto each of my legs and beg me not to go, and my poor wife, who was home with them all day, would have to break them loose one by one. Those days I will never forget for the rest of my life. They were a little sad in some ways, but I have the fondest of memories. These were no leisure times, but when you are young and have a young family to work for, no burden seems to be too heavy, and that great desire to achieve whatever is possible in order to be able to provide a brighter and better life for the ones you love makes it all worthwhile. Although I was never sure what I exactly wanted out of life, since there are so many wonderful alternatives to choose from, and as a result I selected a path and pursued it to the finish line, which bore great dividends. Life has so much to offer in so many different ways. The hardest thing to do is to carve out a path and stay the course, which is the only way to achieve lasting success. When there are children to take care of, it is all about them, and you do not seem to think about yourself.

What becomes most important is that you just want to be in a position to do well for them. Someone once said it is our children that bring out the softer and the better part of us. I was always very lucky with jobs and was fortunate enough to work in the big pharmaceutical industry during a time when there was a great boom and there were new drugs coming onto the market that were providing great profit margins and companies were offering all kinds of opportunities, which give me and all who worked in the industry an opportunity to move around and maximize our earning potential.

I was always very lucky when I changed jobs. The new job always seemed to have a niche where there would be a need for my skills that created a unique opportunity for me to be recognized. I was always able to demonstrate my skills by correcting problems and using my good army organizational skills to build systems and put in place programs that would greatly enhance the business operation.

All this gave me an opportunity to take on higher levels of responsibility with a large staff. I loved the challenge and loved working with people; however, there was still something missing, and I always wanted something more, no matter how full my plate was.

At work I did a lot of training, coaching, mentoring, and personnel development, which is required in middle-management-level positions. This was a part of the job that I enjoyed and had great success with. One of the companies that I worked for did not have a good engineering and maintenance safety record when I got there; mechanics were getting injured on the job too frequently. I thought this was an area where I could make a difference and have fun at the same time. I had just left one of the biggest and best-run pharmaceutical companies in the industry, which had all kinds of safety training programs and had a stellar workplace safety record. So, I built on that experience and developed a safety awareness training program based on the theme that all accidents can be prevented.

I also tied this program in with pay for performance, which put teeth into the program. I had the program approved by corporate safety and the corporate human resources department, which give a high level of support and credence to the enforcement of the program. This program was a great success, and within two years we went from one of the poorest in the pharmaceutical industry on safety to one of the best in class, and from there we went on to win all kinds of New Jersey state workplace safety awards and became a leader in the industry.

Many of our friendly competitors would ask me to give talks on accident-free performance at their plants. This initiative gave me great exposure throughout the pharmaceutical industry and was very rewarding. My next endeavor was to give a little back by teaching the trades at local vocational schools.

For many years I taught two nights a week. This was something that paid very little money, but I really enjoyed the good feeling of giving back. The course I enjoyed most was preparing electricians to sit for their state electrical license. This was a very challenging course where there was a lot of theory, which is an area that tradespeople in general have the most trouble with. My yardstick for how well I was doing was the percentage out of each class that would pass the state electrical license exam on a first try. Since most of the students would have a number of years working in the electrical field, on the first night of class I would always start off with a very basic quiz that gave me a baseline of where everyone was and who in the class would need the most help.

After the quiz it was always obvious that there was a lot of work to do, so my next step was to give a lecture on what was involved and what competencies were required in order to pass the test the first time around. I had everyone's attention. You could hear a pin drop, and I did not mince words.

Since most of the students would do poorly on the first quiz, it created a level playing field; all the students knew they had a lot of hard work in front of them to get done. So now all of them were ready to get down to business in a serious way. After the first quiz, they knew they had a tough road ahead, but I assured them that if they paid attention and applied themselves, they would all get to the finish line. They all worked and studied hard. Each class session started off with a quiz and a critique of deficiencies, and then I would go over each quiz in detail, and everyone was required to do the quiz over if they got a question wrong. By the end of the semester, most of them were ready to go on to the spring semester. The curriculum included theory and the New Jersey state electrical code and how to use the code book and the lockup questions that would be on the New Jersey state exam. After a number of very detailed lectures, then there was the final quiz, where everyone knew exactly where they stood. Each quiz would have final test-related questions to get them ready for the final state exam. The final was 60 percent of the grade, and the combined quizzes accounted for 40 percent. In order for them to pass the state exam, a passing grade of 70 was required on each subject. The first time around in my class, all the students passed the New Jersey state exam except for one who had a learning disability. I worked with the one who had the learning disability and got him enrolled in the state verbal testing program that was available at that time, where he was able to pass the theory and the required code. He was a great hands-on mechanic and knew the daily operations of his trade better than most of his fellow students, and he was also a wonderful, hardworking student who tried so hard.

There was one student in my first class that I will always remember. He was a tall, handsome young man with a little bit of a wise guy attitude. He had just graduated high school but had worked in his dad's electrical business from a young age.

He started working for his dad at the age of fourteen and was very bright. He thought he would have some fun mimicking my accent and acting up in class. I asked him to cut it out a number of times, but instead of cutting it out, it appeared he was revving it up, which was a major distraction for the class.

After deciding I'd had enough. I stopped talking in the middle of a lecture for a few moments, stood up and stared at him, and then with a very stern voice ordered him to come to my desk. While he was at my desk, I walked up to him and ushered him to the exit door, where I opened the door, stared him directly in the eyes, and with a serious voice told him, "If I hear one more blip out of you or any more nonsense, you will be out this door. Do you understand?" When I asked him if he understood, with a very meek voice he said yes. With that I told him to go back to his seat, and he walked back as white as a ghost. The rest of the class was stunned, and I assume somewhat amazed at what had just taken place in the classroom. One of the younger students stood up and clapped his hands while saying "Way to go, Mr. Scollans." For the rest of the night, you could hear a pin drop in the classroom. His name was Joey, and I guess after working with his dad for so many years, he thought he could get away with stuff. Joey was very bright and from that point on a model student who would help others who were having trouble grasping some of the technical theory concepts. I would praise him for his efforts, and he seemed to like the attention, and with that he was back in my good graces, which was easy since I have a soft spot for young people and love to see them do well, and I think Joey saw and appreciated that. During the Christmas break, I was at home in my office doing some work when the phone rang, and who was on the other end but Joey's mother? She asked if I was Mr. Scollans. Hesitantly I said yes, and she went on to say, "Do you remember my son Joey?" I said yes, and I went on to say he was a fine young man, and she should be proud of him.

She said, "Yes, I am very proud of Joey, but the reason I am calling you is that I do not know what you did with him, but ever since he attended your class, he is a different young man and much more respectful at home, and for that I wanted to thank you and tell you how much I appreciate your influence on him."

I said, "Thank you for sharing. Your son is a nice young man who is maturing and will continue to make you proud." Well, needless to say, for me, what a huge relief. I'd thought she was calling to yell at me for traumatizing her son.

When I shared Joey's story with my family, they laughed, and then my youngest daughter, who is a teacher, said, "Dad, you probably did traumatize him," and everyone got a big laugh. I like to think both the young man and I learned from that experience.

As for me, should I have been so harsh? I came to like the young man, and had I had a second chance to be kinder and gentler, that would have been the better option. After the Joey episode, I realized my reaction in dealing with Joey's behavior was subconsciously acting out my old Irish schoolmaster's approach to dealing with students who did not behave, where he would severely punish his students. I thought that I was better than that, and for me, too, this was a lesson learned in controlling my own reactions. Sometimes it is better to stop and think before we go dishing out punishments or judgments that might be in haste rather than well thought through. I should have taken time out and rationally decided how to deal with his behavior rather than making a spectacle out of the young man.

If I had calmly taken him into a quiet place and explained to him that his behavior was unacceptable and would not be tolerated or he could be reported to the continuing education principal or expelled from the program, more than likely I would have gotten the same results. The one thing we all learn going through life is how most situations can be resolved where there are all winners and if possible, no losers, and this can be accomplished when we recognize our shortcomings.

CHAPTER 33

Entrepreneur

I always wanted to have my own business where I could call the shots, or so I assumed. I started an engineering inspection business because I had significant experience in home improvements and some small additions—decks, patios, and so on. Plus, there was the fact that when I bought our first house shortly before my wife and I got married, this was a little six-hundred-square-foot summer bungalow where we more than doubled the size of house and completely renovated the old existing house from top to bottom, and we learned a lot doing most of the work ourselves, and my wife was a great help. This was a great experience, and when I was for the most part all done, my neighbors started lining up and wanted all kinds of home-improvement work done, which got me into the home-improvement business, where I did very well. However, this was hard work, although I enjoyed it and was able to get some young guys who needed extra money to work with me as helpers. There were two in particular great young men who would work so hard, and we got along really well where we enjoyed working together. They appreciated the fact that I would explain to them all aspects of the trade and was always willing to spend time showing them the easy way to do things. I made sure they were well compensated, and they made good money. I was generous to my help and had a philosophy that a good man was worth whatever you could afford to pay him, and a poor worker was worth nothing and could end up costing you money. After a few years in the home-improvement business, I decided to buy up old, run-down houses and fix them up. This was also hard work but turned out to be very lucrative, and we did very well while doing it. A friend of mine who was an attorney wanted to get in on the home-purchase fix-up flip bandwagon, and he would keep asking me to let him in on one of my deals to get him started.

When an opportunity came up, I let him in on a deal where we worked out a very fair agreement. Our first joint purchase was an old, run-down two-family house in Sussex County that required a lot of work, but he had no clue what was required to make the place marketable. I felt he could take care of the legal part of the business, such as closings on the buying and selling ends, and that would save some money. I hit the road running, lined up what had to be done, and did a lot of the renovation work myself, since my partner was not into construction and would not know which side of the hammer to use. I hired help as needed until finally the place was finished and ready to rent. When it came to renting, my lawyer friend did not have any idea what was involved in the renting business. I did all the advertising, and he wrote up the renting leases which are for the most part pretty boilerplate in today's world. My partner was amazed at how much was involved from a legal point of view regarding tenant rights in New Jersey, where in many ways the tenant has more rights than the property owner. My partner was very smart and a quick study when it came to legal issues and not afraid to go toe to toe with the best in the business, a quality I admired. After a few months, the second-floor tenant stopped paying the rent, at which time I called my lawyer friend and asked him to start eviction proceedings; however, his answer was "Ah, Kevin, give her a chance to come up with the money. Maybe she hit hard times." However, we had a mortgage to pay, and the bank did not want to know about the tenant's problems. We knew the tenant had a spotty credit problem, so I immediately started eviction proceedings on my own and called my partner to meet with him and to fill him in on the details. He was a great guy, a friend, and we got on well, and I did not want to strain our relationship, so I started off by saying "You are a successful Jewish lawyer, and I am supposed to be the friendly, smiling Irishman—what is going on? Then I said humorously, "Are you turning the tables where you are being the nice guy who wants to save the world?"

At that he roared laughing and said, "Kevin, you are far more experienced than I am, and you are much better and tougher." He went on to say, "You are a much better businessman than I am, and it would be hard for me to do what you just did." The next day the eviction papers came through, and the county sheriff served the papers to the tenant. She got out before the court date and did not appear in court. The judge told me to wait twenty-four hours before renting, and then we would be ready to roll. Instead of re-renting, my partner and I agreed to put the house up for sale. The market was reasonably good at this time, and the house sold reasonably fast, and we both made a nice profit. My friend was eager to do another deal, but I decided to stay on my own. Partnering with friends is not always the best way to go. I told him to keep an eye open for some deals and we could do it again, but in reality, I did not want to but did not want to hurt his feelings. By this time, I was pretty well established and had enough of my own seed money to do deals, but I valued his friendship. He was a great guy and a good friend whose friendship I valued. I continued to do a number of other deals that were very successful, and by now we had made enough money to take care of our three children's college, which was a very important achievement for my wife and me. This was hard work, and I was getting tired of the hard work of renovating houses, and the renting business is not easy—you must be on call around the clock to take care of any tenant problem that arises. With all that in mind, I decided to do something less labor intensive and more engineering in nature, so I decided to start an engineering inspection business and put my engineering skills and strong trades and construction background together, which was the perfect combination for me to enter the inspection business. I felt confident and comfortable with my decision, and it turned out to be very profitable.

CHAPTER 34

Inspector

This was the right time for me to enter the engineering inspection business. I had a very well-rounded background and licenses in a number of the trades and knew all aspects of the building trades and construction, which is a necessity to be successful in engineering inspection work. This was a great move, and I made a number of great contacts in the corporate relocation business. The corporate relocation company would take over property from the large corporations that would purchase property from their employees who were being transferred to another location, which was usually out of state. I had three full-time inspectors and an office staff, plus myself. My wife was the office manager and did a great job; it was nice to have a member of the family to keep a watchful eye on all aspects of the business since I could not be there to oversee the office functions all the time. This was a wonderful but very hectic time and could be very stressful for all involved. In life I have been very fortunate and could always handle a great deal of stress; it would take an almost catastrophic incident to have any effect on me. Our oldest college-bound daughter worked in our business office during the summer in order to give my wife a break so she could spend more time with our youngest daughter, which worked out very well. For a young girl, our daughter had great business sense, and the customers loved her.

She had a great personality and very good sales intuition, although she would say she did not want to be a salesperson. In business there are always challenging customers that require a lot of attention and are not easy to deal with, but our daughter handled them very effectively as a sixteen-year-old. I would get calls from clients asking me if that was our daughter that they had spoken to and singing her praises about how knowledgeable and professional she was. We were very proud of her.

I was working sixteen to eighteen hours a day, seven days a week, doing inspections, and after spending all day in the field I had to dictate all the inspection report details for the office staff to type the next morning. All reports had to be proofread and corrections made as necessary, since I had the ultimate responsibility for every report that left the office. Although I had a wonderful, well-trained staff, I could have up to ten or twelve reports, each consisting of fourteen to twenty pages, to proofread and correct each night, which was grueling. I would be up into the wee hours of the morning, burning the candle at both ends. The toughest part of the engineering inspection business was dealing with lawyers and realtors. Most of the realtors hate component inspectors, who are very persnickety and are going to find every problem big and small and report on the details. Realtors refer to those inspectors as the deal killers, and no realtor wants a deal killer. Every good inspector tries to keep the deals together, but not at the expense of their client. It is the inspector's job to make sure the client is aware of all findings and their seriousness, in particular if a problem is of a structural nature, including systems and equipment that may be at the end of their useful life. The client needs to know if a system has limited life that could pose a major expense after moving in.

The realtor's philosophy is that if the system is operating at the time of inspection, the inspector should not be reporting on the probability of how long it might last. However, if the new homeowner moves into the house and a system breaks down a few weeks later, the inspector is on the hook and will have to replace the system out of pocket or end up in court, where he will have to have an attorney to represent him. When an inspector misses something big, the word gets out that the inspector is incompetent and tarnishes his reputation for not knowing that the system was at the end of its useful life and on its way out. This is a tough call because the inspector may not know if the system will fail the next day or a year later.

The most competent of inspectors walk a very fine line. If they miss something or do not accurately report on the facts, the buyer will hold them responsible. If the inspector is overzealous and reports something that is not accurate about the property or makes an inaccurate assumption, the selling homeowner will hold them responsible for killing the deal and sue for damages, which could be major.

I have dozens of stories on both sides of these issues but will touch on only a few that will give the reader a flavor of the complexity involved in the inspectors' reporting, where there is very little room for any type of error or omission in the report details—plus anyone can sue for anything they think will stick, in particular if a hungry lawyer is willing to take the case on a percentage basis if they win and no charge if they lose.

One example is when I inspected a property where the septic system failed the dye volume and probe test. My reports accentuated the facts and spelled out all the technical details. A few days after the inspection, my office issued the report, and when the selling homeowners got a copy of my report, the sellers had their attorney call in two other inspection companies for a second opinion. One of the company inspectors certified the system as functional, while the second inspection company inspector indicated that the system was functioning but did not certify the system. When the selling attorney got the two reports, he called my office and was very abrupt and nasty to our office manager and threatened that there would be a lawsuit unless I reversed my findings, since two other certified inspection companies had passed the septic system. As soon as I got back to my office, I called the selling realtor and asked him if he had a copy of the two second-opinion septic reports. He too was quick to say, "You are in big trouble, and the sellers' attorney is one of the best in the legal business—he never loses a case." I asked the selling realtor to read to me each report over the phone.

The first inspector passed the system and certified it; however, the second inspector reported that the system was functioning, used a lot of evasive mumbo jumbo, but would not and did not certify the system. That was all I needed to hear. Now there were two inspectors who would not certify the septic system and one that did, for whatever sleazy, unscrupulous reason I don't know. Now I was loaded for bear and got back to the attorney's office and asked for the attorney who placed the complaint. When he came on the phone, he was very condescending, arrogant, and belligerent and was talking down to me. He got into a dialogue about the other two inspectors and how they were very reputable and well respected in the industry. He went on to say they had both passed the septic system, and he wanted to know what my problem was and if I knew what I was doing. He went on to say, "You have a major liability here—the homeowner is going to sue you for damages for the loss of a sale and all associated costs due to your overzealous, inaccurate findings as verified by the two other inspection companies," and he went on with a lot of legal intimidation. I said very little and only listened until he was finished with his shakedown and intimidation. Now I asked him if he had anything more to say on this issue, and he abruptly said no.

Now it was my time on the stand, and my first statement was "Well, I want you to know that the two inspectors that you picked and sent out to provide you with a certified second opinion…it is they who do not know what they are doing. One of your inspectors certified the system, which is not a septic system—it is a cesspool consisting of a hole in the ground lined with fieldstone, with no leaching field, and therefore not certifiable. Your second inspector may have lost you in his mumbo jumbo, but he did not certify the system. In addition, you should know that, as depicted in my report, when I performed a volume dye and probe test, water came to the surface after about 150 gallons entered the cesspool system."

Now I asked him, "Do you have the two second-opinion inspection reports in front of you"? And he said yes. "Would you please read to me each inspection report in full detail?" At this time, I could hear his voice breaking, and he read both reports per my request.

I asked him if both inspection companies had issued certification for the given system, and he said yes. At that point I had all the information I needed and said to him, "You are a liar. Only one of the inspection companies issued a certification, which means two out of three did not issue certification. You asked me if I knew what I was doing. Well, your handling of this case is pure evidence that you do not know what you are doing as an attorney, and you are misrepresenting the facts and causing me and my office manager undue stress and suffering, and I will hold you legally liable. I will also report you to the state bar association and start proceedings to have you disbarred for lying and misrepresenting the facts on this important business transaction. I will also sue you for punitive damages for the undue stress you put my office manager and me through on this matter." At this point he knew he had a major credibility problem and the possibility of liability lawsuits, and a risk of his license being censured or revoked for his unscrupulous legal action. He now realized he had tried to shake down the wrong guy and tried to bait and switch by saying that I misunderstood what he was saying. I quickly told him, "I fully understood what you said and that you had misrepresented the facts, which is a violation of your oath of office as an attorney representing the public. And you tried to defraud the poor first-time home-buyer by lying."

Now his voice was breaking again, and he stated that he had just had a heart attack and that because of this issue he was about to have another. I replied, "People like you do not deserve to live. You are an arrogant and dishonest person who unfortunately is representing the public." He then begged to know if we could work this out between us before things got out of hand.

I said, "You are the one who is out of hand. "You are a liar, a cheat, and very unscrupulous," and I hung up. That evening around 3:30 p.m., a courier dropped off an envelope at my office with an apology from him stating that he was sorry for any misunderstanding. He went on to say he was just trying to best serve his client and that he would like to come by my office and mutually work out this misunderstanding.

I did not respond and let him stew in his own misery but never heard another word. I am convinced that for him this was a once-in-a-lifetime legal experience; he had never thought an attorney would be challenged and humiliated in this way by a layperson with a funny accent. Hopefully my successfully challenging his illegal shakedown will save someone else from unnecessary suffering at the hands of this unscrupulous attorney.

And then there was Hennery, another very abrupt, obnoxious lawyer who was very big on intimidating his opponent in order to have the upper hand. I had performed an inspection on a property owned by one of his clients, and when he received my report, he was not very happy, so he called my office and spoke to my office manager. He was obnoxious and complained about this nitpicking report that was not based on facts and asked that the inspector call him to discuss some of the stupid discrepancies.

When I called him, he too came off as belligerent and nasty, and right away he started to rip my report apart and make all kinds of claims and threats in order to intimidate me. I let him go on until he was done with his intimidating approach and then asked him if that was all he had to say, and when he said yes, now it was my time to turn the tables. I was never known to run away from a good fight. The first thing I said was "You are arrogant and obnoxious and have no idea what you are doing or talking about. And now let me address each of your erroneous complaint issues." I went down the list, answering and explaining in great detail each of his arrogant, unfounded complaints.

Upon hearing my summary, he said, "Scollans, you will be hearing from me," and hung up with a bang. About two weeks after this encounter, my office got a call from the same attorney asking if the Irish bastard was around and asking to have him call his office.

When I called him, he started off by saying, "Anyone who spoke to me the way you did must really know what they are doing, and therefore I want you to do my work." He gave me his first job, which was for one of his relatives. He wanted to make sure that he was recommending someone that was good and tough, since his relative was also a trial lawyer and he wanted to make sure that he was well taken care of, and from that point on, I was doing all his work. We became good friends. He was a good attorney, and once you got past the gruff, he was a great guy. When I would go to his office, he would close the door, put his feet on the desk, and pull out a few joints, and say, "I know you can be an arrogant bastard." With a big laugh, he would pull out a joint and then say, "Let's relax and have a smoke." The inspector walks a very narrow and treacherous path in order to be successful.

There are four basic sources that engineering inspectors get their work from. Three of them are as follows: realtors, lawyers, relocation companies. Then there are the word of mouth and referrals from a variety of sources: friends, coworkers, church, school, and so on. The best marketing resources are word of mouth and referrals. The only requirement is that the inspector who comes highly recommended lives up to or surpasses the client's level of expectation in performing the inspection and has the ability to explain all findings professionally and in detail. When a realtor recommends an inspector, the inspector is usually hamstrung in order not to kill the deal. A homebuyer should never use an inspector recommended by the realtor.

While there are many wonderful, honest, hardworking realtors who want to do what is right for their clients, there are also those who put pressure on the inspectors to not kill the deal, and as a result many times the inspector gets in trouble.

The reality is that the prospective homebuyer is relying on that inspector's report to play a major role in the decision-making process about whether the homebuyer should buy that house or not. On the other hand, the realtor has probably spent months of his or her own time taking the prospect homebuyer around and looking at scores of houses, which is time consuming.

Driving customers around also costs money on gasoline, wear and tear on the vehicle, and so on, with the only payback being when they sell a property and close the deal.

All realtors shun the deal-killing inspector, and they blackmail such inspectors in every way possible. When realtors are selling houses to close friends or family members, it is then and only then they will recommend the competent inspector who they know will do a good job. When realtors have difficult clients who they know will sue them if they sell a house that has problems not reflected in the disclosure agreement or in the inspector's report or the seller's contract agreement that is where the competent inspector will keep the realtor and themselves out of court. I had one very interesting experience where a realtor that I had never done work for recommended me to inspect a large old three-story house that required a lot of work in Upper Montclair.

When I met the realtor at the at the inspection site, she told me that she had a very difficult client whom she was scared of, and she recommended me because I had the reputation of being the best and toughest in the business, and she told her client all about me. No inspector wants to do an inspection where you know up front that the client will sue for the least little problem not covered in the inspection report. When the client arrived, he was a small, stocky man who came across as very ornery, whose name was Joel.

No sooner had he landed than he started giving me the third degree, asking all kinds of questions about my experience and qualifications, if I had insurance, and so on until I'd had enough.

I told him to stop right there, and I asked him what he was looking for and went on to say, "You have my brochure in your hand that tells you everything about me and my company, and I am sure you have read it."

He quivered, and I could see him thinking, I may have met my match—this guy is tough.

I gave him two choices. "If you do not want me to perform this inspection, you will pay me for my travel time and time spent here with you. If you agree that I will proceed to perform this inspection, then I ask you to follow me around, and by the time this inspection is complete, I can assure you that you will be convinced that I do know what I am doing." By this time, I had turned the tables, and now it was he who was getting a little intimidated, which was exactly where I wanted him to be.

In a somewhat timid voice, he said, "Yes, please proceed, and I will follow you around, if that is OK, to ask questions," and of course I said, "By all means," which made him happy and seemed to make him a little more relaxed.

He soon learned that I was no realtor's puppet but truly a hard-nosed professional who believed in performing the due diligence that I was commissioned to do in almost an anal type of way where there would be no stone unturned. Joel and I started out on our mission, which was a very lengthy, nonstop process that lasted approximately four hours.

This large, very old house had stucco siding with a lot of gingerbread moldings and trim and two layers of asphalt compound shingles over a wood-shingle-on-lath roof where no more than two layers of shingles are allowed based on present-day code and the asphalt shingles should be on plyscore, not on the wood shingles. The third story had a finished attic dormer. I had a protocol that I followed religiously when inspecting a house. The process was to start with the outside, on the roof, and work my way down to the foundation, inspecting the gutters, downspouts, chimneys, siding, windows, doors, grading, signs of a termite or carpenter ant infestation, and any type of visible damage.

I started with the roof, and the first thing I did was to grab my thirty-two-foot extension ladder off my truck rack and extend it to the second-floor level. After I properly lashed the ladder, I then grabbed a second smaller ladder and pulled it up to the second-floor roof level in order to reach the third-floor dormer roofs and the top part of the chimney. Joel followed me up the ladder to the second-floor roof, at which time I could see he was pretty shaky, and his voice was getting higher pitched and squeaky. I said to him in a commanding voice, "Are you alright?" and in a squeaky voice he said, "I think I am OK." I headed up the second ladder and onto the third-level dormer roof, which was about thirty-five feet from ground level. Joel crawled his way to the dormer roof by the chimney. He hugged the chimney and looked scared. It became obvious that he was very scared and was holding on for dear life. It was at this time that I leapt into action, with a level of determination that I was going to perform due diligence like Joel had never seen before. I started with the chimney, where there were major structural impairments. I pointed these out to Joel as I went along and made notes so that I would remember all the detail when it came time to prepare the official written inspection report. The dormer roof, which had two layers of asphalt compound shingles over a single layer of wood shingles on lath, had major structural deterioration and damage. The second roof level also had major structural impairments, which I continued to verbally rattle off so that Joel could hear.

Joel was still on the third-level roof, hugging the chimney. I wanted to make sure he was properly informed verbally as well as in writing. However, at this point Joel did not really seem to care. He was more concerned about his safety and his own well-being. It became obvious that he had a height phobia that was getting the better of him. I came down the ladder to the ground level and started on the exterior inspection of each of the components, where there was all kinds of water and infestation damage, mostly termite. Joel was still on the third-level roof, holding on to the chimney, and had no intention of making a move to come down. I proceeded into the house using a defined protocol for inspecting the inside of the structure, starting with the attic and moving room by room down through the house until I reached the basement.

When I was in the basement, the realtor asked me, "Did Joel go home?"

I said, "I don't know" and went on to say, "The last time I saw him, he was on the third-level roof by the chimney."

She said, "Oh my God, is he still up there?" and she ran out to check, and when she came back, she was a little frantic. Of course, I knew that he could not get off the roof and was like a stranded cat with his fingers dug into that chimney and hanging on.

At this time, I was about three hours into the inspection, and I felt it was time to rescue Joel. By now I was convinced that he had learned his lesson that two people can play hardball and to never take on an opponent until you know how hard a punch he can throw. I ran up the ladders to the third-level roof, and there was Joel hanging on to the chimney with a grip that would require mechanical means to release. By now he was pale in the face and looked like death. I asked him if he was all right and why he was still up there. He looked at me with a very sad look like he was ready to cry and said he could not get down. I told him I was going to get him down, but he would have to listen to me and follow directions. I told him to do exactly what I was going to tell him to do. He looked at me like a scared cat and said, "I don't think I will be able to come down."

Now all I could think of was that I might have to call the fire department to get him down, but I was determined to give it my best shot and try and get him down myself. I came close to him, patted him on the shoulder, and said, "Joel, trust me—I will get you down. Let's get started right now. I will go in front of you and guide you down very slowly, step by step, until we reach the ground." He looked at me and said thanks and started to move slowly down the first ladder. He was horrified.

He would stop every few steps, and it would take five minutes or more to get him moving again. It took twenty minutes to get Joel from the third-level roof to the ground

level, and by the time he got to the ground, I too was exhausted. By the time he reached the ground, he was barely able
to talk, and it was difficult to understand him. He sounded
weak and somewhat despondent and wanted to be left alone.
When the realtor would talk to him, he would not answer her
at all and would just turn his head and look in the opposite
direction. I think he blamed her for not looking out for him.
He was her customer, and that made her very uncomfortable
and scared. She kept saying, "What do I do? What do I do?"
and I would tell her just to leave him alone and I would work
with him. There was something about the realtor that Joel
did not like or trust, although she seemed to be a very nice,
honest lady.

After a half hour had passed, I sat down next to him and
started to go over my inspection findings, but he was not interested and acted like he did not care. His priorities had completely changed, and he was now concerned only about his own
well-being.

He was a different man who now realized he was not an
island, he did need people, and if he had not been rescued
from that high, cold roof, he would not have survived—a scary
thought. He also realized that this was just a house that he was
purchasing and was not a life-or-death type of situation and
there was no reason to overreact about an inspection—just relax and put some trust in people. The reality is that more than
90 percent of inspectors and realtors are good people trying to
do the best job they know how, and the other 10 percent or less
who are sleazy and not trustworthy are a very small minority,
so why not put some trust in people when the vast majority are
good, honest people? I then continued my inspection of the

basement, performing due diligence—the basement is the most important part of any structure. Joel did not seem to care and asked me if I would mind if he went upstairs to sit down. "Of course," I said. "Whatever you wish. You are the boss."

When I said, "You are the boss on this job," he looked at me with a sad look and said, "No, you are."

When the physical part of the inspection was complete, I sat down again at the table in the kitchen to write up all the details of the report, which would go into my final inspection report. The realtor asked Joel what he thought of the inspection, and he replied, "He is a tough man, but he really knows his business," and from Joel I took that as a great compliment.

The realtor went on to say, "I've never met an inspector like him before. He is so detailed. This inspector makes the rest of the inspectors out there, including some I have used, look like rookies." The realtor again spoke up and said, "Most inspectors blow through in an hour, and he is here over four hours, so you know you are getting your money's worth." That made Joel happy, knowing he was getting a good job.

After I finished writing up the report, I said to Joel, "Let's walk through the house inside and outside so I can explain all my findings, but he quickly said, "No thanks. Your report will be fine," and I guess maybe he was not too sure he wanted to go on another scary trip with me.

I issued an invoice to Joel when the physical inspection was complete. In most cases inspectors will not issue a written report until the invoice is paid in full, and some will not discuss their findings until they are paid in full. I handed Joel the invoice. He did not seem to look at the invoice but just glanced and wrote a check; however, the check was for a significant amount—30 percent—more than the invoice, which I brought to his attention.

He replied, "You did a great job, and sorry for me being a jerk." Now I felt like the jerk for leaving him up on the roof in a desperate state as a punishment for what I thought was his arrogant and belligerent behavior toward me when in reality it was Joel's way of doing business. From that day forward until I retired from the business, I would get many great recommendations from Joel, and each customer would tell me how highly Joel spoke of me and would warn them that I was tough and took no nonsense.

Joel was Jewish, so every holiday season, when we would send out Christmas gifts to our good customers and those who referred us, I would send Joel a bottle of the best Irish whiskey, and he would be so pleased and say, "I will have one for St. Paddy's Day on you." I later learned that Joel was a very well-liked and very influential man within his own community and the business world, where he worked all his professional life. I must have inspected homes and businesses for everyone in his family, extended family, and friends.

Joel was a tough businessman who wanted to know what he was getting for his money and what the caliber of the person doing the work was. Joel was a man of character—honesty with the utmost integrity. He had great respect for competent people who did good work. The world needs more people like Joel. Despite his initial gruff presence, he was a man that I learned to respect and admire. He had the courage and decency to recognize his shortcomings; more important yet, he was willing in a very special and dynamic way to make up for his shortcomings in a very honorable and respectful way. I learned from Joel's actions and courage where I could improve and only hope that under the same circumstances, I would have the courage to be forgiving and correct my shortcomings in the way he did. Our inspection company had a great reputation mostly because of our level of knowledge coupled with a very high level of performing due diligence, which earned us the reputation of being honest and the best of the best when it came to reporting the facts in a very clear and distinctive way with total transparency. My wife did a great job in the office and was extremely knowledgeable, and in fact she knew the building inspection business inside out from working in the business when we renovated houses, and I would come home and tell her how customers would sing her praises and talk about how knowledgeable she was and how in many cases she would be the reason some customers would go with our company instead of a competitor.

When I would give her customer feedback, she would be delighted and on cloud nine hearing these stories. This hard-nosed, honest approach did not earn us any business recommendations from most realtors—some would blackmail us whenever they could—but at the end of the day, I could sleep at night and feel good about an honest, well-done job. Some of the realtors who had inroads with the corporate relo companies would complain that they had to disclose the content of our reports, which made those properties difficult to sell; however, this scurrilous approach did not hurt our reputation with the relo companies—they liked our toughness.

Some of my competitors who played into the hands of unscrupulous realtors ended up in serious trouble and paid a heavy price for their disingenuous approach. They hid behind a lack of transparency rather than reporting the facts, which was what the customer was paying for. No matter how diligent and knowledgeable an inspector is, they can miss something when inspecting a home or building, or one can forget to document an impairment which would render the inspector liable should the homebuyer decide to pursue damages. Many judges, if they see the omission as an honest mistake where the inspector forgot to document something, will be very reasonable in their judgment against the inspector. However, if the judge thinks the inspector was in cahoots with the realtor and was hiding some things in order to keep the deal alive, many judges will throw the book at the inspector and the realtor, which gives credence to how honesty is always the best policy in everything we do. We were very successful in the inspection business, which allowed us to send all of our three children to the schools of their choice, which was one of the most important priorities for my wife and me. As a result, all three got off to a good start in their careers. Once a company gets the reputation of being honest and does good work, success follows. Every buyer wants a thorough, honest evaluation with no hidden agenda.

When the word gets around that you do good work, you do not need to depend on unscrupulous, manipulative realtors or lawyers for their recommendations. The good realtors who are honest and want the best for their clients will recommend the good, honest inspector in order to maintain their reputations, resulting in repeat business, which is the key to being successful so that eventually one can build a client base that can sustain itself through the tough times as well as the good times.

One of my most memorable stories about an unscrupulous realtor was about the selling realtor for a house that his sister was buying where I was the inspector.

When performing the inspection, I discovered that the septic system had a serious malfunction. The realtor was following me around as I inspected each component, and I told him about the poor condition of the septic system. However, he did not want me to tell the purchaser, who was his sister, and said that she did not need to know.

He said that if there was a problem, he knew people who could repair the septic system without having to get permits or file any paperwork. I looked at him and said, "How can you do this to your sister?" and he replied, "I need this sale, and I can take care of this problem. There is no need to scare her."

I said, "Look, she is my client, and I have no choice but to report to her all the details; I will also write up the facts in my final report." I went on to say to him, "Note she will need a septic certification for a working system in order for a lender to give her a mortgage." Then he went on to say that he could work this out with the mortgage lender salesperson who was his friend and would do whatever he wanted because he gave him all his mortgage business. I issued my report, indicating a failed septic inspection and including all the other issues that were discovered during the inspection. I never heard from that realtor again, and from that day on we never got any more recommendations out of his office.

It is so unfortunate that there are so many unscrupulous businesspeople who will lie.

In the long run, most of them get caught and pay the price by losing their reputations and many times losing their businesses through lawsuits that have to be paid, and there can also be serious punitive damages that can bankrupt them personally as well as their companies. I loved the engineering inspection business and the interaction with so many wonderful people on all levels, including many wonderful realtors and attorneys. Many became good friends, and they loved to hate the unscrupulous businesspeople who made all the others look bad and painted with the same brush. There were many challenges in the engineering inspection business.

Most of the major challenges were in particular dealing with lawyers, realtors, and prospective buyers; there were always many issues to deal with from a legal as well as a business prospective. The engineering inspection business is one of the most litigious businesses, and if the inspector is not knowledgeable, good at performing due diligence, and good at report writing, more than likely that inspector will end up getting sued. Approximately 90 percent of inspectors go out of business within the first two to three years as a result of lawsuits. Many good inspectors I knew very well left the business because they could not sleep at night worrying about possible lawsuits. If the inspector or the inspection company has a number of insurance claims the cost of insurance will become unaffordable or could be dropped, which would mean the inspector or Inspection Company would be forced out of business.

CHAPTER 35

Judgment

U sing good judgment in everything we do and say is extremely important and can determine our destiny, whether it be in our personal or business life. When someone is not capable of taking responsibility for their actions or admitting to themselves where there is a lack of judgment, in the long run they become the biggest loser and may very well lose ground that they can never take back. All of us have some level of stubbornness, which can be due to our cultural background or upbringing, but it seems to be everywhere. When that stubbornness starts to have a negative effect on the business and you lose respect among those who are important in your private or business life, then that stubbornness can be considered bad judgment.

In the course of life, we all have to fight many battles and make critical decisions. Some we make in order to survive, and some may be defending what we believe and hold dear in our hearts. In politics good judgment plays a part; and getting it right the first time may determine one's future. Judgment plays a large part in how we raise our children and what we expect from them academically and morally, and the list goes on. The judgments we make in raising our children to a great extent will reflect strongly on who they are. All of us at one time or another will err in judgment, but it is how we recover and correct our mistakes that will make the difference. Of all the challenges in life, the most difficult one is maintaining relationships with our spouses, children, grandchildren, and close friends, and an error in judgment can ruin a relationship that may be very difficult to repair. Then there is love of country, for which young people will join the military to fight for their country as so many did during the two world wars and after 9/11, when men left their wives and small children to fight for the country they loved.

There are countries like Ireland where every generation a new breed of patriots rises up. For the past eight hundred years, each new generation of Irish men and women would rise up to rid an oppressive occupier from their land. These are judgments that can be life changing for the individual and their loved ones. I am a big believer in love of country and defending what one believes to be one's God-given right. If your country is not worth fighting and dying for, why not leave and move on to what you consider to be a better place? There is nothing more honorable than to lay down one's life for love of country. When I was growing up in Ireland, although the country was poor and most of the young people had to emigrate to make a living, there was still an uncanny love of country where masses of young men and women would rise up and chase that dawn light of freedom.

Young people were willing to lift up arms and fight to re-move the yoke of imperialism that dominated this little coun-try for hundreds of years, yet the people rarely complained. They were willing to accept their lot, fight, and die for their country's freedom at every opportunity. This was a realism that I always admired in an embattled people. Now that I live in this great United States, I have had the distinct honor and privilege to proudly serve in the military from October 1967 to October 1969. I believe that every American should be called to serve; service keeps our country's military strong and compels us not to take freedom for granted. I also believe that a prerequisite for political office should be military service or its equivalent as a basic indicator that the politician is not solely out to promote his or her self-interest rather than that of the country or community they wish to represent. There is no better example to demonstrate love of country than to show a willingness to fight and die to defend one's country if necessary. Today more than ever before, the whole world is a spotted tinderbox of all types of eruptions—wars, scrimmages—that could spiral out of control with bad political judgment.

CHAPTER 36

The American Dream

Opportunity in America was always in abundance, and I was always eager to pursue all that it had to offer. I must say that good fortune was always on my side, from my childhood in Ireland to my short stay in the United Kingdom and to this day in America.

I believe that we must be ready for opportunity when it presents itself and seize the moment when it comes our way. We must be ready to accept the challenge and have the courage to pursue what lies ahead. In my case I was always ready and willing to take on the task and deal with whatever risks lay ahead. There were many times when I got in over my head, but with the spirit to survive and the will to overcome whatever obstacles lay ahead, I was always able to forge ahead and end up on my feet. Although I started off from a very humble beginning, I had the confidence and the desire to take on the challenge by working harder than most people and building trust along the way.

One of the most important attributes on the way to being successful is trust, where colleagues, peers, and subordinates know that they can trust and believe in you and that you will follow through and do what you promise. This is a credo that is paramount for being a business owner or any type of successful leader.

We all can fail those who believe in us along the way, but like in every other situation, when we fail, we must get up, move on, and work twice as hard to regain that trust and confidence. One of the most important roads to success is by demonstrating respect at all levels. If you are a leader, whether it be at a small operation or large, when subordinates and peers trust and believe in you, they will go the full distance with you in order to help you accomplish your mission, because everyone likes to work on a winning team and with people that they believe in and trust.

There is nothing that is more crippling or destructive to one's road to success than the lack of honesty and integrity. If you do not have the ability to deliver and demonstrate what you say is real, it is then that your peers and subordinates can lose faith in you.

Trustworthiness is like many other characteristics in people: you either have it or you do not, and when it is missing, it can derail one's ambitions when least expected, and people whom you depend on will rise up and walk away. I always worked hard on making sure that I maintained a very high level of integrity among people at all levels, and I know that this philosophy served me well.

My father was a man with great intuition and highly valued trustworthiness. He would always preach to his children that your word is your honor and without it you have nothing, and if you show that you have a high level of integrity, people will more than likely come and want to be on your team. My credo in going through life is to be truthful, and like every other edict my father taught us, it pays great dividends because no one likes a phony.

CHAPTER 37

First US Job

Shortly after starting to work for a small factory that made hammers and screens for milling machines, I befriended a curmudgeonly older Englishman coworker who liked to give friendly advice to young people. He advised me to look for a large company where there would be more opportunity for advancement and benefits, and he named a few large companies. After about six months on the job, I took his advice and was fortunate enough to get into the pharmaceutical industry, where I took an entry-level job. Now that I had my foot in the door, there was plenty of opportunity for advancement. I began to realize that I would need to go back to school if I wanted to get ahead and maximize my potential. I decided that I wanted to get into electronics and signed up with DeVry Institute, which was a two-year associate's degree equivalency program that took three years, four nights a week. This was a wonderful program and was more hands-on than the typical two-year county college degree programs but without all the humanities and only included what was necessary to prepare students to become electronics technicians. This was a great program and, when successfully completed, guaranteed job placement. In my case, a job for a junior electronics technician opened up at the plant where I was working. I applied and got the position in the biomedical technology research labs that repaired and built electronic equipment to support the research projects.

My supervisor, who was a wonderful person, loved to provide on-the-job training for the people in his shop, which was a great opportunity for me, and I learned a great deal that became the basis for my technical background, which I kept expanding on. Then I was drafted into the military service for two years, which was life changing.

When I got out of the service, I came back to my old job, but with a different mindset. While in the military, I had the opportunity to have a great assignment where I had a lot of responsibility for managing people in a number of areas. Now that I was back in civilian life, I was ready to take the business world more seriously and do what I had to do to propel my career ahead. I went back to night school, this time in pursuit of a degree, which was the only way forward in order to enhance my career and have an opportunity to pursue management-level positions. This was a daunting task, since my academic background was spotty, and in many ways very limited, because there were large academic gaps. The first step was that I went to the local county college and met with a career counselor in order to find out what my options were. The counselor was excellent and put me on sound footing. He advised me that my DeVry education in electronics technology, where I had maintained good grades, would allow me to sit for a number of CLEP tests, and if I got a successful grade of C or greater, I would get full credit for these courses. The total number of CLEP courses came to twelve credits—not a lot but better than nothing. However, he also spelled out that I would have to take ten prerequisite mathematical noncredit courses, including trigonometry and precalculus, and success-fully complete each one of them with no less than a C grade in order to make up for my large mathematical gaps that would be required for college acceptance into the engineering technology degree program. Needless to say, this was a big hurdle to over-come, but I was willing to get started and give it my best shot. I was challenged in many ways as I tried to overcome a very steep academic slope, especially in the area of advanced mathematics that I was not very well prepared for, but I never gave up, and when the going got rough, I would buckle down, spending an enormous amount of time studying.

There were times when I had to use the school's on-staff tutoring service to get through some of the difficult math ma-terial where I had large academic voids. This approach paid off when I got passing grades and was able to matriculate and pur-sue my intended program. There was some comfort in knowing that a number of my classmates had a much better academic foundation than I had but were struggling, and unfortunately a number of them dropped out of the program. Being stubborn and hardworking, coupled with my military experience, my army GED results, and my technical school grades provided me with the courage to hang in and keep plunging. Pursuing an engineering degree is like building a house: if there is not a good foundation to build on, there will be a lot of cracks that will require shoring up in order to complete the project, and the same philosophy applies to life in general. Without under-standing and successfully completing all the prerequisite ma-terials, one would find it very difficult and next to impossible to ever complete an engineering degree program, regardless of academic ability. It is amazing what a determined young mind can accomplish when there is a high level of ambition – this ambition helps us not lose confidence in our ability to succeed. I am glad that I had the endurance to be able to advance my education, and it paid outstanding dividends for the rest of my working career, which is one of the many reasons why I am such a big advocate for education. I would be remiss if I did not say how lucky I was to have a wife and family that supported my ambitions during this long quest.

From the day our three children were born, there never was a question of whether they were going to go to college—the only question was which college, and for each of them their education has also paid great dividends. My wife and I were very proud parents when each of them graduated. Although there is no substitute for a good education, the road to success in the business world requires a great deal more.

Large companies' internal politics are part of every management and higher-level position and can be very delicate and difficult to navigate. There are many challenges and hurdles to overcome to have a successful career, which makes the challenge that much more intriguing and brings out the best of our survival skills.

After working in the pharmaceutical industry for over a decade in the trades as part of the bargaining group, it was time to make a break and enter the world of management.

This was a big step in which I left all my friends and the company where I had spent over a decade and started with a new company as an area supervisor.

This new company was also one of the best and largest pharmaceutical and bulk chemical manufacturing companies in the United States. It had a very strong trade union, and there were many union shop stewards walking around looking for a reason to file a grievance against management. This added a great deal of stress to the job, and this caused many maintenance supervisors to avoid going out onto the maintenance shop floor to supervise their staff. These supervisors were literally intimidated by the trade union leaders and would just hand out work orders with little if any direction or accountability. These union leaders were loudmouths, and many if not all were bullies who used their power to intimidate the more timid supervisors. The supervisors in many cases felt that they did not have the support of upper management, so as a result they thought, why get stressed out dealing with the union stewards, who were only looking for trouble to make them feel inferior at every opportunity? One morning around 10:30, which was after the morning break that theoretically ended at 10:20 a.m., I walked out onto the maintenance shop floor and observed one of the technicians in my gang working on his rifle at his workbench. When I approached him and asked him what he was doing with a rifle in the workplace his reply was "Go 'F' yourself."

Since I was new and relatively young, with a funny accent or brogue, he felt I was easy prey to bully and intimidate. I immediately called security and had him escorted off the site. I wrote him up and give him two weeks off without pay, which was in keeping with the union rule book for insubordination and working on a firearm at his workbench. When the union's chief shop steward was informed of this incident, he and his army of shop stewards invaded my office in an attempt to intimidate me, and the chief steward started to yell, curse, and call me all kinds of names. They were taken by surprise when

I immediately issued a direct order to each of them to get out of my office or I would call security to have them also removed from the site. The union officials became mesmerized and confused and did not know what was going on. Who was this brand-new rookie supervisor with a funny accent, and who gave him all this power? What had changed?

With that I wrote up each one of them for abusive and threatening language and gave each of them one week off without pay. This set the stage for a senior management frenzy where they had no idea how to deal with this situation, knowing that I was determined to make my actions stick. The company was extremely busy, operating three shifts twenty-four seven to keep up with customer demands and making all kinds of money, so it did not want any work stoppages. The company was willing to give the union whatever it wanted in return for peace and no work stoppages. So, the next thing I knew, the executive vice president of manufacturing, who was my boss's boss, requested that I come to his office with my boss and his boss, where I found myself being interrogated for my actions until I finally spoke up and asked if I could say a few words. Of course, my direct bosses were horrified that I, a brand-new rookie supervisor, would make such a daring request, but the VP, with a little reluctance, said "Go ahead."

I started by saying, "Are you aware that most of the maintenance supervisors are intimidated by the union leaders to the point where they are too intimidated to go out on the maintenance shop floor?" I went on to say, "Is this what you want? If I do not have the support of senior management in dealing with this type of issue, I am wasting my time as a supervisor." At that point, I suspect, the VP thought that I was about to walk out.

He knew if he did not give me the necessary support I would resign. He also knew that if that happened, then he had completely lost control of the union. He stood up, stared at me, and then stared at my two bosses and said, "Kevin, go back to work, and I will get back to you on this matter." I had no idea what that meant, and when I went home that evening, I told my wife I might be out of a job. A week later the union stewards were back, and there was a high-level union and management meeting that included the union state delegate.

The meeting also included the company labor relations director, the company labor lawyers, and an arbitrator to work out some ground rules. The company, after meeting with the labor relations people and the labor lawyers, took a very hard stance with the union, which came to me as a huge surprise, since all my peers were telling me, "You are fighting a losing cause where management will never support you and will throw you under the bus." The union leaders were reprimanded by the arbitrator and the state union delegate for their bad behavior and warned that their behavior was abusive, and they were put on notice that this behavior would not be tolerated and was reason for termination if it should ever happen again. This was a tremendous setback for the union. All my actions stuck, and they had to regroup to get back their composure.

This left the union wondering whether this was just the beginning and whether I had been brought in to break the union. They were taken by surprise with my in-depth union knowledge and my ability to do handle each situation in a new way.

This happened in such a rapid and direct way, and it was very scary for union leadership. The union leadership became so scared of me that whenever there would be any type of incident, no matter how minor, they would always bring along at least one other union steward. Of course, I would also have another supervisor to cover my end, which they did not like, and as a result they were somewhat intimidated and very nervous.

The union management took a very guarded, low-profile approach to solving every incident and were afraid if they tried to get back at me that I might set them up again for another embarrassment, or worse, fire any one of them who stepped out of line. When they would meet with me, they no longer would threaten to file a grievance but would work toward a more amicable solution. At this point they felt that I had all the cards in my hand and was not afraid (and maybe liked) to play hardball. This was great for me, and I was enjoying the nervousness of the union leadership and would call regular department meetings to spell out and mandate policies that were consistent with company policy and the union rule book. I became a student of the union rule book and used it to its fullest extent, which scared the union leadership.

About two weeks after the incident, everyone was back to work, and things had settled down now. The arbitrator had given the union leaders a slap on the wrist, and they were dealing with an embarrassing situation where not only did the union member punishment stick, but so did that of union leadership. Management was very happy with the outcome. About one month after this incident had passed and the dust had settled, the VP of operations came to my office with my two bosses, which was very unusual. When a VP comes into a supervisor's office, there is something really serious going on. When he walked in, he had a big smile on his face and said, "Kevin, great job," and then handed me an envelope and asked me to read the letter inside.

To my surprise, it stated, "Keep up the good work—we like what you are doing," and although I only had only two-plus months on the job, he awarded me a 6 percent merit raise, and he went on to say, "You are doing a great job. All your customers are very pleased with your work and how you solve problems, so again, keep up the good work, and we are glad to have you on board." I was ecstatic, and my immediate boss, a great guy, said, "Kevin, after work let's meet at the local pub and have a beer. We should celebrate."

Needless to say, the union leadership was lying low and hoping to get something on me so they could get their payback and regain their composure. Their first attempt was when I was showing the union steward, who was at the technician level, how to troubleshoot an electronic instrument where he was having a problem. I helped him make a repair using his tools. The union steward filed a grievance against me for using the tools in the process of assisting him in making the repair. I fought the grievance and won on the aspect that I was only showing the technician how to make the repair and made a strong point that this was a routine repair and the technician, who was a full-fledged journeyman, should have had the know-how to make the repair himself. I documented that the technician was not capable of making a routine repair, so I had to assist him. The technician was one of the union stewards who had rarely ever been asked to perform a task by his previous supervisors, whom he had bullied and intimidated. From that point on, when this union steward journeyman could not make a routine repair, I would remove him from the job, document the incident, and have another technician finish the work. After three documented failures where another journeyman of the same grade had to finish the job that was justification to demote that journeyman by one grade based on the union rule book. A demotion precedent was initiated, and the union leadership was up in arms. This was the first time ever a union steward was demoted for incompetence.

They claimed that this was unfair and unjust; however, it was pointed out to them what was stated in the union rule book and spelled out in detail. If a journeyman technician or mechanic failed to perform a routine task three times and had to be assisted by another technician of the same grade, which was grounds for a demotion, as indicated on page 5, paragraph 3 of the union rule book.

The chief steward said to me, "Are you now studying the union rule book?"

I replied, "You got that right, and you might want to do the same." I went on to say, "I am also a student of state labor laws," which literally sent shivers up the union leader's spine. This was the worst possible scenario: that a management person had become an expert in union rules and state labor laws. The arbitrator would many times ask me to verify a state law—I was not sure if he was just testing to see how much I really knew. When we were dealing with the union, documentation was something that the union leaders were poor at, and when they did document information, they left out important information or omitted some facts that made their documentation irrelevant. I would document each incident in detail when the technician did not know how to make the repair, including the time and date and the equipment name, make, model, and serial number. This in-depth detail drove the union leaders crazy, and they became paranoid that I was only waiting for them to make a mistake so I could capitalize on it.

During the next two situations where the same technician failed to make a routine repair, I removed him from the job and brought in another technician to finish the job. Once I had three incidents properly documented where the technician could not make a routine repair and another technician had to be called in to do his work, this was grounds for a one-grade demotion, which would result in a reduction in pay and would require the mechanic to enroll in a remedial training program. Failure to follow the company policy as spelled out in the union rule book could result in termination.

This was a scary and a very embarrassing situation for the employee; he went out on sick call for a week. I immediately took the necessary action to demote him. Now the union was up in arms, since this technician had been with the company over twenty years and been a shop steward for ten years. They went on to say that as a union steward, he spent less time on repairs and was somewhat rusty.

I simply told them that was no excuse and that nowhere in the union rule book was there such an exemption where union officials should be treated differently than any other employee in the bargaining unit. I went on to say the union leadership had left me with no other choice, since they had filed a grievance when I tried to instruct the journeyman on how to make the repair. He had proved to be an incompetent journeyman and could not perform his duties as required under union rules. The union leadership brought in the arbitrator, who again agreed with the company: since the journeyman technician was not performing his duties as spelled out in the union rule book based on his classification and grade, this was grounds for a grade-level demotion. The arbitrator went on to say that the supervisor had given the technician every opportunity to succeed by assisting him in making the repair. He went on to say that the union leadership could not have it both ways. This was a tremendous blow to the union leadership, and as a result they backed off considerably, especially when it came to me, because they realized that I had worked as a union member for so many years and was an astute student of union rules and state labor laws.

In fact, the company labor relations director would invite me in on labor bargaining meetings to get my input, which was a big thorn in the union leadership's side, and now they realized that by their own arrogance and bullying, they had created a situation that was not going away.

There was one more incident where the union lost ground when a number of union workers were working overtime. This was the first time for me running a big electrical installation project that had a very high organizational priority, and when a number of the union workers went off the site for supper, instead of taking a thirty-minute break, they took ninety minutes, and a number of them came back inebriated. As they were coming back into the plant, I was waiting at the parking lot gate with a security guard.

I ordered them to line up at my office, where I would meet with each of them one on one, included the union chief steward I spelt out, based on company policy, the seriousness of their behavior. Worse yet, the chief shop steward was the ringleader, and the rest of the crew felt they were safe in the company of the chief steward, who used to carry a lot of weight, but not so much anymore. The security guard, a retired New York City police officer, was a huge man—very well built and in great physical shape, with biceps three times the size of an average man's, and although he was a very nice guy, he could be very gruff and took no nonsense from anyone, in particular the chief shop steward, whom he did not like because of his arrogance. He felt that the chief shop steward was a loud-mouthed, obnoxious, arrogant bully and not a nice person, and he was so happy that someone had come along who would take them to task and beat them at their own game. When one of the union members would get loud and angry, he would walk up to him, put his hand on his shoulder, and say in a very stern voice, "Cut it out, buster, if you know what is good for you." As the mechanics entered my office, I would ask them a few questions, and based on how they answered the questions, I would determine how inebriated they were. I felt that many of them were not fit for work, including the union's chief shop steward. I sent each of them home, canceled their overtime, and wrote up each of them for leaving the job site without permission and inebriation. Showing up inebriated while on the clock in itself was justification for severe punishment, including termination.

The company rarely ever dismissed an employee, and as a result the workers knew they would have to do something extremely egregious to get fired, but my record of throwing the book at those who abused the system and were verbally abusive made them very worried, since all of them were trouble-type employees. This was a tremendous embarrassment for the union leadership, and as a result they were willing to negotiate the best settlement they could get and take whatever punishment the company dished out without taking it to arbitration. My boss and senior management were very impressed with how

I was handling the union. They saw that I wasn't afraid to exert my authority and take control of each situation. As a result of having the union leadership on the run, my boss orchestrated a high-level management meeting.

I was asked to give a short presentation to senior management explaining the progress that had been made in reining in the union's bad actors and the approach for dealing with major union issues. As a result of this meeting, my profile increased greatly within the overall organization, and the union leaders were becoming very paranoid, in particular when dealing with me. As a result of my no-nonsense approach, they erroneously labeled me as the one that the company had brought in to bust the union, and from that point forward, when there was a problem in my area, only the union's chief steward and the union president were allowed to talk to me for fear that if others made a wrong move, they might find themselves in trouble.

After the inebriation incident settled down, one evening, as I was leaving the site, I found my truck's four tires slashed in the parking lot. I called my boss, who called the VP, and he told me, "Your truck will get new tires, and you will have door-to-door limo service until your truck is back." Then the VP called a meeting with all the union representatives. He went on to say the local police detective team would investigate the incident.

He made it clear the police would not leave a stone unturned and the perpetrators would be brought to justice, and they would face the full brunt of the law, including dismissal and possible prison time if found guilty.

The police went to work, and the first step was that one of the detectives would meet with each of the suspects and interrogate them for hours. This was grueling. One of the suspects resigned, and it was said that he could not handle the interrogations, which went on for months until they found the culprit. The culprit was fired, but the company dropped all legal charges. After a period of time, the union's chief steward and the union president started to realize I was not out to bust the union but was one who could not be intimidated and would never run away from a good fight. They became acutely aware that I was not going to put up with any nonsense and we came to a meeting of the minds. Then things became very stable, and there were zero grievances filed in my department, which was a big plus for me. As a result of effectively dealing with the union leadership, we were able to reduce union grievances all across the site, which was a major achievement. Up until this point, every year the union would file three hundred or more grievances, and the company would have to settle each grievance by the end of each fiscal year and pay out large sums of money to settle each grievance before going into the year-end labor negotiations.

After I had worked for the company for three years, an opportunity came up with another pharmaceutical company much closer to home, where there was a need for a person with my technical expertise. The company contacted me and made me an offer that I could not refuse. Now I was faced with the quagmire of having to tell my boss, whom I had a wonderful working relationship with, that I would be leaving. He would continually remind me that the two of us made a great team, which I agreed with and was happy to be part of.

As much as I loved my job, there was one concern that I had with my current company. It was a chemical manufacturing facility where there were a number of small factories producing a number of high-demand products, there were some very hazardous chemicals used in the process. Six people in my team of twenty-seven had low platelet counts and were required to go to the infirmary once a week to have their platelet counts monitored.

This was a major concern for my wife, who wanted me out of this company because we had two very young children, and she was a nervous wreck knowing that I too could get sick, and although she knew I loved the job and the people that I worked for, she felt it was not worth the health risk, and of course she was absolutely correct. Her influence had a great impact on my final decision, which was a very difficult one to make.

When I went to my boss and broke the news to him that I was leaving, he was so surprised and so disappointed that I really felt bad. We were good friends—he was a brilliant manager, a great engineer, a great person, and a boss that I respected. At the end of the day, I had to think of my wife and family first, and work had to become secondary. By far the most important thing for me was my wife and two young children at that time. My boss did not make this move easy for me. He offered me a double promotion, including his own position—he would move to a higher level—and offered to match the compensation of the prospective company and then some. All that wonderful recognition that I had garnered made it very hard to pull the plug, but I realized my health, wife, and family had to come first. Before I left the company, management had a going-away luncheon party at one of the local restaurants, and many people, including the union leadership, attended. Everyone that got up to say a few words. Many guests said very nice things that were very complimentary.

To my surprise the union's chief steward got up and was also very complimentary and stated that what he was going to miss most was the honesty.

He went on to say, "Kevin will never back down when he thinks he is right, which he usually is. When you take on Kevin, you better be willing to go to the mat, and you know there will be no surrender." With that comment from the chief shop steward, the place broke out in a loud roar of laughter and applause.

My new position was challenging but completely different in every way, since there was only one very small bargaining group. However, the management's philosophy was to treat all the workers as if they were all part of the bargaining unit in order to keep the union out of all the other departments. When I arrived, the workforce, including supervision, had a very lackadaisical approach to their job. The workforce skill level when I arrived was for the most part very poor, and there was a very poor work ethic that meant the plant infrastructure and maintenance equipment were neglected in many ways, but all that was about to change. After a short time on the job, I had a good handle on the problems and shortcomings and as a result launched a mission that was going to change the way things were done and to a great extent the culture as well. The mission was for the overall organization to become more customer focused and driven and to become the best in class. I understood that this was a very ambitious undertaking, knowing the mentality of the workforce and also knowing their history. They were badly managed and spoiled rather than having a level of accountability for their work and results. With that said, they were all very nice people and very respectful for the most part. I am a big believer in treating people well and with respect but at the same time holding them accountable for their actions and quality of work. I also believe in establishing a level of accountability where the good performers are recognized for their work and the poor performers are required to improve.

Poor performers were put on a performance improvement plan, which nobody wanted to have to deal with. Up until this time, substandard performers did not have any incentive to improve, but that too was about to change. A performance improvement plan was a last resort to get people on board—they had to shape up or they would be moved to a lower-level job. Before I implemented the performance improvement plan, the employee would be given every opportunity to shape up and to get with the program, which would be encouraged. Employees could initiate their own plans, and they would be monitored and mentored as needed. Before rolling out this program, I had a number of meetings with the full workforce spelling out the details and expectations. This was a completely new approach for a workforce that in the past had no pressure and no level of accountability, including first-line supervision. This was a culture shock at best. There was one old-timer in the maintenance crew who was very political and was on a first-name basis with the CEO and all senior management, and they all loved him because he was their mole, or so it was said. This politically motivated mechanic went around telling all the maintenance workers that I would not last three months. He went on to boast that he would see to it that my time with the company would be short lived. All this information was getting back to me, and this was a great opportunity for me to zero in on this guy's activities. The first thing I did was to reassign him to a different part of the facility where he would have no contact with senior management. I also made it department policy that no one could leave the work site without the supervisor's permission. The mechanic's immediate supervisor would give permission when there was a reasonable request. In addition, if employees were found wandering off the job site, they had better have a justified reason, or they would be written up for insubordination, and that could get the ball rolling and be grounds for dismissal.

All our department policies had to be approved by HR and senior management. As I was walking out of a management meeting one afternoon, I saw the same mechanic coming out of an executive office in a building on the opposite side of the site where he did not belong. I approached him and asked him what he was doing off the job site. He told me he was visiting the executive, who had called him. Then I asked him if he got permission from his supervisor to leave his work assignment. He said no, so I gave him two days off without pay in order to let him know that I was serious about enforcing rules. I quickly got the reputation, from the floor level to the highest office, as a tough taskmaster and one who ran a tight ship. People on all levels soon began to understand that I was fair and balanced and was very big on holding workers accountable for their work and actions, though I was also very fair and flexible. I would go out of my way to help people who fell on hard times, whether it be personal or family related, and as a result I began to gain a high level of respect, and a new culture began emerging and transcending across the entire site We became a model for other departments as the department that could get things done with a high level of competence and accountability.

I was very big on recognition and making sure that the people who were contributing were recognized in a very meaningful way. What was amazing was that our politically motivated mechanic came over to my side, and we developed a great working relationship. I think he realized he could have been dismissed, and since he had only a few years left to retirement, that would not have been good for him and his wife, a lovely woman. This mechanic was very talented and became a real asset and over time he became one of my best cheerleaders. And yes, he was a mole. When he came over to our side, he was big on talking about other people and you might say squealing on them, which I did not encourage, since I believe that is not how to build trust, and trust is so important.

He began to realize it was much better having a leader who recognized his talent than one who only played politics. He also realized that I had no tolerance for politics and rewarded only results. From that point on, he became a model worker who could always be depended on, and I would let him know that he was making an important contribution to the department, which made him feel good. He liked to speak up at meetings, but now his approach was more supportive than critical of management. When I'd joined the company, it had had a dismal safety record; workers were getting injured, and the injuries were mostly minor in nature but should have been treated as OSHA recordable. I initiated a safety awareness training program for all the areas under my control. I identified gaps and held two-hour safety awareness training sessions twice a month. These sessions were mandatory: employees were required to attend. The attendees had the opportunity to discuss issues and get answers, while these sessions provided me with the opportunity to document and to set policy that established a vehicle for change to drive the system and accomplish the goals and objectives of the safety awareness mission.

There was an opportunity for a Q&A, but also, I would call on people with questions based on what was discussed in order to make sure everyone was paying attention, and that kept everyone on their toes because they never knew who might be called on to answer a question. I was not trying to trap anyone, and as long as there was a good stab at the answer, it was OK.

This approach was met with skepticism by many, but they all quickly realized that they had to get on this fast-moving train or they would be soon left behind and become irrelevant within the organization. My boss was amazed at the depth and intensity of the initiative and how quickly it was taking a grip. He quickly realized he too had to get on board and get behind the program. The program was making a rapid impact on the organization and was having very positive results in customer-driven performance.

Everyone realized the impact of safety on productivity and how in many areas skill levels also improved; systems that had never worked were now working. There was almost an immediate reduction in lost-time accidents that became evident. It became quickly obvious that this was going to be the hallmark of this organization going forward and a theme that would resonate with senior management.

There was recognition by management on all levels all over the company that this new imitative was having a very positive impact on how this team was better serving customers with a much more positive attitude. Workers were no longer complaining and had a much better customer focus and a better attitude. I was extremely pleased with the results and continued to push even harder in order to have an even greater impact that allowed the department to grow and flourish and meet the challenges of the future, which was picking up speed with new demands that required enhanced skills.

The company had just launched a multibillion-dollar drug and was growing by leaps and bounds; new buildings were planned, and the site buildings' square footage was going to double to accommodate head count, which was also going to increase. This was a great time to be working for the company, where there was great opportunity for those who were prepared and ready to take on new responsibility. I, among many others, was a recipient of the good times in a major way. I got back-to-back promotions—for me this was as good as it gets. After a number of good years when every department got bloated and there were fiefdoms popping up all over the company, a new type of change was in the air. People felt the good times were here to stay, but nothing ever lasts forever.

In the business world, you always have to be ready for the next phase to come. As the old adage goes, in the real world, trees do not grow to the sky.

When change comes, it is usually unpredictable and scary for those who are resting on their laurels. Sure, enough one day there came a crackdown where every position was to be reevaluated using advanced industrial metrics. There was no place to hide, especially for those who abused the system. The company hired a business consulting company to evaluate all aspects of the business, including head count, which is typically where there is always opportunity to cut and reduce runaway cost.

The high-powered consulting company McKinsey was brought in as the consulting firm and was commissioned to perform an audit of every job and every department. Managers had to justify their own positions and each one of their subordinates' using defined McKinsey metrics. The bottom line was that management headquarters in Basel, Switzerland, was going to cut 10 percent of the head count across the board, and it had commissioned McKinsey to justify and document the reasons for the cuts. Each department had to defend its existing head count and justify in detail every position. In our department we were able to justify each position using a previous Quinnipiac University man-hour study that we had completed about six months prior, which was great timing. Although, at first, the McKinsey consultants were not the least bit interested in any study other than its own, the Quinnipiac study went a long way in justifying estimated hours on each job assignment work order, which was a fair and reasonable approach and gave us the tools to effectively present our case. The McKinsey consultant who was auditing the facilities and maintenance organization was impressed with our documentation and backup information; he said this detail was unique. With that said, the consultant recommended that we reduce our total estimated hours by a minimum of 6 percent in order to show headquarters there was a serious effort, which could include outsourced help to reduce operating cost. For our department that was a reasonable percentage.

If our department had not done a good job defending staff, the cuts could have been much more than 6 percent. Some departments were considered redundant and as a result got completely eliminated. In our case, we got away with an overall reduction of just 6 percent, which meant some other department had to pick up the 4 percent that we were able to negotiate, plus its own 10 percent cut. This was the beginning of a squeeze to reduce cost that was going to be ongoing and was about to have a drastic effect on how each department conducted its business.

Budgets were cut 10 percent across the board. There was also a hiring freeze where new positions could be created only when there was new business, such as a new production line or a new packaging line, to keep up with customer demand. A few years later the company merged with one of its main pharmaceutical competitors and became a giant in the industry. Now with the merger, there was another major round of cuts in head count: every department had to reduce staff by at least 10 percent, either through attrition or through layoffs, and some departments were merged, resulting in 30 to 40 percent reduction in that area.

The new buzzword was *synergy*, and every manager had to come up with synergies and show significant reductions in cost. A mandatory 10 percent reduction in budget spending on top of the 10 percent head count reduction was required, and it was up to each manager to find a way to meet these objectives, and if the managers did not meet the required reduction targets, they would be replaced by someone who would. I survived the merger and continued to do well with the company in spite of all the cuts.

However, the company was not the same anymore, and it seemed that you were working for a different company with a different culture.

When I joined the company, I was told by the hiring manager, "As long as you do a good job, this is a job for life," but that quickly changed with the merger. The new organization and a lot of new management resulted in a complete change of culture. The new management philosophy was that the company owes you nothing and you must prove your worth by adding value to keep your job. There was a new approach to control head count by outsourcing everything except very essential functions. During this period my boss asked me to take on a new role where I could mentor and harmonize the facilities and maintenance management at all three sites. This was a lot different from what I had done for many years, but it was a new challenge that I enjoyed. However, about two years after the merger, all production operations shipped overseas, and two of the three plants were closed and mothballed. This brought an end to my harmonization of the sites, so I would have to find something new within one year, which was the amount of time it would take to successfully transition all the products to their new overseas location. During this transition time, I got a call from an old acquaintance who had taken over as the new COO at a biotech company and needed someone with my background to manage the biotech facilities engineering and maintenance and had the necessary experience to develop the necessary FDA documentation and validation for all the manufacturing and building equipment in collaboration with the in-house quality control department. This sounded exciting, and I was committed to taking on this new assignment. As a result of the merger, my old company was offering very lucrative severance packages to those whose jobs were eliminated. Although my job was not eliminated, I more or less saw the writing on the wall, so I went back to my old boss and asked for a meeting with him, which he granted, and I asked him whether, since two of the plants were closing, I could get the separation package.

He was very accommodating and asked me if I could stay long enough to finish all the documentation and projects that I was working on and transition over to my replacement. I said yes and gave two months' notice. When the two months were up, I was told Basel would not support a replacement, so my intuition paid off. The separation package was very generous: I ended up with a year and a half of full pay and medical benefits for life, and I chose a lump-sum pension rather than the annuity. I was a very happy camper and moved on to the next phase in a new career assignment. After spending twenty-one-plus years with the company, I knew this new assignment was going to be a daunting challenge into a whole new world where I knew none of the players other than the COO, who assured me he would have my back until I became familiar with this new global California-based company, where I would have to adapt to the West Coast culture. This was a global position that included three locations: my main office in Philadelphia, a ninety-minute commute away, where there was a production and distribution facility, and two locations in the California Bay Area consisting of another manufacturing facility, research and development, and corporate headquarters; there were an additional two locations in the United Kingdom where egg harvesting was used in the production of influenza vaccines. From a lay point of view, this is where fertilized chicken eggs are placed in an incubator and incubated for nine to twelve days. Then the allantoides of viable embryos are inoculated with the influenza virus.

CHAPTER 38

A Global Position

When the hiring manager called me, the company had a dire need for someone with my credentials and experience. It was truly great timing. This was a global California-based company; however, my office would be in the Philadelphia area, an eighth-mile commute from where I lived. Despite the long commute, the company made me an offer I could not refuse. This was a global position that involved traveling both domestically (Philadelphia and California) and internationally to the United Kingdom. The job sounded very exciting, and I had not done much travel with my current or previous positions, so this would be a new experience.

I accepted the position and loved the job. It was very challenging, but my boss was a great guy and very autonomous, which suited my work style. I traveled and rotated on a weekly basis between Philadelphia, California, and the United Kingdom except when there were issues that required my attention; then I would spend more than one week in a specific location until the problem was successfully resolved. With the continual weekly travel, I accrued significant frequent traveler mileage, a nice perk. My task with the new company was to manage and harmonize the maintenance or facilities organization at each location, including developing the required documentation to meet FDA regulatory compliance. This was a very challenging position that required a high level of knowledge in good manufacturing practices (GMP), quality control, and validations in the areas of facilities, engineering, and manufacturing. All equipment had to be validated and properly documented. I felt confident that all this was achievable with the right team approach. After evaluating the status of each site location and the existing staff, I made some changes and hired a chemical engineering consultant with a PhD who worked with me and traveled with me as needed to each location.

The documentation requirements were to develop the standard operating procedures.

In addition to SOPs, equipment maintenance work orders using a validated computerized maintenance management tracking system had to be developed and approved by the corporate quality control, including a computer maintenance management system. All systems and procedures had to comply with established FDA protocol, and these procedures were subject to an FDA audit at any time during the new drug approval process.

This was a daunting task: several hundred SOPs had to be developed, written, and approved by the company's corporate quality control management within a defined timeline. Once we had all the preliminary concepts in place, the consultant we brought on board was very experienced at developing standard operating procedures and familiar with FDA protocol. The consultant was a chemical engineer with a PhD who could hit the ground running and required very limited supervision. I gave him a few samples of what was required, and he was read to go. We both had a lot in common and worked well together; there was a lot of synergy in our approach, which made for a good team.

We would brainstorm and come up with the best approach to meet deadlines and protocol by partnering and collaborating with other regulatory groups within the company to meet deadlines and remove roadblocks. There were many issues and hurdles to overcome, but with teamwork and a good, common-sense approach, we were able to make progress. The consultant and I became friends; we would travel and dine together, and much of our leisure time together was spent strategizing about our next big challenge. He was also an Episcopalian minster in his church in a small town outside Philadelphia and was very much into religion—somewhat different from me. I am for the most part a doubting Thomas, and that made for interesting conversation.

When working in the United Kingdom and spending weekends working on high-priority projects, he would spend his little leisure time (if he had any) visiting old historical churches.

He was big into ancient church history, and he would try to drag me along.

One beautiful Sunday afternoon in Liverpool, he talked me into going along, and he introduced me to his friend, a high-level Episcopalian minister, a lovely man with a great sense of humor. When I told the minister that I was not into church stuff very much and was something of a doubting Thomas, he looked at me with a big bright smile and in his very posh English accent said, "Without blokes like you, there would not be much need for people like me." The minister was a great host with a very endearing personality. He took us all around the church and explained all the wonderful history that went all the way back to the eleventh and twelfth centuries, and then after we were all done visiting the church sites, he invited us for high tea. The high tea was at his home residence, which was magnificent, with all kinds of delicious bites, and he went on to say that for special Irish guests his wife, who was just as lovely, liked to bring out her home-made scones and other sweets which were all scrumptious. I was not comfortable going for the high tea, but my minster friend whispered that it would be considered unfriendly if we did not go. Well, it was one of the more delightful and interesting evenings of my life. He was so charismatic and charming in every way, and since I was Irish, he told me that he loved the Irish people and had visited Ireland numerous times. His paternal grandmother, whom he loved, was from County Down and was Catholic, and as a result he grew up among a lot of Catholic relatives, and then he went on to say, "That just means we have some different views on the laws of the church, but we all worship the same God, and that is what matters." This man should be a world diplomat, and if he were, he would bring people together from all walks of life.

My minster friend was so happy that his minister friend and I hit it off so well, and I am sure he already knew that the minister knew how to put everyone at ease. I could not believe how comfortable I felt; it was like we had known each other for ever.

I said to my friend, "Your friend has a wonderful personali-ty. He knows how to make you feel at ease with his warmth and enormous ability to engage."

I also said to my friend, "It is no wonder this ministry is such a success, and if he ever comes to the United States, let me know, and I will attend his service—not for the sake of religion but for him." My minster friend was highly educated, with a PhD in chemical engineering and a degree in theology—a wonderful person, but on a different wavelength from most of us when it came to people; his UK minister friend was completely the opposite and was like a magnet when it came to people. The UK minister could win people over without trying; he had an inherent gift of always hitting all their hot buttons that endeared himself to his audience in a very gracious way. On the other hand, my friend could be indifferent when it came to people's feelings. One of the examples that characterizes his personality was when we were at dinner in a restaurant in the city of Liverpool, which is a place I love because the people are so warm and friendly. When we sat down at a nice table to eat overlooking a beautiful garden that had magnificent flora, two gorgeous young waitresses, both with big smiles that lit up the place (college students), came over to our table to wait on us, and because of their beauty and charm we started to talk to them (not sure my friend appreciated their beauty and charm). No sooner had we started to talk to them than he asked if they were going to college, and with big warm smiles both said yes and give us the name of the college, at which time he blurted out of the blue, "How come the college doesn't teach you girls proper English?" He went on to say, "You girls use the word *me* this and *me* that, which is not proper English."

Well, I was never so embarrassed in my life and felt so bad for the poor girls, who were as sweet as could be, and all I could say was "He is trying to be funny—do not pay any heed to him. He is really a very nice man who likes to get a rise out of the youth. He likes to see how you respond so he can get into a deeper conversation." In order to try and soften the insult, I went on to say, "I love the Liverpool people's colloquialisms and the charm that you girls exude. You should never change, and I am sure you are loved by all who come your way." When the girls left, I could not help myself but to yell at him and say, "Why did you do that to the poor young girls who were so nice and friendly and so young, almost as young as your daughter?"

He said, "That is the real me, and sometimes I cannot help it—I always blurt out stupid things at the wrong time." He went onto say, "You admit that you are not religious, and I am a minister who is supposed to work with and help people. I only wish I could be more like you and see the good in young people. What is wrong with me? I want to be able to do just what you did, but there is always something that pulls me in the other direction, and I do not know what it is. I cannot explain, but I always feel so guilty and terrible, like I failed again, when this happens."

He went on to say he had contemplated going for therapy to help him deal with his lack of the ability to connect with people, and worse yet, he felt he turned people away by saying the wrong thing at the wrong time. I said to him, "When those beautiful young girls come back to our table, tell them how beautiful they are and that you are sorry for your silly comment. See how it feels, and look at the girls, and see how good you made them feel, just as if they were your own daughters, and I know how much you love your daughter."

He looked at me for a second, and then the tears ran down his face. When he got his composure back, he said, "You say you are just a little engineer, and I am a PhD. Well, so much for that."

I said, "You are a brilliant man in every way, and you have the background and ability to be whatever you want to be—just work on it." It is amazing when you get to know people really well how the skeletons start falling out one by one, and when the mask comes down, even the most outgoing, brilliant, and charismatic people can have a dark side.

It is not the clothes they wear or to a great extent the things they say—it is who is really hidden behind the mask that we want to see and understand before we can accept that person as a real friend.

After I had worked for the California-based company for two-plus years, the company got purchased by a larger pharmaceutical company that made similar products and was looking for a company to buy or merge with where there would be some synergies. Combining and marketing similar products using one marketing strategy and sales force rather than having two separate groups, including other opportunities, was where they reduced cost.

It was all about the profitability and growth that could be generated with a larger product line.

When a company buys or merges with another company, the end result is always head count reduction, and that is where big money can be saved. This was a dream job where I had great success, made great friends, and enjoyed so much. In these situations, the acquiring company often has people in a similar position, and since they are the acquiring company in control, it is they who decide who stays and who goes, despite their fuzzy claim of equal cutbacks at each company. The acquiring company was very generous and gave all its management team a great severance package, to the extent that if they offered me a job somewhere else in the new company, I could not afford to give up the severance package, including the stock options that I could cash in. While working at the acquired company, I had made several great friends at each location that I would miss. In particular, I loved Liverpool, where I had so many wonderful friends, including the car driver, Harry.

Harry had picked me up at the airport and provided car service during each stay at the Liverpool location. Harry was a real prince whom everyone loved, and as time went on, we became great friends. The first day I landed at the Manchester airport, Harry was there waiting with a big warm smile like he had known me forever. I said to him, "With that big warm smile, you must be Irish."

With a big hearty laugh, he said, "No, but Englishmen also smile." Then he went on to say, "Everyone in Liverpool claims to be Irish, especially on St. Patrick's Day." On the way to the Liverpool hotel, he asked me if I had ever heard of the Beatles, and I said of course I had and that while growing up in Ireland, I had loved the Beatles—they were all around my age. With that Harry said, "My great-grandmother on my mom's side was from Belfast."

A few minutes later, Harry asked me if he could pick me up and take me to the homes where all the Beatles grew up and show me the Yellow Submarine at the Liverpool dock.

I said, "Of course. I would love to. What a wonderful experience that would be."

I will always be grateful to my friend Harry, who always exuded Liverpool hospitality at its best and added to a memorable experience. Harry will always shine as one of my favorite people as I reminisce about those fond memories.

CHAPTER 39

Down Under

The timing was right for a trip to Australia now that I was between jobs and could take as much time as my wife and I wanted. Our youngest daughter, Tara, was a junior in college and had decided to go to Australia for a semester abroad, which was a wonderful experience for her and something she will treasure for the rest of her life. My wife and I availed ourselves of this once-in-a-lifetime opportunity to visit our daughter down under. What a wonderful experience that was! Our daughter was the best host and tour guide ever. My wife and I also loved Australia, a beautiful country with wonderful, friendly people everywhere we went.

Australia was a place I had always wanted to go, and having our daughter there made a dream come true. The trip was so pleasant and memorable that my wife and I will forever cherish it.

The fact that I was off from work allowed us to stay for almost a month, and we wished it was longer, since there was so much to do and everything was so beautiful. The weather was great, and so were the people and the food, and everyone was so friendly and helpful. We would have loved to spend six months there and tour the whole country, but we had a dog to come home to. While there, we visited Cairns in the northern part of the country and the Great Barrier Reef, which was awesome, and traveled around the Cairns area, which is beautiful. Because our daughter had already spent a few months in the country and had traveled all over, including in New Zealand, she was like a native compared to us. She was our tour guide and did an amazing job. What a great place to visit with so many things to do and places to see. Young people are so good at planning and making sure that they can see as much as possible in a short time compared to older folks.

Of all the places that my wife and I have visited, Australia is one of the most memorable, and we would love to go back at the first opportunity.

While there we had the opportunity to visit with my wife's first cousin, Kevin.

We share the same first name. He is a great guy with a beautiful Australian wife and family in one of the outer suburbs of Sidney, an absolutely beautiful area with rolling hills and beautiful spacious homes with gorgeous flora and landscaping. There is very splendid weather, and golfing and outdoor activities are great almost all year round. Cousin Kevin grew up down the road from where my wife grew up in Ireland, and his wife is a native Australian, a great host who makes you feel like you have known her all your life. From the first time we met her and their three lovely teenage children, they could not have been more welcoming. The youngest child was in high school, and two were attending college. While we were there, they appeared to be a model family living the Aussie good life with all the luxuries of this beautiful country.

They treated us like royalty. Cousin Kevin picked us up at our hotel in the Sydney Rocks area and took us to their beautiful home, which they were very proud of and was nice to see.

His wife cooked a wonderful Aussie meal with great Australian wine, and we just had a wonderful day, and at close to midnight Cousin Kevin took us back to our hotel. They were very gracious hosts that just personified everything that is so great about Australia's culture and lifestyle.

I would recommend to anyone who has any interest in seeing down under to seize the moment and take advantage of a wonderful opportunity—the people who are so nice, the beautiful weather, and a country that is so spectacular and vast, with so much to do and see. To make it even more spectacular, their dollar was at a 40 percent discount to the US dollar while we were there.

I am so grateful that our daughter created such a wonderful opportunity for us.

When my wife and I landed at the airport, our daughter was there in all her glory to meet us, and although she had been there only a few months, she looked so different and had grown into a very glamorous young lady.

She had an air of confidence and beauty inside and out, and of course she was overjoyed to see us on Aussie turf and know that we were hers so she could be our tour guide extraordinaire.

There is one part of this wonderful story that I feel obligated to tell our readers. When our daughter decided to go to Australia, my wife and I thought it was too far away.

If something happened, it would take so long to get there or for her to get home, but our daughter had made up her mind that this was where she wanted to go, and there was just no stopping her. When she started preparing for her long trip, she had planned to travel with a male school friend (nothing romantic, just a friend), but he was a rich boy who traveled all over the world. When it was time for our daughter to travel, she found out that her travel mate was in Europe with his parents and would not be joining her until a week later, which give my wife and me great concern because now she would be traveling to this distant land all by herself. I wanted to go with her to get her set up, but she wanted no part of that. She was a college junior and a very independent young woman who was very confident in herself. When she was preparing her travel arrangements, my wife and I went with her to a very reputable, well-known travel agency in the area where we lived and told the agent to make sure that she was going into a nice area and a nice hotel. The travel agent was great and very helpful. When all the arrangements were set and she was ready to go, my wife and I were very uneasy letting her go alone, but she did not want to hear of me joining her. I guess this would not be in line with what an independent, and maybe overconfident, nineteen-year-old young woman has in mind.

My wife and I took her to the airport and went as far inside the airport as we possibly could until we had to part and say goodbye. Only a parent truly understands how hard it is to part and say goodbye to a child who, although nineteen years old, is still your child, but for the most part teenagers do not see it that way.

When she took off, my wife was very sad and in tears. I have to admit I was not tearing up on the outside but was just as broken on the inside. Our baby daughter was off to a distant land where she knew no one and had no idea where she was going other than what the travel agent had told her and us. When she landed in Australia, she gave the address of the hotel to a taxi driver who took her to the wrong hotel with a similar name. When she got to the hotel desk, they did not have a reservation for her but had a vacant room and were willing to put her up. This hotel was not in a very good neighborhood, and she did not like the room. Then she looked at her reservation, which was for a different hotel, and realized that there had been a big mistake. She immediately went to see the concierge and told her what had happened—she was in the wrong hotel, which explained why she did not have a reservation there. The concierge was very nice and told her yes, she was in the wrong hotel, and went on to tell her that she would call a taxi that would take her to the right hotel, and she would also call the hotel to tell them what had happened and that Tara Scollans was on her way there. The concierge was so nice she did not charge her for the night—so helpful in every way.

When Tara got to the right hotel and checked in, she found a phone booth and called home and told us what had happened. I could detect a lot of stress in her voice, and I asked her if she was all right, at which time I could detect a slight break in her voice. I was devastated and angry with myself for letting her go by herself and questioned my own common sense. How could I have let her go all alone?

My wife, who was listening to this part of the conversation, was more than devastated when she heard the whole story. I told my daughter that I would fly out the next morning and help her to get acclimated.

She did not want to hear of that. I also told her if she was not totally happy to make arrangements and take the first flight home, or I would make the arrangements for her.

Needless to say, she wanted no part of that either. Now she was getting back her composure and became very strong very quickly after realizing that we were probably in much worse shape than she was, although I made sure that I did not show any emotion, only concern for her well-being and her safety.

Our daughter is very strong and very independent, and it was very important for her to get through this rough patch on her own terms. I admire her for her courage and chutzpah. As a young man I had come to America all alone, which was similar in some ways, but it is easier for a young man than a young woman. She assured me that she would be all right, and I told her to get an international cell phone right away and to call us every day, or as often as she could, and we could also be in touch with her. This was good for her and good for us, especially my wife. Tara was concerned about the cost of the international phone, but I assured her that we did not care what the cost was—we wanted her to be able to be in touch with us where she could call any time and we could call her, which also made my wife very happy and lessened her worry, at least to some degree. I made it clear I did not care what the cost was to take care of herself and to eat well, and she promised me that she would eat well and take good care of herself. My wife and I gave her a credit card with no spending limit where the charges would go directly to our account so she did not have to worry about having enough money, and in addition she opened a bank account with check-writing privileges so she could pay for her rent and other needs.

Every day for the first few weeks, my wife and I would be on pins and needles waiting for her call. She was wonderful and always called. For my wife and me, the first day and a half waiting to hear from her seemed to be the longest waiting period in our lives.

After the first day's confusion, she was fine and was very upbeat, getting around all over the place to the point where she had blisters on her feet from walking.

On about the second or third day, she met some Aussie college student friends at Sidney University whom she quickly befriended, and they were wonderful and very good to her.

This made us very happy and more at ease, knowing she was adjusting very well to her new abode. Hearing that she had already made friends was like a breath of fresh air. In no way were we helicopter parents that hovered over our children. However, when their safety and well-being came into play, we would want to be there in every possible way, and that is what parents are supposed to do—at least that is what my wife and I were raised to believe. A week later her rooming friend landed, and now she was in control. She knew her way around, had a bunch of new wonderful young friends, and was taking her rooming friend all over—he was amazed at how much she had gotten to know about the city of Sidney in one week. Letting her go across the world all by herself was one of my biggest regrets, and still to this day I get shivers up my back when I think of her first few days there and that first phone call after she arrived. In my opinion I made a major error in judgment, but with that said, all is well that ends well, and I think as a result she was better, stronger, and yet more confident in herself after a somewhat harrowing experience. Now that time has taken care of everything, we are all very proud of her and how quickly she adjusted to her new environment. At the end of the day, this was a tremendous experience for her in every respect, where she learned how to survive in a foreign land thousands of miles away and made all kinds of new wonderful friends.

She loved Australia and traveled all over the country and to New Zealand and participated in all kinds of activities, including bungee jumping, scuba diving, surfing, and a variety of other activities and events.

When my wife and I went to visit her, although she had been there only a few months, we were so amazed by how much she had matured with her beautiful suntan and outward-looking appearance that made us so proud of her.

Her boyfriend, Mike, now her husband, whom she met in college, also visited her, and they traveled all over. He too loved Australia, and having her there before him, as with my wife and me, enriched Mike's Aussie experience; he too traveled to so many places and learned so much about the country. The down under had always intrigued me, and I am so glad I had the opportunity to see so much of it; indeed, it was a once-in-a-lifetime treat. My wife and I are sure having us and her boyfriend, Mike, visit where she was the tour guide extraordinaire is a story she can share with their children and friends.

CHAPTER 40

Freelancing

When I got back from Australia, I started a new gig in engineering consulting for a small pharmaceutical company and got a three-month assignment where there were a lot of problems and big challenges to overcome due to an FDA consent decree. Many of the issues were engineering- and mechanical systems–related, which was an area where I had extensive experience and could add significant value. The executive director of engineering for this rather small, niche pharmaceutical company knew me from a trade organization that I was very active in where he had become very familiar with my background and experience dealing with the FDA. We always hit it off well, and he contacted me and offered me a three-month temporary assignment that lasted fourteen months. When a company gets in trouble with a regulatory agency, the blame game goes into full motion, and everything becomes very political. There are always those who try to take advantage of the situation and start jockeying for power. During my time as a consultant there, I had to be careful to dodge the political minefields while doing my job.

I was brought in to fix the engineering, equipment, and documentation problems, while there were others who did not want the problems fixed. There was one engineer who was brought in as a project manager from one of the company's other facilities to assist in managing the engineering compliance issues; however, he had a hidden agenda and was scamming to get a big job by undermining others who were trying to work through the problems. Although I made great progress and took care of everything that required fixing, the saboteur had a more cynical agenda. His approach was to replace all the equipment with state-of-the-art new systems that would cost tens of millions.

His motive was that he would head up the project and more than likely get a promotion.

However, this would require shutting down much of the manufacturing plant for an undetermined amount of time and would require revalidation of all new equipment and procedures, which could take an indefinite amount of time, since the validation process alone is extremely time intensive and many times engineering adjustments are required to meet very stringent requirements. The plant could be offline for a year or more. Since there was no reason to replace all the equipment, it was more about making the necessary repairs and adjustments to meet the existing validation requirements and properly document all the details and proven results. I ended up sending a scathing report that challenged the scammer's recommendation to the CEO, the COO, and the engineering department, and as a result a high-end engineering consulting company that specialized in pharmaceutical manufacturing equipment design was commissioned to evaluate my report versus the scammer's recommendations.

The engineering consulting company agreed with my findings, and as a result the overzealous scammer ended up shooting himself in the foot and was sent packing back to where he came from in a hurry. However, the cynical saboteur did irreversible damage to a number of good, honest, hardworking, dedicated people in the engineering department. However, the company also had a major restructuring due to the FDA consent decree. New management personnel, including a new CEO, were brought in, and they brought in all their own people, and all the existing management personnel who had any connection with the consent decree were let go. My assignment ended when my boss, who had brought me in, moved on to another company; otherwise, I would have been there much longer.

For me another opportunity became available at a medical device company. I would be working for a service contracting company as an account manager responsible for the facility.

This position became available due to a situation where the client was not happy with the service being provided by the existing account manager and wanted someone new who had the experience to do the job and to take it to the next level. The outsourcing contract company, which was one of the largest in that business, had worked for me, providing similar types of services, at my previous job.

I had a very good relationship with one of the district managers, who had given my name to the other district manager covering the account where the existing account manager had been replaced.

The outsourcing company was about to lose the account when they approached me to take it over. We came to terms, and I was willing to give it a go for one year. Soon after I got there, it became very apparent that the real problem was not the outsourced account manager. When I took over the position, the existing account manager was demoted and was assigned to me on a temporary basis as part of the handover; this account manager was a brilliant engineer with very good overall skills. The real issue, I soon discovered, was the client's department director, who was totally psychotic and was almost impossible to deal with. He trusted very few people and was extremely paranoid and thought that everyone was out to get him. You never knew what type of mood he was going to be in or when he was going to fly off the handle and attack for no reason. He acted like a psychopath, and most of the contract workers were scared of him. He relished having power over subordinates and contractors he controlled where he could wield his authority, intimidate others, and fire people on the spot for no reason. There was something very sadistic about him. He enjoyed having the ability to fire people indiscriminately and display very poor taste, and he had little trust or respect from those he controlled. The previous account manager moved on after about six months, when he found a new in-house job as an engineering project manager. This was another, larger pharmaceutical company, and he thanked me for giving him an excellent personal recommendation. The psychopath director had an unpredictable personality, and you always had to be extremely careful in everything you said and had to make sure that you never brought him bad news. It was very important to praise him and assure him how great and important he was. His wife worked for the same company in another building. She was a nice-looking woman, and he was forever checking up on her. When his wife would go to lunch with someone, he would be on edge until she got back, and she had to call him and keep him assured that she was with other women.

I would take him out to lunch on a regular basis and give him all kinds of positive reinforcement and assurances and make him believe that I was in his corner and would do whatever was necessary to make him look good. His boss was a very nice man with a level-headed personality. He and I had a very good relationship, but he too wanted to hear only good news and had no interest in what was going on in his area of responsibility as long as his subordinates kept the monkey off his back. Although I turned the operation around and got rid of all the trouble employees and brought in competent people who were good workers and made the director look good, he would make comments that he did not trust this one or that one and that maybe we should get rid of them with no just cause or reason, with no other reason than that he did not trust them. I would have to work with him to raise his level of trust in those he was not sure about and reassure him that they were good employees who were adding value to the operation. In general, he was very pleased with the people that I would hire and the tone I set, which was for the most part very positive and results oriented, which he liked and made him look good until again the bogeyman would again appear in his psychotic mind. With great success getting things done and organizing a great team in spite of the trials and tribulations, I had no intention of staying and was making plans for my exit when I got a call from a small pharmaceutical company's HR manager, who was looking for a hands-on engineering project manager that had the wherewithal to solve complex engineering problems and asked if I was interested. The HR manager said he got my name from a colleague of mine who gave a raving recommendation.

However, to this day I have no idea who that person was that recommended me, and the HR manager would not tell me. I had worked out an agreement with the HR manager on the terms and compensation, which I ended up being very pleased with, when he made me an offer that exceeded my expectations. I accepted the offer, and the next day I gave my notice to the service provider's district manager, who went into a panic and told me not to tell the crazy client. The district manager went on to say, "Your leaving is going to be a disaster, since you are the only account manager that he ever trusted and could work with. He never complained about you but would say once in a while 'I hope that you guys [the service provider company] are taking care of Kevin.'" Which he assured him that he was, although that was not exactly true. The service provider's margins were so thin there was little they could do in the way of additional compensation, but otherwise they treated me well and would give me positive feedback on the client and full operational autonomy, which was very nice. I also knew that the contract providers could give to me only what was in the client contract. The contract provider tried to talk to me into staying and came up with a counteroffer that was pretty good, and apparently the client was willing to kick in a little extra contract funding. However, the bottom line was that I did not want to deal with this psychotic client who could blow up and go ballistic at any moment anymore. He was like a walking time bomb every day, especially when the bogeyman was chasing him, which was most of if not all the time.

The contract provider knew that if I left, they were in big trouble with the client, and they also knew that I knew how to handle this unpredictable sociopath and put up with his erratic behavior. The previous seven account managers had failed; some had lasted only a month before the client asked to have them removed from the site like they did something terribly wrong, and others just quit on the spot when they realized what they were dealing with. At least two of the previous account managers were very capable and good, according to one of our best supervisors who worked for him. He indicated that the psychopath did not trust either of them, but then he did not really trust anyone, and I am sure he also had plenty of doubts about me, but I was able to keep him somewhat subdued.

I pretty much knew how to deal with him, or at least it seemed that way, and how long that would have lasted is anyone's guess, and therefore it was better to get out while the getting was good.

Now that he finally had someone who apparently knew how to work with him, this was a real quagmire for the outsourcing company that the client did not trust, and in particular my boss, the district manager. When the DM told the client that I would be leaving, he went ballistic, as they knew he would, and told them that if they could not retain me, they would lose the contract, which was up for renewal in six months. The DM did not want to go through the awful task of going through another seven account managers, or who knows how many, to get someone who could work with him and stay. However, at the end of the day, the psychopath did not want to have to take a chance on a new contract provider that he knew nothing about, and as a result the existing contract provider stayed on. However, the contract provider's contract was cut back such that they would provide only some of the services, and the remainder would be outsourced to other contractors. Keeping the existing service provider on made way for a safety net in case a new contractor might not work out, which was almost a guarantee, knowing the client.

This was a $30 million operational budget that this incompetent, crazy operations director was responsible for. I could never understand his boss, a very nice, relatively young man in his late forties or early fifties, a professional engineer and a VP with a master's in business. How he could not see how dysfunctional this crazy department head had baffled me to the point where I often questioned what the psychopath had on him.

This guy had worked for the Operations and Engineering VP for seven years, which was hard to fathom.

This too was a great and very successful company that was very generous to its direct employees, with a very lucrative compensation package and benefits program, so there was a very low personnel turnover rate. The company PR people and HR liked to boast about their very low turnover rate, which was a very attractive benefit for new hires. I could have gone direct but wanted to move on and be as far away from the psychopath as possible. Now that I was in my late sixties, although I loved working, I preferred to work as a consultant, where there were fewer strings attached and more autonomy. This way, if I did not like what was taking place, I was free to move on and not get caught up in what sometimes seemed to be a dysfunctional organization, where people were bent on sniping at each other with venom and resentment that did not have a clear path to a successful outcome. I had a great run and a great reputation in the industry; there were a number of professional engineering organizations that I served on as the head. My skills were in pretty high demand, so I could move on to the next gig, and it was a nice liberating feeling to get away from this crazy clown who could blow up at any minute for no just reason, so that every day you had to be on guard.

And then there was his propensity to fire good people, who were difficult to replace, on the spot, with no just reason other than that he did not like or trust them.

CHAPTER 41

The Next Gig

I was glad for the opportunity to move on. Although I had liked the job and the challenge of working in this dysfunctional environment, it was time to move on. As I got into the new position, I was finding out that this company was somewhat dysfunctional. It also had many problems, including people problems. They had an old, dilapidated manufacturing facility that they had converted into a biotech clean room facility that they had just built and were having trouble validating the facility production process to meet FDA regulatory requirements. The new manufacturing suite HVAC and utilities systems had issues, including the poorly designed, undersized ductwork from a previous manufacturing operation that had been reused and was not in compliance with the ISO clean room classification standards that were required for this type of facility. The installation contractors had taken shortcuts, and the in-house company engineering director had no idea what was going on. The incompetence of the company in-house engineering director became a major problem. He had hired and fired three engineering project managers before I came along. Each engineering project manager tried to get the systems validated and failed miserably, and then the director fired each of them to protect his own butt. At this point the COO took over the project himself and hired me to run the project and to do whatever had to be done to get the systems validated. It was not until the first week, after I started, that I found out that the engineering director had fired the three previous engineering project managers because they were not able to get the new facility online or validated. The new manufacturing suite startup completion date was eighteen months behind the scheduled due date, and the COO, who answered to the CEO, was under fire and had taken the project away from the incompetent engineering director, which put him on the hot seat. Although the COO had a PhD in chemical engineering and an MBA from one of the Ivy League schools, he did not have a clue about how things should work, let alone how to correct the many in-depth technical problems.

When I started to dig in and troubleshoot the many startup problems, they turned out to be monumental, and the COO did not want to hear about the real facts.

The big problem for the COO was that over time he had given several different stories to the CEO. He had sidelined the engineering director who had fired the three previous engineering project managers and blamed everything on the incompetence of these three project managers this was all on the COO's watch and the project was eighteen months behind schedule. The COO was no better off than where he started. Now another new Engineering director, hired as a project manager, to evaluate the situation just like the three previous ones did. After a preliminary investigation of the issues at hand, I issued a written report and called for a follow-up meeting for discussion. The meeting included the COO and all the appropriate parties, including the heads of manufacturing, validations, and quality. This was a very frosty meeting where there was a lot of blame going around and a very angry COO. Knowing the sensitivity and volatility of the situation, I put together a very detailed, fact-driven presentation depicting all the problems in detail based on my own personal experience and with backup photos and documentation to prove my point. In addition, I proposed an engineering solution, a timeline, and an approximate cost estimate based on a preliminary review. When I presented the facts, the COO, who was my boss, went ballistic and started shouting, "We need a quick fix and not a revamp of the complete system." He went on to say, "You want to redesign the whole system, and that is not going to happen." The project was already 50 percent or more over budget, and therefore this proposal was not acceptable.

I stood my ground and very calmly told him, "If you want this system up and running, validated, and operational, this is what is required."

I went on to say, "I cannot perform any magic, and I wish there were a quick and easy fix, but keep in mind that it is the current situation that got this project in such trouble to start with."

Trying to make a system work that is undersized and not designed properly to meet ISO clean room classification standards and the validation requirements is a recipe for failure; you are throwing good money after bad. I went on to say that it was obvious the previous engineers working on the project had had no idea what was required. They had used contractors to get them what they thought was needed to make the system work, and as a result the company had ended up with a complete cataclysm. The COO did not like my tone or comments but knew that I was speaking from experience and with sound technical authority. To some extent I was saying the reason for the problems was that the company had not been willing to spend the money to have it done right the first time. There is a price you pay to do something right, and that was what I would do if they approved this plan.

He yelled some more and said he had heard all these stories before. He went on to yell, "How do I know that you know what you are doing?"

My answer was "I have the experience and knowledge necessary to make things work." I went on to say, "Here are people you can call to verify what I can do. I have the ability and track record to solve complicated engineering systems problems and know how to make systems work." I went on to say, "If I cannot make it work, then I will quit. I am not a quitter, but you will not have to fire me, and if you do not think I can do the job, I will quit right now."

With that he looked at me with a scared look on his face and said, "You are not going to walk out, are you?"

My answer was "I am not a quitter, but as I already said, I cannot work magic."

Then he wanted more assurance that I would stay the course to make it work, and I gave assurances that I was committed to the project and made it clear that I was a no-nonsense guy. He asked what I meant by that, and I replied, "I think you know" and left it at that.

Then he asked me to give him my final plan, cost, and timeline. He promised he would call me as soon as he could get it approved and said he was putting his trust in me to deliver the project. As soon as he got my plan, he called me and asked me to write up a capital appropriation and to expedite the project.

The total cost to mitigate the problems was $550,000 plus 10 percent override, which brought it up to $605,000. He approved, and now the ball was in my court to get the job done and to get the promised results within the given timeline. I hit the ground running. While going through the approval process, I had gotten all the contractors lined up and ready to go. I also had met with the internal procurement people and made them aware of the project and the urgency to get the work done within the given timeframe. Once the capital appropriation was signed off on, the project moved forward like clockwork in a race to meet or beat the timeline. There were many ups and downs during the mitigation process, and it became very evident that all the systems were undersized or at best very marginal; however, I pushed to squeeze out every possible little bit by making the necessary adjustments—installing booster fans and so on—to meet the required criteria. I had sixteen weeks to deliver the goods, and we worked long, hard hours to get to the finish line two days before the deadline. Before I'd joined the company, my wife had made plans to visit Ireland for my mother's eightieth birthday.

My taking the job had been contingent on my being able to make the two-week trip to Ireland, which was midway through the project. When the COO found out that I was going to be away for two weeks, he had a conniption and yelled, "You will have to cancel those plans until the job is complete."

I stood my ground and said, "This is a family trip to visit aging parents, and no, I am not about to cancel the trip and disappoint my wife, three children, and mother, who are all looking forward to this trip. However, I can assure you that the project will go on per the timeline and I will be available by phone as needed."

He did not particularly like what he felt was somewhat arrogant but knew he had little choice. He also knew that I did not need the job and had other opportunities waiting but that I loved the challenge and had promised to deliver. He was Cuban and loved the Irish and had many Irish friends that he would say never let him down, and maybe that gave him a little comfort. While I was on vacation, we did not miss a beat and stayed with the timeline.

Upon satisfactory completion of the upgrade, I called a meeting and spelled out the results to senior management and took them on a walking tour of what was accomplished. The next step was to work with the validations and quality control groups to perform a validating approval on each of sixty different components, which was required by good manufacturing standards (GMP) before the system could be put into operation. That was paramount. I had a very good rapport with the quality and validations team, and I worked side by side with each of them while making the necessary adjustments along the way to successful approval. During the process, the quality and validations groups appreciated my presence as a technical assistant that knew every nut and bolt in the project and acted as a mentor in many ways. The COO was very pleased and was very generous with his praise, but if the approach had not delivered the required results, there would have been a high price to pay—not just for me but also for the COO, who had no idea of the project's scope and complexity. The next step was to do a production run and again validate the production product results. Having a great relationship with the VP of quality and including him in every step of the mitigation process, where he understood and we both learned a few things on the way, made for a great team and a little comradery—in the evening we would have a beer together.

Sharing knowledge in both directions and working as a team while knowing that no one can do it all alone is a great recipe for success. It is during these types of very demanding times that engineering project managers earn their worth.

When engineers fail to deliver the goods, there is little future left within the organization, and they had better have their résumés ready for the marketplace.

After all this, there came an announcement from senior management that the manufacturing facility that I had successfully worked so hard to get running was now closing down within twelve months because the manufacturing operation would start moving to another state, where they had a plant and cheaper labor and the cost to manufacture the product would drop by 25 percent. This was part of the company's overall effort to come up with synergies to reduce the unit cost of manufacturing goods.

This was a major shock to all of us, including my boss; however, the company offered a very generous package to all its key in-house people who could be counted on for a smooth transfer of the product and all associated equipment. Although I was a consultant, the COO, who now is my friend, put me on the payroll as a direct employee with the same consultant hourly rate in order to include me in the severance package which consisted of fourteen months' pay after the facility officially closed and all the products were successfully transferred. He wanted to make sure I stayed around in the event of any technical issues on either end, at which point he would have me jump in and pull the rabbit out of the hat. It was the COO's job to make sure the transfer of all products went smoothly and in accordance with FDA compliance. By the plant's closing date,

I was sixty-six years of age. The timing for retirement was perfect, and with fourteen months' severance pay, I was smiling.

While we were in the process of transferring the product and equipment to the new location, there was plenty of downtime. In the downtime, I found myself looking for work to keep me busy. It was then that the next big challenge was just waiting around the corner.

There was a research and development facility four miles from the manufacturing plant, where they were in the process of starting up a new high-tech research pilot plant.

The facility was already one year behind schedule, another quagmire for the COO. When it came time to start up the equipment, there were major problems in the engineering design and equipment selection. The project was a $60 million project that was already $10 million over budget and over a year behind schedule for the startup.

The COO asked me if I would be willing to help to get the systems online and ready for startup. He knew by now that I was really very good at starting up complex facilities and that I knew how to dissect problems, improvise, and get them resolved. I was elated and agreed to take on the project.

I immediately dove in, and the more I got involved, the more I realized that this was déjà vu. Just like the previous Manufacturing facility debacle. There were major design issues and omissions in the design. The problem was that I was between a rock and a hard spot and could not talk freely about the magnitude of the problem, since the problems were all on my bosses' watch. The same engineering director who was sidelined off the biotech manufacturing project due to incompetence was now on this project and answered to the COO, and since the project was way over budget and timeline, there was no money to fix the problems, so the way forward would be very difficult. With the in-depth knowledge that I had in this type of work, I had quickly learned that I had to develop a detailed list of the issues, including a basic scope of the work that it would require to correct each issue, including an approximate cost and timeline. Again, this was a major political quagmire for my boss.

By this time. I had developed a very good relationship with the COO—he called me *buddy*, and I really liked him and enjoyed working for him. With a PhD in chemical engineering and an MBA, he was very bright, a very quick study, and always on the ball, which made him very easy to work with. The worst boss you can work for is a dumb one where he never knows what he needs to know. I had to walk a fine line in my approach to addressing each of the issues. My boss was great in every way but not good technically or hands-on, and so I filled in the voids by preparing technical status reports.

When he would go in front of the board of directors, he was well prepared and would laugh and say, "Buddy, they are going to think that I know what I am doing." He was so appreciative to have me there to work out these highly complex engineering technical equipment and very sophisticated control interface problems.

He now knew that I would come up with creative ways to solve each technical issue and the enormous omissions. This was a very challenging time, but I always deal well with stress and enjoyed the work—I buried myself in the detail.

My boss called me into his office one morning and said, "I am so glad that I have you on board, and you are doing great work." He knew that I had the technical resolve to pull the rabbit out of the hat and make things work, and for that he was forever grateful.

Now that he had fully empowered me to do whatever was necessary to get the job done, I was fully in control, and good things started to happen. I took one piece of equipment at a time and determined how each piece of equipment functioned in the overall process and then worked on making it work according to the basis of the engineering design. To make this approach work, I had to collaborate with user groups and department heads to determine what they expected at the process operation level. This approach worked very well, and I was able to make sense of what was there.

The research PhD user group heads and people in general started to gain trust in my ability to make things work, and suddenly there was great support for what had to be done, which brought resolution to all the issues. The user group department heads were all brilliant chemistry and biology PhDs who would say at meetings, "It is nice to have someone who understands and knows what they are doing for a change." While I was solving problems, the original engineering project manager, who was at the director level and was originally responsible for the overall project, was pulled off and given special projects. This guy was very envious of my approach and my ability to solve problems and that I knew how to connect the dots. He could not understand why my boss did not put me with him and have us work together to complete the project. He was a professional engineer with an MBA from the Wharton School. With all the great credentials, he had a reputation for being totally incompetent. He had never successfully completed a project and was always taking credit for other people's work.

The reason he lasted as long as he did was that he was very cunning and shrewd and a big talker who would take credit for other people's work when reporting to his boss. Knowing how this character operated, I made it clear to my boss that the only way I would take on the project, , was if he was completely off the project since he was not capable of bringing anything meaningful to the table and would only get in my way, and my boss totally agreed.

He assured me that I would have complete control and autonomy and that there would be no interference or roadblocks that would impede or slow the job down. Although there were many trials and tribulations due to his incompetence in the design process, I was able to overcome these by redesigning and getting all the equipment started up and online within the promised timeline. Now the boss realized how incompetent this project manager, who was actually a director, really was.

When he allowed the engineering design company and the contractors to place equipment on an open floor without blueprints, P&IDs, or engineering scope of work details, his boss had no choice but to terminate him. By now the manufacturing transfer of all products was satisfactorily complete. The pilot plant was also up and running, and I was in a nice position to collect the generous promised severance and bonus and move on to the next phase of my life.

To stop working is something that does not come easy for me. I love working and enjoy the day-to-day interaction and comradery of the workplace.

For me work provides a challenge, a sense of purpose, and stimulation; there is fulfillment that is hard to walk away from. I cannot remember a time from the age of fourteen on the family farm when I was not working from dawn to dark, always having many irons in the fire at the same time. However, looking at life realistically, I know there comes a day when everyone has to hang up the tools and slide into a more leisurely life.

This is when you have to become creative, using whatever toys and tools or hobbies you have in your tool bag to fill in the big void left by leaving the life you enjoyed, for the most part the only life you know. The good news for those of us who love to work is that there are many things to turn our attention to, such as all the neglected projects around the house that are waiting to get done. I love the outdoors and enjoy outdoor projects and outdoor activities, including golf, jogging, and skiing. My life accomplishments include positions held that went far beyond my wildest dreams. Like most people I have had ups and downs, but fortunately the ups far surpassed the downs, and I have had a very fulfilled life, which I am forever grateful for. I like to say that I've had a charmed life, and if I had to live it all over again, there is very little, if anything, I would change, no matter how many options there were to choose from.

In life there are many options that we can choose from, and to a great extent these choices determine one's destiny. It is important when we choose an option or a path in life to stay with it and to give it everything that we have got in order to be successful. It is also important to leverage all aspects of our expertise and become as diversified as possible by spawning out in as many areas as possible in order to grow and to establish a broad-based career path. Then there is the question of whether you want to be the one who knows a little about a lot or a lot about a little.

CHAPTER 42

First House

When I bought my first house, I had no money but had great friends and people who wanted to help me get into a house. I was in the U.S. Army and ready to be discharged into civilian life, with plans to get married a few months after I got out.

My initial plan was to rent a place until I would get enough money to have a down payment. While home on a weekend, I saw a house for rent in the classifieds section of the local newspaper that was within the range that I could afford, so I called the telephone number, and who was on the other end of the phone line but my next-door neighbor in civilian life, who was a builder and realtor. When he heard my voice and what I had to say, he replied, "Kevin, you are not going to rent this house—you are going to buy it." This man was one of God's noble men; there was just no better. He was always reaching out to help young people. He said to me, "You are going to buy this house," at which time I said, "I am a GI with very little money to buy a house."

The house was a little summer bungalow that was converted to be an all-year-round residence. The house looked like a dollhouse situated on a beautiful large lot. Again, when I told my realtor I did not have money to buy this house, he replied, "Don't worry—I will get you into the house, and it will be yours." Two old, retired ladies who lived in Jersey City owned the summer home, and my friend, the selling realtor, was managing the property for them, but they wanted to sell it because they were too old and no longer using it as a summer residence. With the realtor's assistance, being a veteran, I was able to get a zero-down-payment mortgage, and my realtor got me a great deal on the closing. There was no application fee, and he kicked in his commission as the buying agent he attorney that I used was a man I had used to handle some previous family legal work before I went into the army, another wonderful man.

After my attorney finished the closing legal process, I asked him how much I owed him.

He replied, "You have served your country; therefore, there is no legal charge except for the title insurance and the property survey, where I got you the best possible deal available." I was shocked that an attorney would do such a kind deal for me, and needless to say, after that he got all my business and everyone else that I could send his way until he retired from his law business and as a municipal judge.

I was so happy to be able to get into my first house, and now it was time to have my future wife come out from Yonkers, New York, where she lived and see our home. She was a little disappointed when she saw how small the house was, but I pointed out the beautiful large double lot and said that I would expand the house as we would get money. This was one of the greatest breaks that I ever got, and within a year after moving in, we doubled the size of the house, doing most of the work ourselves, which was a wonderful experience with my wife, who was pregnant at the time with our first child but was helping me every step of the way. When the construction got to the roof, which was a relatively low-pitched roof, five inches on twelve, which is approximately a forty-degree pitch where you can walk without installing scaffolding, she was on the roof helping me to hang rafters and position sheets of three-quarter-inch plywood until our neighbor, who was like a family member and a wonderful friend, yelled at me for having my pregnant wife up on the roof working with me. She loved it, and we were a team, and in those days whenever I was working on the house or working on a car or truck, she loved to be part of it more than working in the house. These times were without any doubt the most wonderful and enjoyable days of our young lives, and I guess you could say we were still honeymooning. Great memories—and although we had no money other than the next paycheck, life was as good as it gets with a great sense of accomplishment.

CHAPTER 43

A Landlord

When I bought my first investment property, we again had no surplus money to invest. When the house next door came on the market for sale, I knew the house was in poor condition and could be bought for a reasonable price. I went directly to the owner and asked him how much he was asking for the house, and when he told me what the price was, I made an offer on the spot and told him that this was a sure deal where he did not have to worry about the deal falling through. Little did he know that we had very little money but were determined to put this deal together with whatever it would take?

The homeowner went home and told his wife about our offer, and she was eager to make a deal, since they were in the process of moving into another house on a lake where she had dreamed of living, where they could use their little boat, which they loved. Within an hour of my making the offer, he came over to our house and said it was a deal. We shook hands, and I told him that I would contact my attorney and draw up a contract, including all the legalese. He did not have much money either, and he asked me if he could use the same attorney that I was using, and I told him that I would check with my attorney, who was the same attorney who closed my first house. When I asked my attorney if the seller could use him as well, he said sure. Our attorney again gave us a great closing deal. The next evening, I told the seller he could use the same attorney, and I gave him his name and telephone number, and he was delighted because that saved him a few hundred dollars. I was not expecting such a quick response on the purchase and had to hustle to get the money. There was a new bank that had opened up in town just around the corner from where we lived, and the CEO was a friend of our realtor. When I went to the bank and asked for the CEO, who met with me, I told him who I was and my story about buying the house next door.

I told him about my realtor friend who had advised me to speak to him and then gave him a little background information, including my accomplishments. The first thing he said was "You are a pretty impressive young man, and I think we can work this out." I told him that I was an army veteran with distinction, and he liked that, since he was a retired army major who had spent twenty years in the service, and I was off to a good start. I told him I did not have much money, so he said, "You are going to need money to do upgrades and closing." I said yes, and he added $5,000 for fixup and closing money, including the full mortgage amount. This was just great; I could start work and have a little money to work with. We hit it off well, and I was saying all the right things, and he gave me the feeling that he trusted me, so I walked out of the bank with a commitment for a full mortgage plus, which was great for an investment property. Now I knew that if this deal went through, I would need the first month's mortgage to stay ahead. I knew that I would not have a penny left over after closing except for what was left of the $5,000 fixup money. I knew the only way I could pull this off was to advertise the house for rent in the local paper a month or more before closing.

Fortunately for us we got a young couple with a child who were being transferred from the Kennedy airport to Morris County so one of them could work as an airport control tower operator on a two-year job assignment and needed a place to rent within the price range that we were asking. The new tenants were lovely people and stayed for the full two-year assignment, which gave us enough time to get our feet on the ground, and in the meantime, we did a lot of upgrades to the outside of the house, which made the property much more attractive, so I could increase the new rent by a significant amount. The increase in rent created a positive cash flow, and we were on our way to become successful landlords. Later on, we bought other properties that were in poor condition and also fixed them up to rent for a period before selling them.

When we got the places fixed up, we rented them for a period of time and eventually sold them for a nice profit. There was one tenant in particular that I will always remember that rented what we called the Lake House, a small bungalow that overlooked the local lake.

The tenants were a nice young couple, newlyweds with no children and ideal tenants—or so we thought. The father of the male tenant was a local accountant who wrote out the first check for the first two months' rent and the security for two additional months, which was great, and we were off to a good start. Approximately three months into the one-year lease, there was no rent check coming, so I called their telephone number but did not get an answer. After placing a number of calls and leaving messages with no callbacks, I decided to go directly to the house with the intention of ordering them out of the house. All my intentions to order them out quickly changed after

I knocked on the door and out came this huge man, about six foot six and about three hundred pounds, with a red bandanna on his head; he looked mean and gruff. He asked me "what the F I wanted", and when I asked him if I could speak to the tenant, he said, "He does not live here, and you should get the F out of here as quick as you can," and he slammed the door in my face. There was a long set of fieldstone stairs with about twenty-two risers from the front door to the street below—I could just see myself being hurled down the twenty-two steep steps out on to the street below. This was a scary thought, and I was glad to get out of there in one piece. I smelled marijuana and expected that there were drugs in the house. The next morning, I called the local police chief, and sure enough the police chief, a great guy, told me that the house was under surveillance. I also filed an eviction notice, which was successfully delivered by the sheriff's department. Two days before the court hearing, they vacated the house, and they did not show up in court, where the judge processed the eviction and told me that I could re-rent the house after forty-eight hours.

There was a friend of mine whom I had done some home-improvement work for in previous years, and we had gotten to know and respect each other. My friend also wanted to get into the real-estate market and buy homes that needed some work, fix them up, and flip them.

He thought that this was a great business, and he begged me to let him in on one of my deals. Sometimes you do things with friends that do not make a whole lot of business sense. This was one of them. I bought an old, run-down two-family house in in a very rural area and let my friend in on the deal as a partner. The house needed a ton of work inside and outside;

it would have been almost as easy to knock it down and build from scratch. I tackled the project, and my partner was of little help, since he had no construction or renovation experience, and therefore I did all the work, including the hiring of contractors when necessary to complete the renovation within a reasonable time frame. When the project was complete, the market was very soft, so we decided to rent the two apartments. This was a rural area far away from the industrial areas, where the tenant clientele was not the best and many of them were Section 8, but we had to rent the place in order to pay the mortgage. My partner, an attorney, came from a very well-to-do family and was financially independent and was in no hurry to rent, but of course I was, since I had to pay half the mortgage and could not afford to have the place empty, so I rented both units and started to collect the monthly rent. After about three months, the second-floor tenant stopped paying the rent, and I called up my partner, the attorney, who did family and real-estate law, to start eviction proceedings, but he saw no rush and asked me to give her some time. My reply to him was "Are you turning the tables on me? I am the friendly Irishman, and you are the successful Jewish lawyer who is supposed to have that dog-kill-dog instinct when it comes to business. He laughed and thought that was the funniest thing he ever heard.

With that I immediately initiated an eviction notice, and when she got the notice, she moved out the next day, which was great, but she left the place in a mess, and I held back the deposit payment in order to pay for the cleanup and the back rent. My lawyer partner thought that was too harsh, but he went along with it when I told him he could give her his part of the deposit. My partner was a wonderful human being, and

I valued his friendship, so we agreed to sell the house and move on, which we did. We made a modest profit, and he was kind enough to compensate me for all my sweat equity, which made the investment a reasonable deal for me, not a big kill but OK.

Lesson learned: from that point on I did not include any investors on my projects. My partner and I continued to be friends, and I am sure he realized that this business was not as easy as it sounds and he was better off practicing law and taking care of his family investments. The business of fixing up houses and flipping them was very profitable when the market was right but there could also be significant financial risk if the market were to take a downturn. We did very well financially, but after a while it was time to move on to something else that was less labor intensive and involved less financial risk where one had to be timing the markets, which is always more luck than good judgment, since no one knows when markets are going to turn downward. The home-improvement business, the investment properties, and the engineering inspection business got us to where we were financially comfortable and could now get involved in other investments, such as the stock market, while holding on to a number of rentals that provided income to the point where we eventually became financially independent. My goal was always to be financially independent by the age of fifty-five so I could retire and take life easy. However, as I got closer to fifty-five, the desire to retire seemed to become less and less attractive. I began to realize that I loved to work and do a little investing, which became a hobby.

It seemed that the more irons I had in the fire, the better I liked it. My wife and children could never understand that side of me, and they would continually say, "You have worked hard all your life—now that you can afford to take it easy, why don't you retire?" But the older I got; the less attractive retirement seemed to be. What would I do with all that spare time? I love to golf, jog, and ski, but all that does not provide the same fulfillment that work does. Some would say I am a workaholic, and to some degree that may be true, but in my way of thinking, at the end of the day, whatever makes you happy and fulfilled is what is most important in order to get the most out of life. A wise man once said that if you love what you do you will never work a day in your life, and I could not agree more.

CHAPTER 44

Love What You Do

When I go to work, there is a purpose, there is the comradery of coworkers, and there are the challenges of everyday business, which I find stimulating and rewarding, especially in situations where there are technical problems that in many cases the team has not dealt with before. When one is managing a large number of people, there are always people issues, which can demand a lot of time. The people end of the business for the most part is one of the most important parts to get right—there can be a devastating impact if there is a bad decision or a bad outcome. You may feel that you have a good handle on technical issues, and that maybe is a strong point, but you must keep in mind that people issues will sink you much faster than technical issues if not handled properly. In the technical arena, there are always outside experts and consultants you can call on if you are not familiar with a particular technical problem who will have the unique expertise to solve problems. Knowing *whom* to call when dealing with a difficult technical problem and having the skills to work collaboratively with experts can be the key to getting the best results. No matter how strong one's technical skills are, it is important to recognize that no one person has all the answers all the time. Having strong technical skills as a manager is very important for gaining the respect of your technical staff and is a key factor in achieving successful results. I always loved the hands-on part of the job—it becomes addictive and hard to give up. There is no better feeling than knowing you can fix it when few others can, which to some extent can be egotistical and self-serving if not properly managed. Being a know-it-all in any line of work does not endear you to those around you, who, when you need to tackle the next major challenge, may take a back seat and assume that you are the one with all the answers. The collaborative approach, where everyone shares in the success of a project, is always the best approach.

Strong hands-on involvement energizes the spirits and the minds of others, which can be challenged if managed properly, and you will know who on your team can be called on to pull the rabbit out of the hat, and that does not always have to be you. Knowing and working with the best people on your team can be very rewarding. Working closely with your most technical people and mentoring while training and developing them to be the best of the best will benefit you as much as them.

It is always rewarding to be the one who pulls the rabbit out of the hat during critical situations that could have catastrophic outcomes for the operation if not effectively managed. I subscribe to the philosophy that when you love what you do and love working with the people on your team, you will never have to work a day in your life. I also believe that the love of work, like love of country, in many ways is a learned behavior that is bred and somewhat part of the genetic makeup. This quality and can-do mentality can also be seen in members of the team who always excel in everything they do, where there is pride that gives them almost a high. My father worked on the family farm up until the day he literally died at the age of seventy-seven, a great patriot who loved his country more than anyone I ever knew, loved his work, and most of all loved his family. All these qualities, in my way of thinking, seem to become learned behaviors, and offspring tend to have similar characteristics. The older I get, the more I see myself following in my father's footsteps, only in a different way, and now I see my children, too, are immersed in what they do. I am glad that my children love their work, and I think it is sad when you see young people who hate their work and, worse yet, do nothing about it other than complain. I cannot imagine going through life hating your work, day after day. Love your work, love your family, and love your country—that is when life is at its best.

When any of the above three items are not fulfilled, life can feel very empty.

This is where young people can stray into a troubled life, and as adults and leaders, we all have a responsibility to help the youth in every way we can. We can help by giving back what we learned from others along the way who were so generous in helping us in achieving a better and more fulfilled life. It is important to be generous in mentoring and sharing our knowledge and experience with the upcoming generation and being a positive force in their lives so that they too can excel and grow in their chosen fields to their full potential and dreams. Love of work is something we have to work at and develop, first by evaluating what we like to do, and when we come up with something that we feel we might enjoy, we should go for it. You must recognize it is only you who can make it happen and do whatever has to be done to make it happen. Making a better life never comes easy and, in most cases requires big commitments in education, self-discipline, and the necessary training; this is a very important message for the youth. Once you decide what type of career you wish to pursue, you will need to hit the ground running to be ready for the challenges that lie ahead. There is no easy road to a successful life unless you are born with a silver spoon in your mouth. You must be prepared to pay your dues at all levels and prove yourself to be better than your competition. On the basis of these beliefs, I recommend that you start preparing and developing a plan and a skill set that will fit your goals and will put you on your way to a successful career. Love of family comes pretty naturally to most people; however, when you are dealing with family, just like with people in general, there will always be the one who wants to challenge the status quo, and to some extent this person can be rapacious, always looking to be the top dog and creating friction and disparity among family members. Recognizing that we are all different and how boring life would be if we were all the same is a good place to start. It is our own individual qualities that make us who we are and that we know are most important.

When you take the high road and can be the arbitrator rather than the dissentious one, you will feel a lot more accomplished and somewhat rewarded. Love of country for most people is also a natural reaction to the place where one was born and raised; there is an etched linkage in one's brain that creates an attachment to one's place of birth that is somewhat the childlike attachment to one's mother. This attachment creates an inner defense mechanism where the love of country is so great that we will fight and die to protect the land of our birth. I would find it very difficult to trust a person who did not love their country. This is the reason why military veterans are on the top of the list when it comes to hiring by most companies large and small. When I was hiring staff, I always put military service at the very top of the list to be considered and valued in an applicant, providing that the veterans served their country honorably, and if they served with distinction, that weighed even that much higher. For the most part, those who serve with distinction are the go-getters and will perform no matter what the job is. Honoring our veterans and looking out for them is more than a national obligation—it should be everyone's obligation, since they have put their own lives on the line to protect all of us and our freedom. After the Vietnam War, there was a lot of whining about how the returning veterans were treated, and for the most part, the querulous never spent a day in the military. My brother was discharged from the army in 1967, and I was discharged in 1969. Maybe there was no ticker-tape parade, but I can say without any hesitation the welcome-home mat was everywhere, and since my fiancée and I were planning to get married shortly after my discharge, friends and neighbors were there to help at every turn, and the GI bill was fabulous. As for my brother, he has a similar story to tell, although he spent a year in the rice paddies and jungles of Vietnam, where his unit suffered big losses that he rationalizes could be expected in this type of war.

For the most part, he never talks about the bad times but always talks about the great comradery and friendships and great stories when on R&R with a big smile on his face—no whining and no resentment on his end either. When he came home, we had a huge party for him at one of our favorite Irish pub restaurants, where there was a full house—somewhere around two hundred people. There was an abundance of great food and everything you could drink; there was also a donation bucket for the veterans, and there were several hundred dollars donated. At the end of the night—actually early morning—I approached the owner of the premises, Bill, a noble man, and asked him what I owed. He replied, "This is on us—your brother served our country." Although we knew Bill well and his wife, whose brothers were our friends and had gone to the same school in Ireland, we could not accept this generous offer. The bill had to be very high because there was a full selection of good food, plus all you could drink and a three-piece band. I guess the cost back then would have been $1,000 to $1,500 or more. Again, when I approached Bill to pay the bill, he said, "You owe me nothing—your brother served his country, and now you are on your way to do the same, and this is just a little of our appreciation."

I went on to say, "I would not have asked you to do all this if I knew you were not going to charge."

"Well then," he said, "give me one hundred dollars, and I do not want to talk any more about it." The pouring out of generosity, where it seemed everyone wanted to be there for the young soldiers who had served or were serving their country, made me very proud of our adopted country and its wonderful people. If I were a young man, I would be honored and glad do it all over again. As for the reasons and politics of war, that is for the people we elect to public office to deal with and hope they are making the right decisions. There is no greater love for country than the will to fight and die to protect its freedom, honor, and glory. For those quislings who burn the flag, shame—they are not worthy of being American citizens.

CHAPTER 45

Volunteering

As a big believer in giving back to the community and civic causes that have given us so much, I felt it was time to get involved, so I became active in many civic and local government activities. My wife Kathleen and I, being both from Ireland, and me from so near to the Northern Ireland border, signed up to get involved with Project Children as area coordinators for our local area. From the 1980s through the 1990s, we were responsible for the placement of 25 to 30 children a year for about eight years, which adds up to somewhere between 250 and 300 children that came through the program and into our local area. Most of the children came from the war-torn parts of Northern Ireland and ranged in age from eight to fourteen. They were mostly Catholic and some Protestant and nondenominational children who were equally accepted and loved by all. My wife and I would recruit and approve host families that were interested in taking a child for the summer. This process was very involved so that we could make sure that the host families were suitable candidates and could take care of the child and welcome them into their home and family as one of their own. This was approximately an eight-week commitment during the summer. Over the years my wife and I hosted eight of the children, not including my wife's nephew and my nephew and niece, from Ireland, who also stayed with us for the summer. This was a wonderful experience and a wonderful period in our life where our three children got as much benefit from the program as the Irish children because they built lifelong, close relationships with their cousins and these children, who also spent the summers with us. Although the children of Project Children were very young, they had learned so much about their culture and the effects of the horrible war that it had robbed them of their childhoods. It was very important that the host family took the child to the church of their religious choice. It was stressed that the host family refrain from religious discussion; religion should not be a dinner-table topic unless the child raised the subject, which was very rarely the case, and if they did so the families were not to encourage the discussion. There was an orientation meeting that all host families were required to attend that went over all necessary details and how to deal with children when some of them might have been exposed to the traumas of war and could have nightmares and other issues. We had one host family whose child was not working out. Although the host family were very qualified, lovely people, the child was not happy. They had one child of their own, a girl who was two or three years older than the Project Children child, and they were very generous and good to their little visitor. They took their daughter and their visiting child to Disney World during the first week and were very generous, but all the little girl would do was cry. When they got back from Disney World, out of desperation they called my wife and me for help, which was the right thing to do as spelled out in the instruction packet given to them when they picked up the child. We invited them to come to our house, and we would talk to the little girl. The little nine-year-old girl's name was Angela, and she was a gorgeous little girl from a Protestant family who were also lovely people. When Angela arrived at our house, she instantly stuck like glue to our youngest daughter, who was around the same age. The two of them disappeared to the basement rec room, where they became inseparable, and when it was time to go home, Angela started to cry and wanted to stay with her newfound friend. This was a difficult situation, and all my wife and I could say to the host family was to leave her with us for a week and see how things worked out. The host family was devastated but happy that the little girl was now happy. The host family's daughter was older and for whatever reason did not connect with her visitor from Ireland. At the same time, we had a little nine-year-old Catholic boy, a little spitfire and very pro-IRA; his dad, a freedom fighter, was serving a jail sentence. For the first two weeks, the two did not communicate, but after a while, playing in the swimming pool, they broke the ice.

Now they both participated in a lot of fun activities that my wife organized and supervised, and the two became friends until it was time for them to go back home.

My wife and I sat the two of them down and praised them for how well they were getting along and how they were now friends. We went on to suggest that since they were both from Belfast they should get together when they get home, but both said, "Oh no, that would get us in big trouble." Sad but true—they had both been brainwashed in a hate culture where there were no winners. During this period, our two oldest children were attending Morris Catholic High School, but the little girl, Angela, hated the name Morris Catholic and would not say

Morris Catholic. An adorable, very sweet, innocent little girl, but that is what brainwashing of any type does to children. At that time, it cost Project Children $750 in airfare for each child, and then there was medical/emergency insurance for each child that was expensive. Project Children brought over nine hundred children to the United States. Most of the children went to families in the New York tri-state area, and a few went to Washington, D.C., and Boston. As area coordinators, we were expected to assist in raising funds to cover the cost of each child that came into our area.

My wife and I ran two major fundraising events, one a dinner dance where we would get three hundred or more in attendance, which was always a great success, and a high-end golf outing, which was always a big success, where large and small companies would buy a foursome with very generous sponsorship. We would have contests for getting closest to the pin and having the longest drive, with two high-end cars, one on each of the three-par holes. We also sold mulligans, which was a big moneymaker, for five dollars and three for ten. We would also raffle off big donations such as foursomes fully paid at high-end golf courses, golf clubs, golf bags, and so forth. There would also be a fifty-fifty where the winner would get half the take in another big moneymaker.

Many times, the well-to-do would be very generous winners and donate back their winnings.

Mulligans for five dollars and three for ten dollars were a big hit; we would make $2,000 to $3,000. The Project Children supporters were very generous, and there were a number of very generous large company sponsors.

There was one young very successful trades contractor, a friend, who would sponsor a beer cart consisting of a large four-seat golf cart with two kegs of beer and other beverages, driven by two young, very gorgeous girls, and they would bring in up to $2,000 to $3,000 in tips alone, which would go into the profits and then my friend would tell me, "Do not worry about the girls." He would take care of them. One was a niece, and the other was the daughter of close friends. Every year the golf outing would sell out, and we would have forty-four foursomes and end up turning away another ten foursomes who did not get their money in early enough. All the golf fundraising activities brought in thousands of dollars in profits. All of the above efforts involved a lot of work and effort. If a golf tournament is not managed correctly, it can lose money rather than make money, since the operational costs are very high. This was all very exciting and a wonderful time in our life, and our children were old enough to help in many ways, so we had a wonderful committee of hardworking, reliable workers. After having a number of very successful outings, we hired a golf management company that took over a lot of the mundane setup work, and recruiting golfers and fundraising became the primary responsibility of the golf chair and the committee. My wife was a tireless worker and did an extraordinary job putting the golf programs together and managing all incoming and outgoing accounts such as accounts payable and receivable, including dealing with the many issues that would come up on a daily basis. We were also responsible for the twenty-five to thirty children assigned to host families, should any issue arise, as well as our own three children.

The coordinators had to deal with everything from home-sick children to medical and personal issues and in some cases host-family issues, which for the most part, were very few but had to be dealt with whenever something came up.

I served on the township zoning board of adjustment for many years and chaired the board, which I enjoyed and which was a wonderful experience that prepared me well for things to come. I learned the ins and outs of how the town management system and the political system worked and were run, including a lot of valuable information about the local people and their communities. The zoning board of adjustment had an inter-esting makeup of people, each unique in their own way, with only one female, which was something I set out to change. The basic criteria for each board member involved evaluating each application and doing all the necessary due diligence in order to make a fair and equitable decision based on the zoning require-ments for the specific area while always taking into account the greater good. The diligent board members would visit the prop-erty to gain a full knowledge of it and the associated application in order to be better prepared to evaluate and make sound judg-ments. In addition, the diligent board members would look up similar applicable case law judgments in the land, using Cox Book in order to strengthen their position, when it came time to deliberate and vote on an application while keeping in mind that the BOA is a quasi-judicial body.

I am a huge believer in due diligence and fact-driven deci-sions, rather than waiting to see what fellow board members have to say, although sharing opinions and having open discussion to form consensus is a very important part of what is required of all board members. The well-informed board members that do their homework and dig deep to find the facts and necessary details are the heart of every board, and quickly gain respect and trust from their colleagues.

During my time on the zoning board, I learned a lot about procedures and how the township operated and the different levels of responsibility. There is a lot involved and a lot to know and learn about how the neighboring municipalities and the county boards come together in the zoning and planning process as needed. I also learned the ins and outs of the county political structure and how the county political system was intertwined with the local boards, which was very interesting. When the time was right, I decided to run for the town council, which was a four-year commitment.

Once elected to office, you can pretty much stay in office as long as you wish if you go along with the status quo and the party line, do not make waves, and support the old political oligarchs, but that is not who I am. I challenged the status quo and evaluated the merit of each decision in great detail, and with my technical background and time on the zoning board of adjustment, I was well prepared and had a high level of understanding of all functions of the local government. Then there are always those who like to hear themselves talk but bring nothing to the table—almost shameful. One of my major objectives as a fiscal conservative was to reduce property taxes; however, many of the council members were in bed with many of the local municipal services and did not want to hear about reducing services or any type of shared services that offered an excellent opportunity to reduce municipal operating costs. One council person was very adamant that he wanted all the municipal services to stay the same and fought constructive change just because the local fire department had responded to an emergency at his house. This kind of thinking is why we have runaway property tax across the state of New Jersey. Sharing services with neighboring towns and the county can significantly reduce operating costs. Failure to break this paradigm will continue to burden every property owner's tax into the foreseeable future.

In politics everything is local, and so is reducing property tax, and if the local governing body is not willing to change the status quo, the continuation of higher taxes is inevitable and here to stay until existing municipal regimes are replaced by more conservative progressive governments that are smarter and willing to challenge the old, protected paradigms. The county and state governments only want what they can get from all the local governments to fund their lofty handouts and political pork-barrel agendas. It is obvious for the most part that the affluent towns in northwest New Jersey like their lifestyle and are not willing to make major changes by sharing services or using shared-services programs. There is so much that can be done with sharing services if there is the will to do so, and some of the more progressive towns have come a long way in doing a great job; consequently, property-tax payers have saved a significant amount of money. All this takes leadership and the ability to bring people together to break down paradigms and to develop and pursue new and better long-term ideas and goals to meet the challenges of the present and future.

I have been so fortunate to live in this great oasis for over half a century, raising a family while living the American dream to its fullest. From a humble start with the normal ups and downs of life, I've had the good fortune to come to live in this wonderful community. With that said, there is not one thing from the day I was born to this day I would want to change; we can always build on our achievements and be a voice for good.

I can only hope that the same opportunities and good fortune will be there for future generations so that they too will only have to work for it and believe in the great rewards of hard work. I have been graced with many wonderful opportunities and had the opportunity to serve this great country's military with distinction, where I was awarded the U.S. Army's Fifth Brigade Certificate of Achievement. I served on a number of very important public/civic boards, including the Denville zoning board and town council, the Morris County Municipal Utility Authority's solid waste advisory board, and the Denville Volunteer Council, where I was the VP and junior awards chair. I was also the Morristown St. Patrick's Day parade marshal chair and was honored to be the 2023 parade starter. This was a great event where my wife, three children, five grandchildren, and friends marched with us up South Street in the beautiful town of Morristown to the melodious sound of dozens of pipe bands, school bands, and so on. Then we went on to the grandstand that overlooks Morristown's beautiful Green and its floral beauty, where honorees' names were called out by the parade committee. It is always nice and rewarding to be honored by your own fraternity brothers, and the community where we have lived for almost sixty years. In 2024, I was selected by the Denville Volunteer Council as the volunteer of the year at the annual awards dinner. This was an extravaganza of speeches and awards; I received a plaque and a proclamation from the mayor of our town. There were close to a hundred family members, guests, friends, and neighbors in attendance; a tenor vocalist friend's melodious voice serenaded the audience, and a pipe band friend with his melodious pipes added a special tone to the festivities. A night to remember. I am proud of my Irish heritage and proud to be an adopted American. God bless America.

About the Author

Kevin Scollans, a native of Southern Ireland, was raised on a farm along the Northern Ireland border during the 1940s. Known for his rebellious spirit, Scollans embraced adventure and travel, eventually pursuing the American Dream. Despite growing up in a time of economic hardship, he always managed to be resourceful, a trait that served him well during his time in the US Army. If not for a chance encounter with a special lady, he might have made the army his career. Today, Scollans reflects on a life filled with good fortune and hopes for the same in the afterlife. His book, *Wild and Hearty*, mirrors his own adventurous spirit.

Milton Keynes UK
Ingram Content Group UK Ltd.
UKHW021119111124
451035UK00016B/1116

9 798822 954168